Acclaim for Ruth Reid

"Ruth Reid is skillful in portraying the Amish way of life as well as weaving together miracles with the everyday. In this book, she writes a beautiful tale of romance, redemption, and faith."

—BETH WISEMAN, BEST-SELLING AUTHOR OF THE DAUGHTERS OF THE PROMISE SERIES, REGARDING *A MIRACLE OF HOPE*

"Ruth Reid pens a touching story of grace, love, and God's mercy in the midst of uncertainty. A must-read for Amish fiction fans!"

—KATHLEEN FULLER, BEST-SELLING AUTHOR OF THE HEARTS OF MIDDLEFIELD SERIES, REGARDING *A MIRACLE OF HOPE*

"Reid gives readers the hope to believe that there are angels with every one of us, both good and evil, and that the good angels will always win."

—ROMANTIC TIMES REVIEW OF *AN ANGEL BY HER SIDE*

"*An Angel by Her Side* brings together not only a protagonist's inner struggle, but the effect on the character from outside forces. In short, the reader rises, falls, grows, and learns alongside the story's champion."

—AMISH COUNTRY NEWS REVIEW

"Reid has written a fine novel that provides, as its series title claims, a bit of 'heaven on earth.'"

—PUBLISHERS WEEKLY REVIEW OF *THE PROMISE OF AN ANGEL*

"If *The Promise of an Angel* is anything to judge by, it looks like she's going to become a favourite amongst Amish fans."

—CHRISTIAN MANIFESTO

"Ruth Reid captivates with a powerful new voice and vision."

—KELLY LONG, BEST-SELLING AUTHOR OF *SARAH'S GARDEN* AND *LILLY'S WEDDING QUILT*

"Ruth Reid's *The Promise of an Angel* is a beautiful story of faith, hope, and second chances. It will captivate fans of Amish fiction and readers who love an endearing romance."

—AMY CLIPSTON, BEST-SELLING AUTHOR OF THE KAUFFMAN AMISH BAKERY SERIES

A Miracle
of Hope

Also by Ruth Reid

A novella included in *An Amish Miracle*

The Heaven on Earth series
The Promise of an Angel
Brush of Angel's Wings
An Angel by Her Side

A Miracle of Hope

The Amish Wonders Series

Ruth Reid

Thomas Nelson
Since 1798

NASHVILLE   DALLAS   MEXICO CITY   RIO DE JANEIRO

Published in Nashville, Tennessee, by Thomas Nelson. Thomas Nelson is a registered trademark of Thomas Nelson, Inc.

Thomas Nelson, Inc., titles may be purchased in bulk for educational, business, fund-raising, or sales promotional use. For information, please e-mail SpecialMarkets@ThomasNelson.com.

Scriptures taken from the Holy Bible, New International Version®, NIV®. Copyright © 1973, 1978, 1984, 2011 by Biblica, Inc.™ Used by permission of Zondervan. All rights reserved worldwide. www.zondervan.com.

Publisher's Note: This novel is a work of fiction. Names, characters, places, and incidents are either products of the author's imagination or used fictitiously. All characters are fictional, and any similarity to people living or dead is purely coincidental.

Library of Congress Cataloging-in-Publication Data

Reid, Ruth, 1963-
  A Miracle of Hope / By Ruth Reid.
    pages cm. -- (The Amish Wonders Series)
  ISBN 978-1-4016-8829-5 (Trade Paper)
  1. Amish--Fiction. I. Title.
  PS3618.E5475M57 2013
  813'.6--dc23

                    2013023672

Printed in the United States of America

13 14 15 16 17 RRD 6 5 4 3 2 1

A Miracle of Hope is dedicated to my brother, Paul Droste. Anytime I write about woodstoves or cutting wood, I can't help but recall the winter you moved in with me. I couldn't seem to get the woodstove to hold a fire or keep the pipes from freezing. Then you arrived and cut a different wood to burn. It was so hot inside the house I had to open the windows to get air. I love you! (Oh, and I'm sorry you came back from Colorado to learn I had sold your car for $15.)

Glossary

ach: oh
aemen: amen
boppli: baby
bruder: brother
bu: boy
daed: dad or father
denki: thank you
dochder: daughter
doktah: doctor
dummkopp: dummy
Englischer: anyone who is not Amish
fraa: wife
greenhaus: greenhouse
grossdaadi haus: a second house on the property where the grandparents live
grossdaadi: grandfather
guder mariye: good morning
gut nacht: good night
gut: good
hiya: a greeting like hello

icehaus: ice house, where food is kept frozen

jah: yes

kaffi: coffee

kalt: cold

kapp: a prayer covering worn by women

kinner: children

kumm: come

mamm: mother or mom

mammi: grandmother

maydel: girl

mei: my

nau: now

nay: no

nett: not

onkel: uncle

redd-up: straighten

Schtecklimann: a go-between; someone who acts as a messenger when a man wants to seek approval from a woman's parents for their daughter's hand in marriage

schul: school

sohn: son

wedder: weather

wilkom: welcome

wunderbaar: wonderful

yummasetti: a traditional Amish dish made with ground beef and noodles

Chapter One

I *promise my name—not my heart.*

Lindie Wyse recalled the words in Josiah's letter that detailed the terms. Not that it mattered what the marital arrangements were. As her older brother, Eli, had pointed out, she couldn't possibly expect more. All she had to offer any man was a marred life.

Eli leaned closer. "It's going to be okay," he said, repeating what he had said shortly after they boarded the bus last evening. Several hours later his tone still lacked certainty. "Cedar Ridge is a smaller district than ours. I think you'll like the people." He paused briefly, then continued when she failed to respond. "I met many of the members at Caroline Plank's funeral. Josiah was out of sorts coping with his *fraa's* unexpected death . . ." His voice droned on, sounding like a far-off woodpecker hammering away on a rotting tree trunk. "The winters are longer than ours. You did pack your wool socks, *jah*?"

Lindie nodded mechanically, a trait she'd only recently acquired. She lent an ear but remained silent. She hoped her brother's assumptions were right. Eli had hardly mentioned

1

Josiah Plank in the three years since his wife's death. It wasn't until her brother returned last month from what he called "a business trip" that he spoke about his childhood friend again. When Eli and his wife, Margaret, talked about Josiah, it was as if they were trying to set Lindie up on a pen-pal courtship. She discovered a few short weeks later that they were arranging much more than a distant courtship. They were setting her up for marriage.

Over the past few months, Lindie had carried the weight of the members' scornful stares. Nothing had hurt worse than when Moses, the man she loved, rejected her, or when his sister, Mary, openly rebuked her. Even after Lindie knelt in confession, the church members' estrangement continued. So did the gossip. She was plagued with nightmares and shrouded in shame. Her life would never be the same, yet the looming question wouldn't be pushed aside.

Could God's mercy extend far enough to reach her?

Daylight crept over the horizon. She leaned forward to peer through the window. Since the majority of their travel had been during the night, she'd missed the change of scenery. Northern Michigan had plenty of trees. Snow too. The farther north they traveled on I-75, the more a snow-covered roadside replaced the brown carpet of grass. She sank back against the vinyl bus seat, pulled her cape tighter against her neck, and watched as the landscape passed in a blur.

A few hours later the bus rattled over the steel grates on the Mackinac Bridge and Lindie's thoughts returned to their approaching destination. She'd overheard some of the other passengers chatting about the Great Lakes, but she hadn't envisioned anything so vast as these open waters. Her settlement was near lakes, but nothing as massive as the Straits of Mackinac. As they reached the end of the bridge, entering the Upper Peninsula, she craned her neck for a full view. The extensive distance that now separated her from her family took root in her mind.

Her stomach curdled at the thought. She lifted one hand to cover her mouth, held her belly with the other, and willed herself not to vomit. A moment later the queasiness subsided. She leaned her forehead against the cold, damp window and closed her eyes. She wished she was moving so far away for another reason— any other reason—than to escape her old life. Pride goes before destruction. The scripture in Proverbs was true. Only she never expected one bad decision would lead to such a hard fall.

"It won't be much longer *nau*," Eli said, then added, "Are you all right?"

She didn't risk responding. Even the motion of a slight nod might aggravate her stomach. She certainly didn't want to be covered in vomit when she met her soon-to-be husband for the first time.

꒰

Josiah Plank took a seat on an empty bus station bench. He propped his elbows on his knees, then buried his face in his hands. None of this seemed real. It certainly didn't seem right. Agreeing to marry a woman he knew little about was crazy. Normally he'd weigh the cost. This just proved how unstable he'd become since Caroline died.

She didn't know him either, other than from things Eli might have said.

She . . . He drew a blank on her name. Perhaps his lapse in memory was a sign. Eli's little sister was just a kid, maybe ten, when he saw her last. Their Ohio settlements were too far apart to belong to the same church district, so their families weren't close. Even since he'd moved to Cedar Ridge, contact with his friend had been sporadic. Eli had made the trip for Caroline's funeral, but they'd talked about the lumber business, and nothing about either of Eli's sisters.

He didn't want to embarrass himself or the girl by stumbling over her name when he introduced her to the bishop. Josiah dug his hand into his pocket and pulled out the letter he'd received two days ago. He scanned down to the bottom of the page. *Lindie.*

"Lindie Rose Wyse." Fire rose from his stomach and shot up the back of his throat. He stood. He needed to find a drinking fountain.

He jammed the folded letter into his pocket, his fingers touching loose cash. He pulled out the money and made a quick count. Enough to purchase a return bus fare. He shoved the money back into his pocket and went in search of water.

Jah, he owed her that much for coming to his senses. She would be glad he did too. *She*, there he went again. "It's Lindie," he said to himself as he pressed the fountain lever and bent to take a drink.

Behind him, a bus squealed to a halt, its compressed air brakes hissing before the door opened. He studied each passenger as they disembarked. The area crowded with newcomers and a hum of greetings spread among the people. Josiah inched forward. Perhaps she'd changed her mind.

He glimpsed a woman in an Amish dress stepping off the bus. His breath caught. Eli had given an accurate description of his sister: early twenties, small frame, average height, and bright-red hair. He shook his head. What Eli hadn't told him was that she was beautiful. With those features, she would have distracted every unmarried man in her district. So why had Eli asked Josiah to marry her?

Eli exited the bus next, reached for his sister's elbow, and guided her toward the building. It only took a moment before Eli's hand shot up in a quick wave.

Josiah swallowed hard. He wasn't ready for this, but he weaved through the crowd in their direction anyway.

"*Gut* to see you, Josiah."

Eli extended his hand and Josiah shook it. "*Jah*, you too."

"This is *mei* sister Lindie." Eli nudged her shoulder.

"Hello." Her voice barely reached a whisper. She kept her head lowered and slightly lifted her eyes to meet his, but the moment she did, she glanced away.

"It's nice to meet you." He turned to Eli. "Was your trip *gut*?" Small talk. He hated every minute.

"It was a long ride, ain't so, Lindie?" Eli nudged his sister but didn't receive a response. He readdressed Josiah. "The *wedder* is much colder up here. Across the Ohio state line, we still have leaves on the trees."

"We had a few flurries last night." He lifted his gaze to the cloudy sky. "We'll probably have another snowfall tonight." That wasn't unusual for November.

Eli shifted his feet. "So what time is the bishop expecting us?"

A raspy noise, something between a cough and a gasp, escaped Lindie's mouth, but she continued to look down.

Josiah hadn't anticipated Eli rushing the wedding when they had only just made introductions. He took a moment to settle the quiver in the back of his throat. "He's probably expecting us any-time *nau*." He wished Lindie would speak up. Josiah cleared his throat. "Lindie," he said, hoping she would look him in the eye. She didn't. "The bishop will wish to speak with you first." *Unless you say something and we end this now.*

She nodded.

"If it's okay, Eli, I would like to talk with her alone," Josiah said.

"I'll get her packages."

She jerked up her head. Her blue-like-Lake-Superior eyes watched her brother, while Josiah tried to count the tiny freckles sprinkled across her nose.

"It's okay," Eli said to his sister. He waited a moment, then joined the throng of people waiting to claim their bags.

Josiah motioned to a bench in a less crowded area. "Let's sit."

She hesitated, peered over her shoulder in Eli's direction, then, with her head lowered, shuffled to the far side of the concrete bench.

He sat on the opposite end. The space between them might indicate they weren't a couple suited for one another. Josiah twiddled his thumbs, not sure where to begin. "You got *mei* letter, *jah*?"

She nodded.

Of course she had. He'd received a note stating she understood and accepted his terms, but he wouldn't be satisfied until he heard it straight from her. For all he knew, Eli might have responded on his sister's behalf.

"You probably know Eli's *fraa* and my *fraa* were second cousins. The four of us attended many of the same weddings and became friends. After I got married, *mei fraa* and I moved up here with her family to start a lumber mill." He paused, unsure why he was telling her this. If it was to ease his guilt for entering into an agreement he now wanted out of, it wasn't working. "I met you once . . . I think you might have been ten. Do you remember?"

Lindie shook her head and a red spiral curl fell out from under her *kapp*. The loose hair dangled in front of her face. Her teeth chattered and white breaths escaped her mouth. She burrowed deeper into her cape.

The midmorning sun shimmered on the red ringlet. He forced himself to focus on his boots.

"I'm *nett* going to ask what kind of trouble you were in. Your *bruder* believes you need a fresh start . . . But I'm thirty-two. At least ten years older than you. Why are you willing to marry me under my stringent conditions?"

She looked him straight in the eye. But before she spoke, the pinkish color drained from her face. She covered her mouth and bolted to a trash can a few feet away.

He stood, pulled a hankie from his pocket, and walked up beside her. When Eli had hinted of his sister's disgrace, Josiah had assumed the unthinkable and stopped Eli before he could share details. Her failure to come home one night led to repentance and that was what mattered. She finished vomiting and he handed her the cotton cloth.

"*Denki.*" She wiped her mouth.

"There's a drinking fountain over there." He motioned to the side of the building and she hurried in that direction.

Josiah scanned the thinning crowd for Eli. He stood beside four reused apple boxes all tied closed with twine. If he noticed that his sister was sick, Eli didn't appear worried.

After a long drink, Lindie lifted her head. Although some of the color had returned to her cheeks, she still looked pasty.

"If you like, I'll buy you a return ticket home," he said.

Josiah expected some hint of relief to wash over her, but instead, he noted quite the opposite. She looked terrified. And that added to his confusion. He tipped his head to one side so he could look her in the eye.

"Lindie, why are you here? Your *bruder* talked you into this, ain't so?"

Eli joined them. "She's here because I know you'll take *gut* care of her." He turned to Lindie. "Wipe your face and get ahold of yourself."

"If you don't mind, Eli"—Josiah's voice hardened—"your sister and I have more to talk about." He flicked his head at the boxes. "You should stay with the packages." Josiah waited until Eli was out of earshot before asking, "Is he preventing you from marrying someone else?" *Like the father of your unborn* boppli*?*

"*Nay.*" He strained to hear her words. She glanced at him a half second. "There is no one else."

He sighed. Prior to her arrival, he'd convinced himself this was a mistake, but in the half second that she acknowledged him, he saw hopelessness. "Are you sure you don't want to go home?"

"I'd like to stay." Her demeanor contradicted her words.

"I said in *mei* letter I would give you *mei* name, but *nett mei* heart."

She nodded.

"I'm *nett* capable of falling in love again. Your *bruder* is mistaken if he's told you otherwise. Even in time, I won't." He paused a moment. Though harsh, the truth needed to be spoken. It was important for her to give some sign of acknowledging this.

She didn't.

"Will you at least lift your head and look me in the eye?" The moment she did, he regretted being so direct. Her tearful blue eyes held a sorrow he wasn't prepared for.

He scanned the area. Other than Eli standing beside the boxes and a handful of people still loitering, they were alone. He looked at her. "This isn't something I would normally discuss . . . and I certainly don't intend to embarrass you. Do you understand what a marriage of convenience means?"

She didn't blink as tears welled.

He had to stress the final point. "That means I'll give you a roof over your head and provide for you. Nothing more."

She squared her shoulders. "And in return, what do you expect from me?"

"I told you in the letter." Didn't she say she read and agreed to the terms? "I have a young *dochder* who is deaf. I can't have her running around the sawmill. In addition to caring for her, I expect you to cook, clean, and keep up the laundry. Things a *fraa* would handle. Also, Eli said you can do record keeping."

"*Jah.* I kept track of the income from my sister-in-law's vegetable stand."

Her bottom lip trembled and he groaned under his breath.

"I want to be straightforward with you. The winters are long and hard. You don't know loneliness until you've suffered through cabin fever." This wasn't the place for a woman in a weakened condition.

She bowed her head, wringing her hands.

"Lindie, will you please stop looking away?"

She met his gaze.

His chest expanded with a deep breath. "A loveless marriage might be unbearable. Going through the motions of marriage without—without love . . . You might grow to despise me." He paused a moment. "If this isn't what you expected . . . I'll buy you a ticket home."

Chapter Two

Things *a* fraa *would handle.* Lindie was sure those were his exact words. That meant more than household chores. Of course a man would expect to have liberties with his wife—it was biblical—even if he didn't love her. Besides, he seemed to emphasize how lonely life would be *going through the motions* of marriage.

A brisk breeze sent a chill down Lindie's spine as she stood outside the bus depot. Shivering, she hugged herself.

Josiah stepped into the wind and, without asking, placed his hands on her shoulders, turning her to face him. A kind gesture to block the wind, but his touch caused her to flinch.

He dropped his hands. "I'm sorry."

A gust of wind pulled at her *kapp,* exposing her ears to the numbing cold air. With the ground covered in snow already, how long would it be before she experienced what he called cabin fever?

Another wave of nausea washed over her, and she fought to control it.

"Does the father of the *boppli* know you're about to get married?"

She coughed, almost launching what little stomach contents she had at him. How could he have figured it out when it took her two months after the sickness started? She had thought it was due to stress.

Josiah's brows rose ever so slightly. "He doesn't know, does he?"

"Nay." She sucked in a breath.

He shifted his feet and crossed his arms over his chest.

Josiah had indicated he wouldn't pry. She needed him to keep that promise.

"You said you weren't going to ask." She probably sounded too stern for someone in her situation, but if she didn't challenge him now, more questions would follow.

"Jah, that is true. I did say that." He looked down at his boots, then back at her. "I trust you have a *gut* reason to withhold such vital information."

"I do."

He stared at her a moment, then waved Eli over to them.

What was he going to do, have Eli explain her predicament? She hadn't even told her brother all the facts.

Eli sprinted over and stood beside them. He buried his hands in his armpits, shivering. "Have you two worked things out?"

Her brother couldn't really believe things would be worked out in less than fifteen minutes, could he? She diverted her attention to the slush buildup on the cement platform.

"I'm going to leave you alone so she can tell you her decision," Josiah said.

Lindie lifted her head and watched Josiah as he crossed the platform and stopped next to her belongings. He was too handsome to settle for someone damaged like her, especially if he was as kind as Eli had made him out to be.

11

"How did your talk go?"

"He offered to buy *mei* ticket home."

"I figured he would."

Her chest grew heavy. Had Eli hauled her almost as far as Canada to prove that her life was too marred for any man? The truth was hard to swallow. "You knew he would change his mind after he met me?"

"He wants to give you every chance to change yours." He shifted his feet. "I wouldn't have agreed to this arrangement if I didn't believe he would treat you *gut*. Since his *fraa* died, he's had no one to take care of his *dochder*." Eli squeezed her hand. "This will all work out."

"I'm scared," she whispered.

"That's understandable. But this is your only chance for a decent future."

In other words, her brother wasn't giving her the option to leave. That didn't surprise her. After she'd refused to share her whereabouts on the night she hadn't come home from the singing, he made it clear he wouldn't tolerate waywardness. At least he wasn't reminding her again of the mess she'd made of her life.

Eli patted her shoulder. "*Kumm*, let's tell him you're ready."

Without uttering a word, she walked beside her brother and they joined Josiah.

"We can go meet the bishop *nau*," Eli said.

Josiah's gaze held hers. For a moment, she thought he might back out of the arrangement. Then he stooped to grasp the twine tied around two of the boxes. "The buggy is this way."

Her brother grabbed the other boxes, and she trailed them both to the corner of the bus station's parking lot where Josiah had tied his horse to a lamppost.

Lindie climbed inside as they piled her belongings in the

back. Being squeezed between the boxes in the backseat didn't leave her much of a view from the side opening. What little she could see of the town looked small. A few old houses converted into antique shops, a spa and salon. Stores she wouldn't frequent. The grocery store's parking lot buzzed with activity, and several cars were parked at the Cedar Ridge Restaurant. Lindie hadn't seen any other Amish buggies. Over the years she'd heard stories of how some areas were so unwelcoming that the Amish folks rarely went into town because they didn't feel safe. She hoped Cedar Ridge wasn't such a place.

"How's the farming around here?" Eli asked.

"*Nett* so *gut*. Too much limestone plus the season is short."

Lindie slumped on the bench. She didn't like the idea of not putting in a large garden.

"Some vegetables grow all right. Others do better if they are seed-started in a *greenhaus*. The woods are full of mushrooms to pick."

Mushrooms weren't part of what Lindie considered a pantry staple. She wasn't fond of the spongy fungus either.

It wasn't long before the pavement ended and the hilly gravel road took a few sharp bends. It must be a beautiful drive when the fall leaves were still on the trees. But even now, the snowy hillside was breathtaking.

Josiah pulled back on the reins and the horse slowed. Lindie sat straighter on the bench at the sight of the steep hill ahead. She held her breath as they climbed, then exhaled slowly as they neared the crest. From the peak, the landscape stretched for miles. She closed her eyes during the descent. Even so, her body slid forward on the bench as the buggy dipped downward.

"This is a little tricky." Josiah worked the reins.

She couldn't imagine how hazardous the roads were after a

heavy snow, or worse yet, an ice storm. In their settlement, the landscape was mostly flat, and even then, it was dangerous to be on the roads in the winter.

They crossed two more tree-covered hills before a clapboard-sided farmhouse came into view. The buggy under the lean-to identified this house as Amish.

Josiah pulled back on the reins and veered his horse into the driveway. He stepped aside as she climbed out of the buggy. "You sure about this?" he whispered.

Didn't he know she couldn't change her mind? She had no place to go. "I'm sure," she replied without looking him in the eye.

"You look white again." He started walking.

"*Jah*, I imagine I do." Her knees wobbled too as they climbed the porch steps. She wasn't sure whether to blame the steep incline or the pending talk with the bishop.

The door opened at the same time Josiah raised his hand to knock.

"*Kumm* in." The woman stepped aside as they entered. "Gideon is waiting for you in the sitting room." The woman's welcoming smile and the sweet aroma of apple pie offered a morsel of hope. Perhaps the settlement wasn't aware of Lindie's circumstances. She'd kept the truth hidden within her own district and the members practically shunned her. She didn't dare think about how this new community would treat her once they knew.

Josiah pulled his hat off his head, clutched it against his chest, and led the way.

A blast of dry heat from the woodstove warmed her face as she followed Josiah into the sitting room.

"Bishop Troyer, this is Lindie Wyse and her *bruder*, Eli." Josiah's voice quivered as he gave the introductions.

"It's *gut* to see you again, Eli. And to meet you, Lindie."

The bishop directed her and Josiah to the ladder-back wooden chairs positioned side by side in the center of the room. "Have a seat."

She did. His authoritative tone reminded her of the meeting she'd had with the bishop in her district prior to the church service where she knelt in repentance. She would rather walk barefoot over shards of glass than relive that experience.

"Josiah, sit beside her." The bishop turned his attention to Eli. "You can wait in the kitchen while I talk with them."

Eli had thought Josiah would treat her well . . . *A chance for a fresh start*. She bowed her head and stared at her brown, wrinkled dress. After riding a bus all night, her clothing wasn't as neat as she would've liked, nor was it the traditional royal blue that women wore for their wedding.

"State your intention," the bishop said to Josiah.

"Lindie . . ." He paused and regarded her as if giving her another chance to change her mind. When she made no move, he cleared his throat and continued. "Lindie and I would like to be married."

The quiver in his voice was gone—she didn't detect a hint of hesitation.

"Usually the wedding takes place in the bride's district." The bishop's tone was more a question than a statement.

"That is true," Josiah said. "But since it would be difficult to travel with *mei dochder* and I didn't want to be away from her too long, Lindie was willing to forgo a large wedding. Her *bruder* has also given his approval. He's one of the ministers in their district and he has a letter from their bishop as well."

Her stomach muscles clenched. Would the letter give a full account of what led up to her kneeling confession?

The bishop turned to her. "Have you been baptized?"

15

"*Jah.*"

The bishop stroked his beard as he studied her.

She swallowed the acid coating her throat. "I made *mei* commitment to God and the church." She understood his need to verify her testimony of faith. Like any bishop, he would refuse to marry them if either had not been baptized. Intermarrying with unbelievers was strictly forbidden.

"And *nau* you wish to make a lasting covenant with Josiah?"

"*Jah*," Lindie said, sounding less than convincing.

After a long moment of intense scrutiny, the bishop shifted his stare to Josiah. "The man is the head of the woman just as Christ is the head of the church."

Josiah's Adam's apple moved down his neck.

"In the union between a husband and *fraa*, they shall become one flesh. Only in death shall the covenant between man and *fraa* be terminated." The bishop studied both of them.

From the corner of her eye, she noticed Josiah lower his head.

"You may join hands," the bishop said before walking out of the room.

Josiah held out his hand and she took it. Needles prickled along her spine. His hand was dry and calloused. A hard worker. Any woman would be pleased to find such a man. She cast a furtive glance his way. His posture was board-straight, his chin set. If it hadn't been for his dull expression, one that no doubt matched hers, she would have found him quite handsome.

The bishop's wife and Eli followed the bishop back into the room. Her brother folded his arms in front of him and stood a few feet to the side of her chair, while the bishop's wife stood on the opposite side.

Bishop Troyer cleared his throat. "Are you both willing to enter wedlock as God has commanded?"

"Jah," she and Josiah said in unison.

The bishop placed his hand over their clasped hands. "Before God, do you take Lindie as your *fraa*? Do you promise that you will not depart from her, but will care for her in affliction, in sickness, and in health?"

"Jah."

"And do you take Josiah as your wedded husband? Do you promise before God that you will not depart from him? Will you remain loyal during all times, even in sickness until death?"

"Jah," she answered to each of his questions.

The thrill of waiting for the *Schtecklimann* to arrive at her parents' home to announce a certain young man's marriage intentions was stolen. Since her parents were gone and she'd lived under Eli's roof, he was her parental figure and the go-between. He'd certainly given his consent and made all the arrangements—only she hadn't been part of the planning.

"May God be with you and bless you with offspring, through Jesus Christ. *Aemen*." The bishop released his hand from theirs. "Go forth in the Lord. You are *nau* man and *fraa*."

Josiah withdrew his hand.

Tears trickled down her cheeks. It wasn't uncommon for the bride to cry on her wedding day, but her tears were shed for a different reason. She had only learned of the arrangements after Josiah had agreed. Instead of having weeks to plan and frolic in all the cooking and sewing preparations, she'd had only a few days. Even then, it didn't give her much time to pack the contents of her hope chest.

She swept the back of her hand over her cheeks. Eli had pressed her about her whereabouts. Unmarried women had a reputation to uphold. He reminded her that as a minister, he was accountable to the bishop. She finally confessed to spending

Ruth Reid

the time with an *Englischer*. He pointed out how disappointed their deceased parents would be. How mortified he felt as her brother.

The humiliating situation created a string of accusations. None of which she would answer—not completely anyway.

"I'm Rebecca Troyer," the bishop's *fraa* said. "*Wilkom* to our settlement." The plump woman with the salt-and-pepper hair extended her arms and gave Lindie a welcoming hug.

"*Denki*."

"This is far from home for you. I hope the adjustment won't be too difficult."

"*Denki*." Lindie smiled. Her first genuine smile since arriving. Rebecca's hug felt maternal. Maybe she would find someone in this foreign land who would make her feel at home.

"I'll put the kettle on for *kaffi* and we can have pie while you tell me a little about yourself."

Josiah cleared his throat. "Perhaps we can visit on church Sunday. We need to get Lindie's *bruder* back to the bus station."

The weight of his words hit Lindie like a cast-iron pan. It wouldn't be long before her brother would leave and she would be alone. Hundreds of miles from family . . .

A hand touched her shoulder. "We need to go," Josiah said. "Eli's bus leaves in an hour."

His face was distorted by her blurred vision. She didn't see him as her husband, but as a stranger.

Rebecca walked them to the door. "We'll get together for *kaffi* soon."

Lindie blinked a few times before facing Rebecca. "I'd like that."

She caught a glimpse of Josiah's frown in her peripheral

18

vision. She hoped he wouldn't disapprove of her eagerness to form a friendship.

Neither Josiah nor her brother spoke on the way to the buggy. Once again, she climbed into the back. This time, before they reached the steepest hill, she closed her eyes until the road leveled. It was snowing when they reached the bus station. Not the pretty, fluffy flakes she liked to catch in her mouth. This was sleet. Cold and wet, but at least it would disguise her tears.

"I'll miss you," she said.

"Send me a letter once you're settled."

Normally her brother rejected showing emotion in public, but he held her like this was their final parting.

Eli peered over his shoulder at Josiah standing a few feet away. "Let me have a word with your husband before I leave."

Your husband . . . The words rolled over in her mind as Eli lumbered over to where Josiah stood. *Josiah Plank's* fraa . . . *Josiah's Lindie.* Her new identity would take getting used to.

The men talked in low voices. Her brother said something and Josiah nodded. Then Eli dug his hand into his pocket, pulled out an envelope, and handed it to Josiah.

Lindie's breath caught. Before leaving home last night, Eli had made a comment that he couldn't forget the cash for the trip. She foolishly assumed the money was for travel expenses.

The men shook hands, their business transaction completed.

Her arranged marriage had come at a cost.

Chapter Three

A chill settled over Lindie's bones. Her brother's bus rounded the corner on Elm Street and she sniffled as it disappeared. Josiah offered her his hankie.

"*Denki*," she squeaked. She dabbed the soft cloth against the creases of her eyes, then used it to wipe her nose. The overcast sky added another level of dreariness to her mood. So did wearing clothes soaked from the icy rain. She couldn't recall any woman who had cried tears of grief on her wedding day.

"I have some things to talk about with you, but we can do that on the way to the *haus* if you're ready," he said.

She wasn't ready. But standing any longer in the sleet wasn't the answer either. They would both catch pneumonia. She dried her nose with the hankie again. His eyes followed her hand as she shoved the hankie into her cape pocket.

"I'd like to wash it before I return it," she said before thinking. Of course she would wash it. From now on, she would be washing all of his clothes.

He motioned to the parking lot. "Let's go before the roads get too slippery."

Her stomach seized up as they approached the buggy. *Please, no more hills.* She'd already made a public spectacle of herself when she hung over the trash can at the bus station. She didn't want that embarrassment repeated.

Neither spoke again until they were inside the buggy and heading out of town—in the same hilly direction as the bishop's house. She sucked in a breath and secured a hold on the side of the bench.

"Don't be surprised if the church members ask a lot of questions. Getting married without a formal announcement will raise some brows," Josiah said, guiding the horse.

She'd seen her share of raised brows lately from the members of her home district. Ones from strangers wouldn't cut as much.

Josiah's face contorted. "I ask that you *nett* tell anyone we married for convenience." He dropped his line of vision to her belly. "So when is your *boppli* due?"

"May tenth."

He opened his mouth, looked again at her belly, then focused on the road.

Perhaps he now regretted his request to conceal the arranged marriage. At three months, she wasn't showing—yet. Her body wouldn't stay this size much longer. Tongues would wag, but they'd be directed just as much at him.

A few moments of silence passed. "*Mei dochder* doesn't respond well to strangers. She's unpredictable. It might take her awhile to get used to you."

His daughter wasn't the only one who needed time to adjust.

She gripped the edge of the bench to keep from jostling around as they traversed the hills. At least her stomach wasn't rolling like it had earlier. She had eaten a sandwich on the bus hours ago but had lost any vestiges of it. Lindie didn't want to think about food.

She peered out the window opening, but the tall pines and dense clouds hid the sun and made the surroundings look gloomy.

"How large is your settlement?" She'd only counted two farms with buggies in the driveway and they were separated by *Englisch* homes. In her district, several Amish houses shared the same acreage and dozens were clustered within a few miles radius.

"It started with ten families. *Nau* we have eight."

"We have over a hundred families in Middlefield." Due to her district's growth, they'd divided, then divided again. It made staying in touch with people difficult. Besides the massive attendance for weddings and funerals, she hadn't seen some members in years.

In the clearing ahead, the bishop's house came into view. But before reaching the Troyer farm, Josiah slowed the horse and turned right onto a narrow road. Shadowed by thick woods on both sides, daylight disappeared. She tightened her grasp on the bench as they approached a wooden bridge. The buggy wheel took a little dip and she bumped into Josiah.

Her face heated. "Sorry." She slid away from him and clutched the edge even tighter.

"I should've warned you. This bridge could use some repairs."

The road wasn't in much better shape. The mixture of dirt and crushed stones gave it a washboard texture. When the lane ended, the horse veered left without any reining from Josiah. Once the buggy cleared the patch of spruce pines, a log home came into view.

"It's small," he said, sounding apologetic.

"It's very nice." She especially liked the idea of sitting under the covered porch while she shucked corn or shelled peas.

"*Denki.* I like it back here. It's peaceful."

Isolated is how she would describe it. That would take some getting used to. Fellowship was the glue that kept her settlement together. Then again, maybe she would welcome the isolation.

"Whoa, Molly." Josiah stopped the horse next to the house and jumped out. He went to the back of the buggy and opened the hatch.

She surveyed the homestead as she climbed out. A small slat-board barn and horse corral stood to the left. On the right were two long barns. They reminded her of the chicken barns on some *Englischers'* farms back home, but instead of aluminum siding, Josiah's were constructed of wood. Smoke curled up from a stovepipe on the barn roof.

"You heat your chicken coop?"

He shook his head. "That's *mei* wood shop." He pointed to the barn without a smokestack. "And that one is the lumber storage barn." She supposed it made sense to have a heated barn to work in, but it seemed strange he would keep a fire burning while he was away.

Mud sucked her shoe into the earth. She jerked her foot out and shook it. Had she been looking where she stepped, she would have spotted the path of cedar shavings. But even the ground beneath the wood chips was soft.

Josiah grabbed two of the boxes. "I'll *kumm* back for the other ones." He headed for the house.

She followed him onto the porch, but paused when he opened the front door. Maybe she should wait for an invitation. After all, it wasn't her home. Not yet.

"You're going to get *kalt* standing on the porch," he said.

It wasn't the warmest welcome, but an invitation nevertheless. She stepped inside and removed her muddy shoes. The wooden floor chilled her stocking feet, though her toes were already numb. One of the first items she planned to unpack was her wool socks.

"This is the sitting room." He kept walking as he spoke. "In here is the kitchen." He pointed with his elbow as he passed the entrance and continued down the hallway.

This wasn't the time for a tour. She was more concerned over where he was hauling her things. Her heart raced so fast some of the beats seemed to jump over themselves.

Josiah stopped at the end of the hall, opened the door on the right, and stepped inside. He lowered the boxes to the floor. "You'll want to get out of those clothes."

She gasped. "Why?"

He crinkled his brows, eyed her from *kapp* to stockings, then looked at his clothes. "Aren't your clothes wet? I know mine are."

Undress? In front of him? She couldn't breathe. She hugged herself and looked down at the floor. She felt his stare.

"I'll bring in your other boxes." He shuffled out of the room.

Her view of the wooden floor blurred. She wiped her eyes, then looked around the room. A large dresser, a table with an oil lamp on it, and a double-sized bed made up with a gray-and-black patched quilt.

A burning sensation climbed the back of her throat. It was normal to feel nervous on one's wedding night—but she was sick.

Lindie bolted out of the room. She nearly ran into Josiah in the hallway as she made her way to the front door. Outside, she rushed to the far end of the porch and bent over the railing just as her stomach revolted in dry heaves. She straightened, but only for a moment before the nausea returned. She hunched over the railing, but still nothing came up. Her ears rang and sweat beaded along her brow, yet her teeth chattered from the cold.

A minute passed, then the door creaked open and Josiah came up beside her. "You've got it bad, don't you?"

"Jah." She pushed off the railing.

"I'll help you get into bed." He looped his arm around her shoulders. "I put your other boxes in the bedroom."

She lacked the strength to object to his assistance. *"Denki."*

Josiah guided her and didn't release his hand from her back until she was seated on the bed. "May I?" He pointed to the boxes.

She shrugged. As her husband, he didn't have to ask. *Ach,* what was she doing married to a stranger?

He pulled a pocketknife from his pants pocket, cut the twine binding, and squatted beside her belongings. He sifted through two of them before he rose to his feet, a nightdress in his hand.

"You can change into this," he said, handing her the garment. "I'll warm a glass of milk for you." He left the room, closing the door behind him.

She trembled as she clutched the nightdress in her hands. She wasn't ready for this night. The clang of pots and pans jolted her senses. She unfastened the pins from her dress, set them on the dresser, then climbed out of her wet clothes and into the cotton nightdress. Hearing footsteps stop outside her door, she scurried to get under the covers.

A soft tap sounded.

She pulled the covers up to her neck. *"Jah?"*

"May I *kumm* in?"

"Jah."

The door creaked open and Josiah entered. "Here's the warmed milk." He set the glass on the lamp table beside the bed. "Would you like anything else?"

"Nay, denki."

"I'm going to reheat some soup for supper. I'll bring you a

cup when it's ready." He crossed the room, then paused at the door. "Are you warm enough?"

"I'm fine, *denki*." He must've confused her trembling with shivering. She wasn't cold now that she had changed out of her wet clothes, just leery of his expectations. After all, it was their wedding night.

⌁

Doubts filled Josiah's mind. He should've insisted they wait longer to marry. He tried to rationalize the swift decision but found it impossible. Josiah pulled his coat off the hook and slipped his arms into the sleeves. He wanted to give Lindie some space. Besides, he needed to put the buggy away, feed Molly, and tend to the other livestock. But first he would check on his daughter. Usually the moment he pulled into the yard, Hannah came bouncing out of the lumber barn.

He hoped Simon hadn't had any problems with Hannah. Lately his daughter tended to wear down her grandfather's patience. Simon didn't have the stamina to keep up with her, especially when she wandered away, which she was doing more and more of these days. The doctor had told Simon last year that his hip needed replacing. Now that the weather had turned cold, his limp was more pronounced.

Now Lindie would care for Hannah while Josiah worked to get the lumber orders out on time. And Simon wouldn't have to watch over his granddaughter. It wouldn't be long before things would start to run smoothly around here.

Josiah trekked across the yard toward the lumber barn. His boots dug into the muddy ground. He made a mental note to toss another layer of wood chips on the path. He didn't mind dirt on his boots or even tracking mud into the house, but he hated how mud messed up his buggy. These fluctuating temperatures caused the mud-caked wheels to make the buggy unbalanced, which interfered with Molly's ability to pull it. He looked forward to the ground being frozen solid.

He pushed the barn door over the track and stepped inside. Simon's living quarters, the *grossdaadi haus*, was attached to the back of the barn. The same place Josiah and Caroline lived when they first were married, and up until Hannah was born. But his in-laws insisted they swap places since the space was too cramped for a growing family.

He tapped on the wooden door.

"*Jah*, it's open," Simon called out. He looked up from reading the *Budget* newspaper as he sat in the rocking chair next to the woodstove.

Hannah sat at the small kitchen table drawing on a sheet of paper. Usually she sensed his footsteps by the vibrations on the floor and would look up from her activity. Not today. Her concentration held steady. She was either upset or preoccupied with her picture.

Josiah crossed the room toward Simon. "How did it go?"

"She ran off twice. The first time she wasn't gone long and returned on her own. The second time I found her in the woods. I gave her two swats with the willow for *nett* minding me." He shook his head. "You've got your hands full with that child."

His hands were not only full, they were tied. He expected his father-in-law to quote the scripture about not sparing the rod, spoiling the child.

Simon held his tongue. Perhaps he was in pain.

"I'm sorry you had to chase after her. How did your hip hold up?"

Simon shrugged. "I'm thankful it didn't give out and leave me in the woods."

Josiah had tried everything he could to reach his daughter, but had failed. He'd even resorted to spanking her when he found her waist-deep in the duck pond. He recalled the dazed look on his daughter's face as if she were oblivious to the frigid water temperature. The ducks had all flown south for the winter. His daughter was eight years old, unable to swim, and didn't have a plugged nickel's worth of sense.

Nothing seemed to reach Hannah since her mother had died. To complicate matters, Hannah hadn't uttered a word in three years. She'd managed to block everyone out as though she were both deaf and dumb. For all he knew, she was. The doctors certainly had no answers for what had happened to her. At first they thought she suffered irreversible head trauma, but later the diagnosis changed to a severe case of emotional trauma. Either way, his daughter was lost.

Simon folded the newspaper. "What kept you so long in town?"

"Remember I told you that I'd found someone to care for Hannah?"

"*Jah.*"

"I was working out the arrangements."

"Will this woman be able to keep up with Hannah? Those other women didn't last."

"Mrs. Zook did the best she could." Her health wasn't much better than Simon's—only it wasn't her hip but her heart that gave her trouble. Ellen Yoder was different. Widowed and raising four young boys, she managed his daughter fine. However, once she pointed out how they'd both lost their spouses and it would be easy to merge their families, he had retreated. Fast. It wasn't difficult to do since Simon didn't care for Ellen. He made it clear that he didn't like the way she intruded, or how she assumed that the role of Hannah's mother was already hers. Josiah didn't think Simon would like anyone stepping into Caroline's place. And he agreed, which made it even more confusing how quickly he'd decided to marry Lindie.

"Well, hopefully Hannah will treat this one differently." Simon sounded like he didn't believe his own words. He gingerly shifted in the chair, grimacing as he moved.

Josiah hoped Simon would treat Lindie differently too.

Hannah looked up from her paper. She dropped the pencil on the table and moved toward her father.

Josiah gathered her into his arms and hugged her close to his chest, then pulled back so that she could read his lips. "Want to help feed Molly?"

She smiled and took his hand once he lowered her to the floor.

He spoke over his shoulder as they left the room. "I'll bring you out some supper when it's ready."

"Don't forget the paper." Simon pushed off the arms of his chair and stood. He wobbled a few steps forward.

"You didn't have to get up."

"*Jah*, I can't sit too long without getting stiff." He extended the folded paper to Josiah.

He took the paper as he did every week. Only he couldn't remember the last time he actually sat and read the news. Anymore, the paper sat on the table until he chucked it into the burn pile. The paper worked well for starting the morning fire in the cookstove, although he limited it to one page since the ink tended to cause a buildup of creosote in the chimney. He didn't want any gummy substance to coat the pipe and cause a house fire.

Josiah placed his hand on Hannah's shoulder and guided her outside. As usual, he did all the talking as they completed the chores. Then, as they did every night, the two of them prepared supper. He wasn't sure if he should trust her to take the meal out to Simon alone, but he wanted to give Lindie a cup of soup and slice of bread, and he wasn't prepared to introduce his daughter to the woman lying in bed.

He wrapped a mason jar filled with soup in a dish towel before handing it and a partial loaf of bread to Hannah. "Take it to *Grossdaadi*," he said, opening the door and motioning to the barn.

She took little steps over the cedar chip pathway.

He prepared Lindie's meal and carried it to the bedroom. He knocked, waited for her response, then opened the door. "I brought you some soup."

"*Denki.*" She clutched the quilt so tight around her neck that her knuckles lost their color.

The warm milk must not have worked. She was shaking. He should have gotten her out of the sleet the minute it started. He set the bowl on the lamp table and grabbed the empty glass. "Do you want more milk?"

"Okay," she whispered.

"Warm or cold?"

She shrugged.

"You don't have to be timid around me."

"Cold, please."

"I'll be back in a minute." He hurried to the kitchen and poured a glassful of milk, then brought it to her.

"*Denki*," she said.

"You'll want to keep this door open."

Her eyes widened. "Why?"

"The temperature dips down at *nacht* and it gets *kalt*. If your door is closed, you won't get much heat from the woodstove."

"I sleep better when it's *kalt*."

Josiah shrugged. He had a feeling warm or cold, they both had a sleepless night ahead of them.

Chapter Four

A soft touch tickled Lindie's head, pulling her from sleep. She forced her eyes open and blinked as daylight filtered through the curtains. It took a moment before she could focus on the child standing at her bedside. Lindie cleared her throat. "*Guder mariye.* You must be Hannah."

The stone-faced girl stared.

Remembering Josiah had said his daughter was deaf, Lindie wasn't sure how to communicate. She exaggerated her smile, but the universal gesture of friendship did nothing to alter the girl's expression.

The dark-eyed child pivoted on her heel and left the room.

Lindie flipped the wool quilt back and climbed out of bed. The wood floor, cold against her bare feet, sent a shiver straight through her. She should have taken time last night to find her wool socks in her belongings. She hunted down her stockings and hurried to pull them on. Josiah had been right about the drop in temperature. Hard to believe this was only November. Compared to Ohio, it felt more like the middle of February. She felt a pang of homesickness.

Lindie put on a black dress and pinned the front closed. She certainly didn't feel like a *fraa*. She hadn't even told her friends she was leaving Ohio to get married. A marriage in name only was hardly what she'd dreamed about. In her dreams, she would be married to Moses.

Lindie touched her belly. Flat. If it wasn't for the sickness, she wouldn't have suspected she was pregnant. She had prayed that wasn't the case, but the lot she'd been given proved that her prayers were in vain.

She slid down the wall to sit on the drafty floor. Alone. Married to a stranger. Living in a settlement where she didn't know a soul. Only a few months ago she and Moses had spoken privately of marriage. Tears welled. She wouldn't ever escape the consequences of her rash decision on that night—her womb would soon swell with the constant reminder.

"I don't even know what to pray, Lord," she choked out.

Thy will be done. She had prayed that before and look where it got her. She couldn't very well pray for God's will again if she wasn't willing to accept it.

God, you didn't answer when I begged you to set me free of the anguish. Vomit rose in her throat. She pushed off the floor, shot out of the bedroom and down the hallway.

"*Guder mariye,*" Josiah said as she raced past the kitchen.

Lindie propelled herself out the front door, bent over the porch railing, and vomited across the snow. The muscles between her ribs spasmed. Soaked in sweat, Lindie shuddered as the hard wind penetrated her core.

God, can't you see that I need help?

The screen door creaked open, then snapped shut.

Footsteps stopped behind her.

Josiah draped her cape over her shoulders.

"Denki." She forced a smile.

"You must be starved after sleeping through yesterday."

"What?" She'd never even slept in late, let alone missed an entire day.

"I figured you were exhausted after your long trip."

A stiff breeze flapped the wool cape and gave her chills. She tugged on the corners of the heavy material as a shield from the next gust. If only she'd slipped on her boots. The porch boards, wet from melting snow, were cold against her stocking feet. She balanced her weight on her right foot and lifted her left, then switched.

Josiah peered down at her feet and smiled. "The winter dance."

She wasn't sure what he meant. In her district, people weren't allowed to dance. The elders had even forbidden some of the traditional youth games due to too much body movement.

"You better *kumm* inside where it's warm."

Jah, this dancing, as he called it, wasn't helping her stomach settle. She followed him into the house.

Hannah peeked around the kitchen corner and he communicated something using hand movements. The child disappeared behind the wall without responding.

"How old is your *dochder?*"

"Eight." He led her into the sitting room and over to the chair next to the woodstove. "Have a seat." He grabbed the iron poker, turned the handle on the firebox, and opened the cast-iron door.

She eased into the rocking chair and looked down at her folded hands. "Don't you want me to start breakfast or something?" She still couldn't believe how long she'd slept. Josiah must think he married a woman with idle hands. She hoped the nausea passed soon so she could show him she wasn't lazy.

He stirred the hot embers, then reached for a piece of wood. "Hannah and I ate a bowl of cereal. You can make a bowl or there are eggs in—"

The young girl poked her head around the wall, then snapped back.

"Excuse me." He latched the fire opening, then crossed the room and disappeared into the kitchen. A moment later he reappeared in the sitting room with Hannah clinging to his side. "This is *mei dochder*, Hannah."

"*Hiya*," Lindie said.

Josiah bent down to Hannah's eye level and signed while talking. "This is"—his hands stopped, and the girl's brows crinkled—"Lindie. Show her where things are in the kitchen, please."

Lindie wondered if he would introduce her as his wife.

Hannah stared at him for a moment before turning her chocolate-colored eyes to Lindie. She turned back to her father and signed.

He shook his head. "Not today. I want you to stay inside and help." He rose from his squatting position and placed his hand on her shoulder, turning her away from him and toward Lindie. "She reads lips," he said.

The girl wiggled out of his hold and stomped toward the kitchen.

Josiah stopped her before she left the room. His face hardened and his hands moved rapidly. He paused a moment, then repeated the same hand gestures.

Hannah's brows knitted.

Josiah pointed to a wooden paddle hanging from a nail over a rolltop desk, then signed something else.

Lindie wished she could crawl under the rug. She scanned

the room. Its contents were simple and sparse. She stole a peek at Josiah, who was still speaking with rapid hand movements. She turned her attention to the wooden desk and chair next to the door. It took up most of the space on the wall opposite her. Off to her right, a wooden bench adorned with two small patchwork pillows sat in front of a large window.

To avoid embarrassing Hannah, Lindie continued to scan the objects in the room. Across from the bench were a lamp table and another rocking chair that matched the one she was sitting in. A worn braided navy rug took up the center of the room and was a mismatch to the forest-green curtains covering the window.

Lindie watched as Hannah passed by, shoulders slumped and looking at the floor as she walked toward the bedrooms.

Josiah mumbled something under his breath and returned to the woodstove. He tossed in a piece of oak, scattering the fiery embers. "You should be warm in a minute."

"*Denki.*" Lindie looked down at her wet stockings and wiggled her toes.

"*Mei dochder* challenges *mei* patience." He gazed at the empty hallway.

"Be thankful you only have one."

His head snapped up, eyes narrowed. One harsh word and she would dissolve into tears. A heavy knock diverted their attention.

Josiah didn't move.

An elderly man entered. He eyed Lindie, then directed his words to Josiah. "I heard the truck going over the bridge. It should be here any minute."

"I'll get *mei* coat." Josiah turned to her. "This is Simon, *mei* father-in-law." He looked at the man. "This is Lindie"—he cleared his throat—"*mei fraa.*" He walked to the door, grabbed a pair of work gloves from the wall shelf and his coat from the hook.

"It's nice to meet you," she said.

Simon nodded, his expression stiff. He pinned his son-in-law with the same look before turning to the door. "I'll wait for the truck."

Josiah lowered his head. His shoulders rose and his chest expanded as he drew in a breath. The door closed behind Simon, and Josiah exhaled.

"I left a sign language book on the table. You'll need to study it in order to communicate with Hannah." He shoved one hand into a leather glove. "I sent her to her room. See that she stays in there for an hour." He opened the door, but paused. "And when the hour's up, make sure she doesn't go outside unsupervised."

Josiah was pleased to see the truck pulling into the yard. He didn't want to discuss his marriage to Lindie with Simon yet.

His father-in-law slowly made his way over. "I expected you to tell me last *nacht* that you got married."

Josiah swallowed. "You knew?"

"Last week the bishop told me of your plans."

Josiah continued to the lumber barn and, once there, unlatched the door. He wasn't going to ask Simon for more details on that conversation. Instead, he shoved the wooden door across its track and waited for the truck to back into place. Even though he pretended not to be interested, he couldn't help but wonder if everyone in their district had been made privy to the details of his marriage. Not that he had told anyone, including the bishop, the exact details.

"I am one of the ministers." Simon broke the silence.

He kicked at a wood shim and it skipped over the snow. "I'm

sorry. I should've told you myself." He wished the bishop had told him that he and Simon had talked. Another reason to keep closemouthed about his and Lindie's arrangement.

"Well, given your situation . . ."

Josiah understood that his father-in-law was unable to continue. He didn't want to talk about his situation either. Josiah waved at Hal as he climbed out of the truck cab.

Hal, a stocky man in his late sixties, ambled to the back of the rig where Josiah and Simon stood. A much younger version of Hal, his teenaged grandson, leaped down from the passenger side.

Josiah wished Hal would cut the engine while they compared paperwork. The truck's exhaust fumes irritated his throat. He turned and coughed into his gloved hand.

Hal handed Josiah the paperwork. "They wanted me to tell you this was a partial shipment. Apparently Badger Creek had some bad weather and couldn't get to the trees."

"I heard talk of the ice storm and wondered how it would affect them." Badger Creek was another settlement, sixty miles north. They supplied the pine lumber he used to build pallets and the maple, oak, and ash he used to build furniture. He usually ordered enough in November to get him through the entire winter.

"They said it will be at least another week."

"That's fine. I have an order of Christmas wreaths to finish anyway." Josiah scanned the invoice. Everything appeared in order.

"That works fine for me too. I'd just as soon recline in my easy chair and watch U of M."

Josiah assumed Hal was talking about football, but up in their neck of the woods, most *Englischers* talked about hockey. Not that

Josiah was a fan of either sport, though he found it interesting when Hal would arrive with the radio blaring a football game. Hal had been squawking about retiring and sitting in his recliner since Josiah and his father-in-law started the mill ten years ago.

Hal's grandson opened the rear of the trailer and dropped the ramp. A few minutes later he drove a mini-forklift out with the first pallet of wood stock. With Simon showing where the wood should be stacked, the order was unloaded in minutes.

Josiah signed the invoice and handed it to Hal. He coughed again into his hand.

"Catching a cold?"

"No, it must be something in the air."

Hal shrugged. "You have anything to send out?"

Josiah shook his head. "Not until after Christmas. But I picked up a new account. Is Ohio too far for you to drive?"

"Depends how often. I still want to retire one day."

Josiah smiled. "Probably four times a year."

"Oh, that ain't nothing. Me and the boy can handle that run," he said, heading to his rig.

"Gut." Josiah figured it wouldn't be a problem when he arranged with Eli to supply wood for his banister business.

Hal shot a wave out the window as the truck rolled out of the drive. Josiah coughed hard to clear his lungs.

"Maybe you're catching a *kalt*." Simon slid the barn door shut.

He shook his head, although he had been feeling run-down the past several days. Stress. And the night before last he noticed a rash had broken out on his chest. He'd attributed most of that to Lindie's arrival. At least he'd prayed it was only stress. Now he wasn't so sure. Three times this week he had woken up with night sweats.

Josiah coughed again. "I need something to drink. Do you want *kaffi*?"

"*Nay, denki.*"

Josiah didn't just need something to wet his throat, he wanted to check on Lindie and Hannah.

♒

Lindie couldn't restrain her curiosity. The envelope Eli had handed Josiah at the bus station lay in plain sight on the kitchen table propped up against the saltshaker. Dare she count what it had cost to marry her off? The sign language book rested on the table also. She should work on learning how to communicate with Hannah. But she reached for the envelope instead and flipped it over. Sealed. Its thickness conveyed a large sum of cash. Money her brother perhaps had to borrow. She wished more than ever that she'd never tried to attend that singing. But wishful thinking couldn't turn back time.

The door creaked open and Lindie dropped the envelope and stepped away from the table just as Josiah entered the kitchen. He coughed into the crook of his arm as he crossed the room, then pulled a glass from the cabinet.

She breathed easier. He didn't seem to notice that she'd been inspecting the envelope.

He gulped the water, draining the glass. "Where's Hannah?"

"She hasn't *kumm* out of her room."

Lines deepened across his forehead and he darted toward the hallway.

Lindie followed as far as the kitchen entrance, stopped, and craned her neck around the wall.

40

Josiah continued toward the bedrooms and disappeared into the child's room.

Lindie wrung her hands. She hoped she hadn't said anything to get Hannah in trouble with her father.

A few moments later Josiah exited the room, his facial expression relaxed. He smiled as he approached Lindie in the hall. "Hannah's fine."

"Were you worried about her being alone in her room for so long?"

"I was worried she'd slipped out of the house unnoticed. She doesn't handle change very well. I thought maybe she went off to the woods."

"Alone?" The hair on Lindie's arms stood on end at the thought. "You need to tell her that's dangerous."

Josiah gave her a less than enthused look, but said nothing.

"She's okay to stay in her room?"

"She's fine. She's drawing a picture." He grabbed the envelope from the table, then turned to leave.

"What do you want me to make for lunch?"

"I'm *nett* fussy. If you don't find what you need in the pantry, canned goods are in the basement, and meat is in the *icehaus*," he said over his shoulder as he left the room.

She inched toward the sitting room. Hiding behind the wall, she caught a glimpse of him seated at the desk.

Josiah opened one of the drawers with a key, placed the envelope inside, then relocked the drawer. He sat there a moment, his elbows resting on the desk and fingers massaging his temples. Then he pushed back the chair and looked toward the kitchen.

Lindie spun around and leaned against the wall. As his footsteps drew closer, she scurried over to the sink, grabbing the glass off the counter. She was filling it when he entered her peripheral vision.

Josiah's mouth twisted as he scanned the counter.

Either her hands had turned clammy or the glass was sweating, but it nearly slipped from her grasp. "Thirsty?" She handed him the glass and grabbed the dishrag. The counter was clean, but she wiped it down anyway. She would do anything to exhaust some of her nervous energy.

"I haven't met your mother-in-law yet. Do they live close by?"

"*Mei* mother-in-law is deceased, and Simon lives in the *grossdaadi haus*, which is attached to the back of the workshop."

"It must have been hard for Hannah to lose her *mamm* and *mammi*." Lindie was a teenager when her parents died. If she hadn't been so close to her sister-in-law, despair might have overtaken her. Lindie was grateful that Eli and Margaret had taken her in.

"*Jah*, Hannah has had a lot to cope with." His face grimaced and he looked away. A moment later he said, "I suppose I better get back to work."

"*Jah*, me too." She continued cleaning the counter until he left the kitchen. Curious if she could see the *grossdaadi haus*, she stepped to the window. Black smoke billowed from two stovepipes extending from the roof of the workshop. The farthest pipe must be the woodstove in Simon's place. From where she was standing, she couldn't see anything that indicated a house was attached to the barn. She started to move away from the window when a woman driving a buggy came into view.

Chapter Five

Lindie rose to her tiptoes and craned her neck, trying to get a better view out of the kitchen window. Josiah waved at the driver and walked over to the buggy. A dark-haired woman in her midthirties climbed out and greeted Josiah with an overly friendly smile.

Lindie hadn't heard him mention having other relatives who lived in Cedar Ridge besides Simon, but she and Josiah hadn't spoken much either.

The woman wore a coy expression and kept her head bowed. She stood so close her shoulder practically touched his. She wasn't acting like a relative. Obviously she wasn't aware that Josiah was a married man now. Did he not notice that the woman was flirting with him? He walked around the back of her buggy.

They were standing close enough to the porch that their conversation would have drifted inside. If only the weather was favorable to open the window.

Lindie sighed. How could she consider eavesdropping on her new husband?

Josiah rounded the corner of the woman's buggy, a large wicker laundry basket in his arms. Following close behind him, the woman carried a covered baking dish.

Lindie moved away from the window as the woman followed him up the porch steps. Muffled chatter about how the woman knew he liked the meal she'd made was drowned out by the sound of stomping feet at the door. Lindie strained to hear Josiah's reply, but his voice was too low.

The front door creaked open.

Lindie grabbed the wet dishrag and began scrubbing the counter.

"*Denki* for the meal. I'll take it to the kitchen," Josiah said.

"Well, ah . . . I thought maybe—"

"Simon is expecting me back in the barn." He didn't wait for the woman's response. "I appreciate you stopping over with the laundry and supper," he said, softening his tone. "Let me walk you to your buggy."

Let me tell you I'm married was what Josiah should be saying.

A few moments later the door opened again. This time his heavy footsteps marched closer to the kitchen.

Lindie continued scrubbing the counter.

"You don't have to make anything for supper."

She lifted the rag. "That was thoughtful of your sister. Why didn't you invite her in for *kaffi*?"

"She's *nett mei* sister."

"Cousin?"

He shook his head.

Lindie resumed scouring, as if beet juice had stained the countertop.

"Weren't you cleaning the counter a few minutes ago?"

She shot him a sideways glare. "I thought this was what you

wanted from our arrangement. Someone to clean and cook." She stared at the dish on the table. "But I guess you don't need someone to cook after all, do you?"

"*Nett* tonight." He motioned to the sitting room. "And you don't have to catch up on the laundry either. Hannah can put her clothes away, and I'll sort through mine and Simon's when I *kumm* in later." He eyed the counter. "I suppose you won't stop scrubbing until you strip the finish off that surface, *jah*?"

She tossed the rag into the sink and planted her hands on her hips. "Why did you marry me? You seem to have all your needs taken care of."

He stared at her a moment.

Another man wouldn't allow his wife such boldness without rebuking her. Still, she wouldn't be made a fool of.

He closed the gap between them. "According to your *bruder*, you needed a fresh start." He turned away, then stopped. Facing her once more, he said, "And what makes you so sure *all* my needs are taken care of?"

Lindie swallowed. She didn't have the nerve to ask what he was referring to, and yet he raised his brows as though prompting her to say something. Her eyes burning, she blinked several times to clear her teary vision. Her brother paid Josiah to marry her—what more did he want?

She sprinted past him, out the door. Somehow she had to gain control of her emotions. They were playing havoc with her stomach.

"Lindie," Josiah said, stepping onto the porch. "I didn't mean to make you cry. I know being pregnant does some crazy things to your—"

"How much did *mei bruder* pay you to marry me?"

"What are you talking about?"

"Eli gave you money to marry me. How much did you charge for a marred *fraa*?"

His brows furrowed and he cocked his head. "It's too *kalt* out here. Let's talk inside."

"I must know so I can pay *mei bruder* back. I'll find a job. You can just tell him— Oh, what does it matter. Tell him you sent me away."

Josiah snorted. "Why would I send you away? We made a covenant before God. Until separated by *death*. Remember?" He reached for her arm and she flinched. "*Kumm* inside."

Lindie bowed her head. She should have kept her mouth shut.

Wives, be submissive to your husbands . . . The Lord had a good reason for reminding her of that command. She had a duty to her husband and was failing.

This time when he gave her arm a tug, she didn't resist.

Josiah guided her to the sitting room and stopped in front of his desk. He opened the drawer, removed a key, then unlocked the compartment where she had seen him put the envelope. "Are you talking about this?"

She nodded.

He handed her the envelope. "See for yourself."

She hesitated.

"It's all right. Open it."

Reluctantly, she emptied the contents in her hand. Along with the stack of twenties was a note. She handed him the money and unfolded the paper.

A few lines into the message, she wished she could seep into the floor. She peered up from the note. "He's ordering a shipment of elm wood?"

"Finding trees unaffected by the Dutch elm disease in Ohio is rare."

She'd never seen his pupils so large. So consuming. Yet she didn't detect any sign of judgment. She folded the paper. Her voice would fail her if she tried to apologize.

Josiah tapped the wooden chair. "Have a seat. I'm going to show you how to log his order into the book."

She tucked her chin against her chest and eased into the chair. Eli hadn't mentioned purchasing lumber.

Josiah crouched beside her and tilted his head so that their eyes met. "You're *nett* marred in *mei* eyes."

Tears wet her cheeks. She pushed them away, but they continued to flow like an undammed stream. If he knew about her past, he would change his mind.

Josiah held out his hankie. "Things will get better." He choked on his words as if he was trying to believe that himself. He turned his attention to the desk and pulled out a thick, leather-bound book from the drawer.

"We need to set up Eli as a new account." He avoided her eyes as he flipped through several pages, stopped on a blank sheet, then handed her the pen. "I'll walk you through entering the information." And he did, line by line, explaining as he went in a gentle but businesslike tone.

Perhaps he was referring to bookkeeping when he spoke of needs not being met. She did her best to listen carefully to the instructions, but she couldn't stop her mind from wandering back to his statement. *You're* nett *marred in* mei *eyes*. Even Moses, who had claimed to love her and wanted to marry her, couldn't say those words.

"There really isn't much to keeping the records straight," he said. "Of course this is somewhat backward. Usually the orders are filled and delivered before the account is paid." He flipped a few pages in the log. "See, this account hasn't been reconciled yet.

The far column is blank because the invoice hasn't been paid." He looked her in the eye. "Do you have any questions?"

She had plenty, but none that pertained to bookkeeping. "*Nay*," she said just above a whisper.

He closed the ledger. "Is there anything else you want to talk about?"

She swiped her dress sleeve over her wet face. "What do you want from me?"

"Just what I told you at the bus station." He scratched the back of his neck and started to walk away, but turned around. "I need you to watch *mei dochder*. If you could concentrate on caring for her, I'll be happy."

"Okay." He wasn't asking much. She could certainly fulfill that request. Children always flocked to her at gatherings.

"I forgot to give you this." He reached into his pocket and pulled out an envelope. "It arrived in the mail today," he said.

"Denki." She looked at the letter addressed to Lindie Plank. Seeing her married name in print seemed surreal. She waited until Josiah went outside to open the letter.

Dear Lindie,

You probably haven't settled in yet, but I wanted to send a letter right away. I miss you already and you have been gone only a few short days. What do you think of Josiah? Is Hannah still quiet? I ask because she didn't say anything when Eli and I had attended Caroline's funeral. I wish things had been different and I could have been present for your wedding. But someone would've had to watch Solomon and besides that, the bus fare is so much. I've been praying for you to have an easy transition to married life and to living in northern Michigan. How are the members? Have you made new friends? Please tell me everything. I'm anxious to hear how well everything is going. Write when you can.

Margaret

Soft footsteps entered the room.

Lindie smiled at Hannah. The girl glared. She didn't appear to like that Lindie was sitting in her father's desk chair.

Lindie crossed the room and knelt to the girl's level. *"Hiya."* She reached out for the girl's hand to give it a pat but Hannah crossed her arms. Her hair needed a good brushing, but this wasn't the time to tackle that matted mess.

Hannah's steely eyes shifted from Lindie to scan the room.

"Are you looking for your father?" Lindie asked once the girl's eyes fell back on her.

Hannah's brows crinkled.

"Are you"—she pointed at Hannah—"looking"—she pointed to her eyes, but realized even talking extra slow, she wasn't communicating very well. She lifted her index finger and darted into the kitchen. She snatched the sign language book off the table. Flipping through the pages, she walked back into the sitting room. She tried once again but had a difficult time holding the book open while manipulating her hands to form the letters.

Hannah clasped her hands behind her back.

Once Lindie finished spelling out "father," the girl turned and walked away. Lindie rubbed her temples. *Practice patience.* This was going to be more difficult than she thought, especially if Hannah continued to ignore her.

She set the book down and looked at the letter once more. She missed Margaret. She wished she were home.

⌇

Josiah hiked to the barn. He'd gotten into more than he'd bargained for with Lindie. She may have needed a fresh start, but he didn't have the ability to offer her any more than that. He wasn't in a stable state of mind to fix his own problems, let alone anyone else's. Besides, he wasn't sure what Lindie had run from—other than being an unwed mother.

Had he prayed about it more, he most likely wouldn't have made such an illogical decision. But he had panicked after finding Hannah dazed in the pond. He would have given anything to provide his daughter with a normal, balanced life. And a mother. He had only reached that desperate decision a few short hours before Eli had made his outrageous suggestion.

"Your *dochder* needs a mother. *Mei* sister needs a husband. It only makes sense." Even reciting Eli's words aloud didn't offer clarity. Now he was married to a woman who'd been hurt by another, and who would probably cry throughout her entire pregnancy. He didn't like that she referred to herself as marred. She had made choices that changed the course of her life. But so had he.

It didn't matter now how distorted their reasoning was for rushing into marriage. They had both agreed.

They took vows, made a covenant.

Josiah reached the barn and yanked open the door. His chest tightened as he forced a breath, which brought on a coughing fit.

Simon stopped hammering and looked up from his work. "You should have that cough looked at."

"Later." He grabbed another hammer from the workbench.

"I've got to fill these orders for the Christmas wreaths. We don't want to lose our new customers or the city's contract for next year." Cedar Ridge's city officials ordered cedar bough wreaths to hang from every lamppost on Main Street each year. Along with the regular accounts, this year he picked up several independent businesses as well, making this his busiest winter yet.

As he unraveled the chicken wire, the jagged end snagged his finger and it started to bleed. It was a lot of blood for something that looked no deeper than a scrape. He jammed his finger in his mouth, then removed it. It continued to bleed. He pulled out his hankie and wrapped it around his finger. He would apply salve later to keep the area free from infection, but right now he needed to wrap the chicken wire around the wood-framed wreath.

Simon stopped pounding. "Was that a buggy I heard earlier?"

"*Jah*, Ellen Yoder brought the laundry by and left a dish for supper."

Simon finished attaching the chicken wire, then looked up. "Did she meet your *fraa*?"

Josiah shook his head. He hoped he hadn't been rude when he kept Ellen from going past the threshold, but he wasn't up for introductions. As it was, he didn't know Lindie and he wasn't prepared to answer questions.

"Don't you usually pick up the laundry from her place?"

"I'm sure she was on her way to a get-together." Rebecca, the bishop's wife, most likely spread the news of his unscheduled wedding. Knowing Ellen, she probably delivered the clothes so she could gather more information to feed to the women's circle. Josiah loaded his arms with the cedar boughs that were piled on the floor, placed them on the worktable, then scratched his abdomen. The wood's natural oils had caused him to itch ever since he cut and hauled the boughs out of the woods. The rash had spread. Now it wasn't just on his stomach and chest, but his sides, and part of his back. The areas he couldn't reach were the worst. Sometimes he would rub against a post like a horse.

Simon pounded the stubborn section of chicken wire into place. He pushed that one aside and grabbed another wood-framed wreath. "I wish you would have thought about what this stress would do to you."

Josiah shrugged off the comment, hoping his father-in-law wouldn't dwell on what was done. Stress was part of the adjustment period, but nothing compared to what he experienced when Caroline died or the hours he spent by Hannah's hospital bed, waiting for some sign that she would wake from her coma.

"I don't want you to wear yourself down again."

"It's *nett* the same." Josiah's clipped response stifled further discussion.

They worked in silence until mealtime, then lumbered toward the house. Simon's limp appeared more pronounced today. Josiah walked slowly in case his father-in-law's hip gave out.

Lindie stood on the porch, her back facing them, her hands clutching the railing.

Josiah tapped Simon's shoulder. "Give me a minute, will you?" He waited for Simon to go inside, then he approached Lindie. "Everything okay?"

"Supper is ready. I reheated the food your woman friend brought over," she said without facing him.

"Let's go eat while it's hot." He half turned, but stopped when she didn't budge. "Something's wrong. What is it?"

"I just need some air."

He moved closer to get a glimpse of her face. Sullen. "Homesick?"

"*Jah*," she whispered.

He'd warned her it would be a hard adjustment. The letter she received probably made her miss her family.

Josiah caught a glimpse of Simon standing at the window. He entered the house alone and braced for Simon's comment.

"I didn't realize how hungry I was." Josiah patted his stomach. "How about you?"

"*Jah*, I'm ready to eat." He flipped his thumb over his shoulder. "Doesn't your *fraa* know it's time to eat? Most women work hard to please their husbands."

She needed time, but Simon may not understand that. The Lord knew she had more to adjust to than any other newly married woman. Besides, at twenty-two, she was still young. Unlike Caroline, who became a wife and mother naturally, Lindie stepped into a role she didn't want—at least not with him.

Lindie wasn't prepared for marriage and motherhood. His daughter's snarly hair was proof of that. Hannah sat at the table, her dress wrinkled and prayer *kapp* missing. He wondered if Lindie had even tried to do something about his child's unkempt appearance. But if he asked Hannah why she wasn't wearing her *kapp*, Simon would have something to say about that. As it was, Hannah and Simon's relationship was strained. His father-in-law believed a child needed nonverbal clues, such as not being included in table conversations, to learn that inappropriate actions like running off wouldn't be tolerated. Josiah wasn't sure Hannah learned anything but ways to retreat even deeper into her own world.

Josiah peeled the foil away from the glass dish. His mouth watered. Ellen had gone out of her way preparing a tender pot roast with mushroom gravy and red potatoes. He looked out the window. If Lindie didn't come in soon, Simon would expect him to insist she get in the house. Josiah didn't want to enforce his authority. It was unrealistic to believe their arranged marriage wouldn't come with some wrinkles. Homesickness for one, remorse another.

Josiah took his place at the table. Hannah sat on his left and Simon at the opposite end. Josiah tried to peek out the window without Simon noticing. Lindie hadn't moved. Did she realize she was holding up the meal? In a few minutes, the fading sun would limit his ability to see outside. Then he'd never get her attention without knocking on the windowpane. That would only rile Simon up over the matter, which wouldn't be good for any of them. Lindie wouldn't be long. If not hunger, the drop in temperature should bring her in at any moment.

Hannah wiggled in her chair.

Simon cleared his throat. "So how does Hannah get along with your new *fr*—"

"Her name is Lindie." He didn't want Simon's reference to be how Hannah learned the news. He turned his attention to his daughter, who was staring at him. Her expression was blank. He smiled warmly at her, but the gesture failed to elicit a response. His child's empty stare cut through his heart. He wished he knew what hid behind those big brown eyes of hers.

Simon heaped a spoonful of potatoes onto his plate and passed the bowl to Josiah. "What is she doing outside anyway?"

Josiah shrugged, then forked a chunk of meat and lowered it onto Hannah's plate.

"It seems as though mealtime would be important to your *fraa*."

Josiah stood. "Let me get you some *kaffi*." He didn't want to discuss this now, especially not in front of his daughter. She could read lips. Although she hadn't shown any interest in joining conversations lately. Even though she was born deaf, she could talk some. But she had chosen not to since her mother died.

With his back turned from them, Josiah explained, "I haven't told Hannah that Lindie and I are married."

"The child's bound to suspect something. The woman is living under your roof."

Josiah jerked around. He blew out a breath; she hadn't been watching her grandfather's lips. Josiah raised his brow in an effort to remind Simon this was something he didn't wish to discuss. Not now.

Simon wasn't one to take advice from others, especially not his son-in-law. "The child's already troubled in the mind."

His father-in-law wasn't saying anything new. Hannah required the same level of supervision as a toddler. And that was something Lindie was supposed to do.

Josiah squeezed his eyes shut for a moment and then reached inside the cabinet for cups. He had enough problems. To top it off, Lindie didn't seem to have enough sense to come in from the cold, or eat for two. She was certainly putting him in an awkward position in front of his father-in-law. The woman was homesick and he was miserable. He needed to pray now that his decision didn't cause Hannah to retreat further. He'd lost his wife. Was it too much to ask God to give him back his little girl?

Simon cleared his throat.

Josiah looked over his shoulder as Lindie wandered into the kitchen. Her red button nose and rosy cheeks masked her pasty complexion and gave her a nice winter's glow. Josiah averted his eyes. She was nice to look at. And under a normal covenant of this sort, a striking wife was a welcome distraction. But he couldn't allow himself that luxury. He needed her to partner with him in making this arrangement work.

"Have a seat," he said, picking up the coffee cups. "I'll bring yours to the table."

"Denki." Her answer was faint. Perhaps Simon's scowl had intimidated her.

They were silent the remainder of the meal. Simon was the first to clean his plate and leave the table, mumbling something about turning in early.

Lindie poked at her food.

The only one who didn't seem affected by the tension in the room was Hannah. But that was about to change.

Chapter Six

Lindie had no more than showed Hannah the brush when the girl flung her arms wildly and raced off to her bedroom. Lindie didn't feel cut out to be a mother. She had to try another approach to reach the child.

Her stomach roiled and she darted out to the porch. Was she going to be sick every morning? She wished Margaret lived close by so she could ask her sister-in-law if this was normal. It didn't feel right. But nothing did. She guessed her insides were rebelling so much today because of all the crying she'd done during the night. How do you stop thinking about home? Even Josiah seemed beside himself not knowing how to help her. The situation wasn't going to change. She needed to accept her new life.

Jesus, I'm so lonely. She lifted her face toward the sun and closed her eyes. *Is all this a mistake? Hannah refuses to communicate, Josiah is tolerant, and Simon hasn't uttered a word to me since our introduction. He's made it clear he doesn't like that Josiah married me.*

Lindie had no clear purpose. Josiah was self-sufficient. Hannah hid in her bedroom most of the time, and when they were in the same room, she ignored Lindie. Studying the sign language book was of no value if she couldn't practice the gestures with someone.

Lindie squinted from the sun's reflection off the snow. This was the first day since her arrival that there weren't any looming snow clouds. It looked like a good day to catch up on laundry.

She went inside, kicked her shoes off at the door, and hurried down the hall toward the bedrooms. It wasn't long before footsteps tromped down the hall.

"Lindie?" Josiah knocked on the door. "Are you in there?"

"*Jah*, you can *kumm* in."

He opened the door and poked his head inside. "Were you planning to rest for a while?"

"*Nay*." She bent down and collected the pile of dirty clothes. "I'm going to do some laundry. Is your friend doing your clothes, or should I collect them from your room?"

He stepped inside the bedroom. "I plan on telling Hannah about our marriage and I had hoped you would join me."

"*Ach*, I'm *nett* sure that's a *gut* idea." She wouldn't be able to follow the hand gestures. She hadn't yet learned the whole finger-spelling alphabet, and certainly hadn't progressed to words. Why would he need her there? She scanned the floor for more clothes even though she was sure she'd collected everything.

He sighed. The weight of disappointment in his tone wasn't lost on Lindie. He crossed his arms over his chest.

"I can't force you to take on a role that should *kumm* natural," he said.

She clutched the clothes against her chest. "And what role are you referring to? It's obvious I've failed to meet your expectations, but please clarify if it's the role of taking care of Caroline's child or her husband."

"This isn't about me. We had an agreement about Hannah."

A MIRACLE OF HOPE

He groaned under his breath. "Lindie," he said, stretching out her name pathetically. "Don't you think it would be best if we talk with her together? She needs to know that"—he cleared his throat—"we're married and . . . you're her . . . new . . ." He turned his head and coughed into his hand. *"Mamm."*

Lindie tried *not* to concentrate on how difficult it seemed for him to say those words aloud. Still, it hurt. Her mouth quivered as she tried to force a smile.

How much would he tell Hannah about their marital conditions? She was too young to understand what a marriage of convenience meant. Yet wouldn't she question why they didn't share the same bedroom? Had he prayed for wisdom? Children learned from example—even poor examples. No parent would want their daughter trapped in a loveless marriage.

"Will you?" he said softly.

She swallowed hard through her throat's tightness. "If you believe it's wise."

"Jah, I do."

She needed to support them. After all, they were in this mess together. The laundry could wait. She tossed the clothes into a pile on the bed. "You don't expect me to talk, do you? I don't know any sign language."

His jaw clenched. "Talk slow and she'll read your lips."

Only if she wants to.

He rubbed the back of his neck. "I'll translate for you."

"Okay."

Josiah took a step, then turned back to face her. "Let's pray first." He reached for her hand and led her to the side of the bed where they knelt together.

"Father God, I ask that you give me wisdom and guidance in what to say to Hannah. Sometimes she's unreachable . . ."

Lindie peeked at Josiah when his prayer fell silent. Tears collected in his closed eyes and wet the creases. *Lord, give him strength.*

"Aemen." He opened his eyes, blinked a few times, then swept his shirtsleeve over his face. "Ready?"

⁓

"You are not making sense." Josiah signed the words as he spoke them. "Slow down."

The child's eyes narrowed as her fingers flew in quick hand motions.

Lindie bit the inside of her cheek. She didn't relish being the topic of a conversation she could only follow by trying to decipher facial expressions. Why wasn't Josiah translating his daughter's words? She studied the wood grains embedded in the table.

"Yes. She and I are married."

Lindie looked up and forced a smile, but Hannah still glared.

"Can you welcome Lindie to the family?" Josiah nodded, encouraging his daughter to agree.

Hannah fisted her hands.

Message received.

Lurching forward in his chair, Josiah gestured without verbalizing the words, leaving Lindie lost.

Hannah shoved away from the table and bolted off the seat.

Josiah jumped up and grabbed her arm to prevent her from leaving the kitchen. He circled her around to face Lindie, knelt in front of the child, then signed and said, "Apologize."

Forcing Hannah to accept her was too much. Lindie stood. "Please, Josiah, give her time."

The child's empty stare tore at Lindie's heart. She wasn't sure she could have accepted a new mother if her father had lived to remarry.

Josiah tapped his daughter's shoulder, made a few hand gestures, and stopped when Hannah covered her eyes.

Stomach acid washed up the back of her throat. She dashed past them and out the door. But once outside, inhaling the cold air helped the queasiness subside. With her arms folded across her chest, she paced up and down the length of the porch. The cold air bit, and yet she couldn't bring herself to go back inside. She made another pass to the end of the porch and stopped at the corner. This marriage was a mistake. She squeezed her eyes closed. "*Ach*, Lord, Josiah's probably saying the same thing."

"That we're in a jam?" Josiah closed the door behind him.

She jolted.

He crossed the porch and stood beside her. "*Jah*, I said that too." He leaned down, rested his forearms on the railing, and sighed. "Neither one of us thought this out."

She huffed and turned her back on him.

"I remember our conversation at the bus station. You were given a choice."

He didn't know her brother very well if he believed Eli had let her choose.

"Lindie," he said, moving in front of her. "It doesn't matter how we got to this point. We took vows in front of God, and we're in this for life."

"It isn't just about us."

"She'll get used to the idea." As though finalizing the statement in his mind, he nodded. "She will." He smiled. "I still believe in miracles."

Miracles took faith. Something she'd lost a significant amount of over the past few months. She marveled at his ability to hold on to any morsel of hope after everything he'd gone through. For his sake, she hoped for a miracle, because she didn't see this marriage working any other way.

※

Josiah burned off most of his frustration mucking out the horse stall. Hannah hadn't accepted Lindie, and Lindie hadn't accepted her new role. The stress was too much. He started coughing and had to stop shoveling to catch his breath. Sweat rolled down his face and stung his eyes. He went to reach for his hankie, then remembered he hadn't replaced the one he'd given Lindie to use.

Simon stepped around the corner. "I heard you coughing over in the milking area. You need to see a *doktah*."

Josiah couldn't think of that now. He had other problems to worry about besides his failing health. "Maybe I'll get a chance next week."

Simon leaned against the half wall. "You better *nett* put it off."

He had to. What if Doctor Ethridge wanted to run tests again? He already had enough to cope with. He leaned the shovel against the wall and picked up the wheelbarrow handles. Simon opened the stall door for Josiah, and thankfully, his father-in-law didn't follow along to continue his lecture.

Everyone coughs when he has a cold. He wasn't going to fret over the possibility that it might be more. And he wouldn't live in fear. Although he agreed with Simon on one thing—he was under too much stress. He dumped the contents of the wheelbarrow on the compost mound.

Josiah had given Hannah enough time to cool down. He left the wheelbarrow and strode across the snowy lawn to the house.

Dishes clanked in the kitchen as he passed through the sitting room and down the hallway to his daughter's room. Hannah was sitting on the bed, and when he sat on the edge of the mattress, she stuck her thumb in her mouth and stared at the wall.

Josiah tapped her shoulder. "You should give Lindie a chance," he signed once he gained her attention.

Her bottom lip puckered, her thumb never leaving her mouth. "She's your new *mamm.*"

Hannah shook her head and turned her back to him again.

God, how should I respond to her disobedience? If I allow these actions to go unpunished, will she become even more unruly? Josiah waited a few moments for Hannah to turn around on her own. When she didn't, he had no option.

He traipsed to the sitting room and removed the wooden paddle from the nail on the wall.

Lindie came out of the kitchen wiping her hands on her apron. "Were you able to get her to understand?" Her eyes widened when she looked at the paddle. "Please, Josiah, give her time."

"She turned her back in the middle of *mei* signing. I cannot allow her defiance."

Lindie reached for his arm. "This is all new. For all of us. Please, don't do something you might regret."

He eyed her hand grasping his arm. "Are you familiar with the verse in Proverbs that instructs prompt discipline?"

"I'm familiar with the scripture."

"Then leave me to do what I must do."

Her grip tightened. "You said you believe in miracles. Give her time to *kumm* around on her own."

How long would that take? His patience was wearing thin. But perhaps Lindie was right. He hung the paddle on the wall on his way outside. He needed air. Instead of going back out to the barn and having to dodge Simon's questions, he tramped through the field. A brisk walk through the snow should calm him, or exhaust him. And at the moment, he didn't care which.

~

Four days after Josiah told Hannah about their marriage, the child still refused to communicate. Lindie understood why the girl would reject her, but now she had stopped signing even to her father. Josiah rubbed his forehead frequently as though the entire ordeal had given him a continuous headache.

Lindie had managed to keep her distance, afraid she would say something wrong and cause more problems. But today it appeared she didn't have to say anything to get under his skin. Every cabinet he opened and shut caused her to flinch.

She set the stack of recipes written on index cards on the table and stood. "What are you looking for?"

"A glass." He turned his head to cough, shielding his mouth in his bent elbow.

"Your cough doesn't sound very *gut*. Are you okay?"

"I will be once I drink some water."

She looked away from his piercing glare and opened the correct cabinet. "I moved them," she said, reaching for a glass.

"So I see." He shifted his stance.

She ran the faucet and handed him a full glass. "It didn't make any sense having the glasses on the left when everyone is right-handed." Most men wouldn't care how the woman arranged the kitchen, but Josiah frowned as he held the glass up to his lips.

"Is this a problem?"

He set the glass down. "It won't be after you return everything to its rightful place."

Her mother used to rearrange the cabinets regularly, and Lindie couldn't recall her father ever getting upset. She didn't understand why something this minor would provoke such an inflamed response. She straightened her shoulders. "Why don't you tell me what you're really upset about? This isn't about my moving the dishes, is it?"

The sluggish movement of his Adam's apple as he drank made it look as though he was having difficulty swallowing. He set the glass on the counter, cleared his throat, then opened his mouth as if to say something, but stalked out of the room instead.

She took a step in his direction and stopped. *The right words at the right time will turn away wrath, but the wrong words at the wrong time will feed the fire.* These handed-down words of wisdom had worked for her mother. Growing up, Lindie had heard her mother quote the saying under her breath often. Lindie repeated her mother's words aloud. "It's better to hold your tongue than to say something you'll regret." This wasn't the time to be confrontational. She needed to try to fix things.

If her mother were alive, she would know how to advise her. Then again, she wouldn't want her mother to know what her life had become. Lindie sank down on the chair. So much for trying to make the kitchen more functional. She looked around the room. It would take hours to put everything back. Time she didn't have if she was to have the meal ready when Josiah and Simon ended their workday.

Lindie scanned the recipe card for chili, then collected all the ingredients except hamburger. Josiah had said the meat was in the *icehaus,* and hopefully she would find a pound or two of ground beef. At the door, she slipped on her cape, then remembered Hannah. Lindie didn't want her to be confused if she came out of her room and found the house empty. She wasn't sure how to convey to the girl that she was running out to the *icehaus* for meat, but she had to try.

Hannah sat on the floor, huddled in the corner, with a pad of paper on her lap. She didn't look up from her drawing as Lindie entered the room, or when she crouched down beside her. Lindie studied the picture, speechless at what she saw. Hannah had drawn a deer standing near a cluster of birch trees. The shading detail was thorough. No one would believe a child had drawn the picture.

She tapped Hannah's arm, then pointed to her picture. "That's beautiful." Even though she spoke slowly, Hannah's eyes narrowed.

Lindie pointed to herself. "I"—she smiled wide at the little girl—"like"—she pointed at the drawing. "I like your picture."

Hannah's despondence unnerved Lindie. Behind those dark brown eyes was a lonely child. Lindie understood that emptiness too well.

The girl pretended not to read lips, and Lindie wasn't about to let the child think she was frustrated. Lindie smiled again. "I'll be back in a few minutes." She stood and turned for the door, not expecting any response. The hem of Lindie's dress caught and she looked over her shoulder. Hannah was holding on to it.

The girl released the dress, pointed at the picture, then made a few hand gestures Lindie couldn't decipher.

She certainly didn't want to discourage Hannah. She looked again at the picture and smiled. "*Jah*, it's beautiful."

A slight lift at the corners of Hannah's mouth encouraged Lindie, but as she squatted next to her, Hannah stuck her thumb in her mouth and turned away. Not wishing to pressure Hannah, she stood back up. If she gave Hannah time, she hoped the girl would warm up to her eventually. Later, when she had a few extra minutes, she would spend more time with the sign language book. But right now, giving her space was more important. Besides, she still needed to find the ground beef. Before leaving the room, Lindie glanced again at Hannah, who hadn't changed positions. Lindie had made some progress. That should please Josiah. Maybe it would even lighten his mood.

The cold air nipped at her face as she crossed the snowy driveway. Next to the long pole barn stood a small shack. Since the other small outbuildings had firewood stacked up along their sides, she figured this was the *icehaus*. She unlatched the door and used her hip to nudge it open. The dark room would hold only two or three people. Frozen water jugs lined the walls. A few blocks of ice surrounded the food packages on the bench top. She wished she'd thought to bring a lantern since there were no windows. The opened door didn't allow much light. She wouldn't be able to read the markings on the brown paper packaging. After a few minutes of searching, her hands began to stiffen. She selected what she thought could be hamburger. If it wasn't, she would figure out something else to make with the meat.

Back in the house, she discovered the package wasn't beef, but ground venison. She hoped the deer meat cooked up the same. She fed the stove a few pieces of wood so the meat would brown up quickly. A gamey deer scent filled the air. A few hours later the pot of chili was still simmering on the stove.

Josiah entered the kitchen. "Simon will be in shortly."

"This is ready." She stirred the chili as he washed his hands at the sink.

"Where's Hannah?" He dried his hands on a dish towel.

She set the ladle on the counter. "I'll go get her."

"*Nay*, wait." He reached for her arm. "I want to talk with you a minute."

"I didn't have time to change the cupboards back to the way they were, but I will, after supper."

"Caroline was left-handed," he blurted.

"Ach." Now it all made sense. Why hadn't it crossed her mind that he would defend Caroline's arrangement?

"I'm going to try harder," he said. "Please have patience."

She nodded. Chili bubbles splashed onto the stove. Thankful for a distraction, she grabbed the pot holders.

Josiah stopped her from reaching for the pot. "Let me lift it." He moved the sputtering chili.

"I'll go get Hannah." Lindie hurried down the hall to Hannah's room and opened the door.

It was empty.

Chapter Seven

Lindie darted out the door behind Josiah. Why hadn't she checked on the girl when she returned from the *icehaus*?

"I'll find her." Josiah pointed to the house. "Go back inside where it's warm."

"I'm *nett kalt*. I want to help." She needed to help. This was her fault.

"Fine." He stomped toward the pasture gate, his breath coming in thick, white puffs.

Lindie looked across the field. Empty. Where had the child gone? She cupped her mouth around her hand and called, "Hannah," then listened for a response.

Nothing. She called again.

Josiah continued walking. His long-legged stride forced her to jog to keep pace. When he came to the wooden, split rail fence, he crawled between the timbers of the fence, then waited for her.

She lifted her dress midcalf and swung her leg between the rough-cut timbers, catching her prayer *kapp* on the fence. She couldn't straddle the fence and pull her *kapp* loose at the same

69

time, at least not without ripping the material or losing a chunk of hair.

"Hold still." Josiah squatted.

His warm breath fanned her face as he worked his hand over the board.

"Ouch." He jerked his hand away and examined his index finger.

"Are you okay?"

"It's nothing." He brought it to his lips.

"Let me see if it's bleeding."

He pulled his finger out of his mouth, but didn't show her the wound.

She wasn't thinking clearly. Even if he'd cut his finger through to the bone, she couldn't do anything about it with her head still caught in such an awkward position. "*Nett* this minute, but you might need a tetanus shot if you cut your finger on a rusty nail."

"I'm fine. It wasn't a nail." He shrugged it off, shaking his finger. Then he reached over her again. After a few short tugs, he worked the cloth free from whatever had snagged her *kapp*. He clutched her elbow and steadied her as she climbed the rest of the way through.

"*Denki.*" She readjusted her *kapp*. "I probably should've used the gate."

"That's what most pregnant women would do," he mumbled under his breath as he stomped away.

She was doing nothing but slowing him down. Her feet sank into the snow as she hurried to catch up to him. She cupped her hands around her mouth and called for Hannah again.

Josiah smirked.

She ignored him and repeated the call, her voice strained. His expression hadn't changed. Why was he looking at her like that?

"You do remember she's deaf, *jah?*" he said.

Lindie dropped her hands to her sides. "What a *dummkopp* I am."

He continued on course.

A few minutes later they reached the end of the pasture. Lindie spotted a fence. She wouldn't make the same mistake twice.

"You better stay on that side."

He didn't need to look so disgusted. "I can make it."

"There isn't a gate." He lowered his gaze to her belly and scowled.

She flinched. So, he thought she couldn't do it simply because she was pregnant? She would be happy if climbing a fence were the most difficult thing she'd face while married to him.

He crawled through with ease.

Lindie lifted her foot to the bottom board. Grabbing hold of the top board, she pulled herself up. If she couldn't crawl between the boards, she could climb over them.

"*Ach.* You don't listen, do you?"

"I can do this." But even as she spoke, he wrapped his hands around her waist and lifted her down. In his arms, her muscles tensed and the air left her lungs. He released his hold the moment her feet landed on the ground. It took several seconds to regain her composure.

Is he blushing? Lindie bit her lip to keep from smiling. She sucked in a breath and made a subtle move to touch her own warm cheeks. She hated it when her face betrayed her. *He hasn't noticed?* He seemed to make a point not to look her in the eye.

She straightened her dress and when she looked up, he was stalking toward the woods. She hurried to join him. "So what makes you think she went this way?"

"I'm following her tracks." He pointed to the small footprints in the snow.

Having only his back to stare at, the tracks she saw were his. She would remember this if Hannah disappeared again.

Josiah's long strides made it impossible for her to use his tracks to avoid bogging down in the ankle-deep snow. Her shoes were soaked and she couldn't feel her toes, much less wiggle them to keep the circulation flowing. At least her hands were tucked warm inside her cape.

He stopped.

"Is something wrong?" Lindie leaned to one side and looked around Josiah. She saw no path cutting through the dense woodlands. "Do you think Hannah would go in there?" She shuddered.

"*Jah*, I know she would." He ducked under a low-hanging branch.

Lindie followed. The lighting was dim and long shadows caused the hair on her arms to stand on end. A branch snapped, and she flinched.

Josiah continued, but she froze. Eyes closed, her heart hammered her ribs with an unsteady beat. Blood whooshed in her ears. Just like the night she sped through the woods. Only not the same. This was daytime, hundreds of miles away. And leaves covered the ground, not snow. *Focus on this moment.* Still, the scent of dead leaves from that night filled her senses, cloaking her with memories she wanted to erase.

A gunshot rang out.

Lindie jolted. It sounded close. Eyeing the direction of the shot, her heartbeat quickened.

"Stay here." Josiah ducked under a low-hanging limb and disappeared into the dense forest.

Lindie wrapped her arms around herself and made a

circle, scanning her surroundings. *Lord, please keep Hannah safe.* Branches snapped in the distance. *Me too, God. I'm so afraid.* She squeezed her eyes closed and silently recited, *Even though I walk through the valley of the shadow of death, I will fear no evil.* She repeated the scripture multiple times before calling out, "Josiah!" She looked one way, then the other. Nothing. She needed to focus.

Look for tracks.

She spotted Josiah's heavy boot prints and moved in that direction. She pushed a pine branch out of her path and it snapped back, launching the snow that had collected on the needles. Tears spilled down her cheeks. "I will fear no evil . . . for thou art with me," she said aloud. Crossing over a fallen log, she slipped, but kept her balance by flailing her arms. *"Ach,* Josiah, why did you leave me alone?"

She followed his tracks several more feet until they led to a steep hill. She paused to catch her breath before trying to tackle the uphill hike. The cold air tightened her lungs and she coughed.

The transverse climb wasn't as difficult as Lindie had anticipated. She only slipped once and caught herself from falling by digging the toe of her shoe deeper into the side of the hill. Lindie regained her footing as Josiah appeared at the top and reached out his hand.

"Denki." She swiped the snow from the front of her dress.

"I thought you were going to wait."

Lindie winced at the scowl on his face.

"You should have returned home." He tramped forward, only to stop a few feet later. He turned his head both ways as though trying to determine which way to go next. "Stay here a minute," he said, plowing through the snow. He looked back at Lindie and waved. "I see her."

Lindie motioned for him to go. She didn't want to hold him up any longer. "I'll catch up." As soon as she caught her breath.

Hannah sat under a large tree, seemingly in her own world, as she twirled a crinkled reddish-brown leaf by its stem. Where she'd found the leaf in the snow-covered woods was beyond Lindie. She drew closer, but not so close as to invade their privacy. She needed to move to keep the blood circulating in her nearly frozen feet.

Hannah jolted when her father clasped her arm. She stood.

"I told you not to leave the house without asking." His forehead wrinkled as he repeated his verbal scolding with precise hand movements. "What did I tell you about running off?"

Hannah's hands remained tucked at her sides. She looked away, demonstrating no remorse for her conduct.

With his hand, Josiah turned his daughter's face toward his and with two fingers, pointed at his eyes and said, "Don't turn away from me when I'm speaking to you. Why did you disobey my instructions?"

Her empty stare seemed to reach beyond him.

"Lord, have mercy," Lindie whispered. Her father would have taken her to the woodshed had she shown the same defiance at that age. At any age.

A few feet away, branches snapped and a deer stumbled through the thicket of tall pines and collapsed.

Hannah ran toward the wounded animal, but Josiah stopped her. He signed something that made her mouth quiver and look at the deer longingly. He tapped her shoulder. When she faced him, he signed something else.

A hunter dressed in orange, following the same path as the deer's through the underbrush, came into view. Josiah lifted his hand to signal Hannah to stay and approached the hunter.

Lindie overheard Josiah say something about hunting on private property. However, she was more concerned about Hannah as the girl inched toward the fallen deer. Before she could reach the child, Hannah had knelt beside the deer and placed her hand on the animal's neck. Her mouth moved, but Lindie could hear no words.

The doe was lifeless.

Lindie edged closer. Wild animals, especially wounded ones, were unpredictable. Deer blood covered Hannah's hand. Lindie tapped the child's arm, but she kept her eyes closed.

A limb above them cracked and Lindie instinctively leaned over Hannah. A small ice-coated branch, no bigger than Lindie's arm, fell to the ground less than a foot away. She tugged Hannah's arm. This time the girl looked at her with penetrating eyes and lifted her hand from the animal's gunshot wound.

The deer stood, sniffed into the wind, and flicked its white tail. Lindie gasped when it sprinted a few feet and paused near a cluster of birch trees. Hannah's drawing was a perfect depiction of the deer standing in front of the trees. So perfect, it seemed almost eerie that a child so young could have drawn with such precision. Lindie studied the group of trees. The peeling white bark, the angle the trunks leaned, it all matched her drawing exactly. The deer twitched its tail again and leaped into the underbrush.

The sound of crunching snow neared. Josiah's attention was fixed on Hannah.

"You will be punished," he said and signed at the same time.

"Nay." Lindie crossed the distance to meet him. "Please, don't."

"Stay out of this." Josiah walked past her to reach Hannah. He cupped his daughter's shoulder with his hand and nudged her forward.

"Did you see what happened?" Lindie didn't wait for his response. "The deer got up. She laid her hands on it and I saw her mouth moving. She was praying."

"It will go off into the woods and die."

"*Nay.* I don't think so." She shook her head. "I think it was already dead when she laid her hand on its wound." She motioned to Hannah. "Look at her hand. It's covered in blood."

Josiah stopped Hannah, looked at her hand, then knelt and gathered a handful of snow.

"Please, don't be upset. I think she did ask permission," Lindie said as he washed Hannah's hand with snow. "She drew a picture of a deer." Lindie pointed to the birch trees. "Standing in front of those exact trees. When she showed me the drawing, she also tried to communicate something."

"When did she do that?"

"Earlier. She must've thought I had okayed her leaving. But I was trying to tell her the picture was beautiful."

His jaw tightened. He rubbed the blood off his hands in the snow, stood, then nudged Hannah forward.

"Don't you see? She might have asked to *kumm* here. Maybe to draw more pictures . . ." *Or lay hands on a fallen deer.* "I don't know. But she made the effort to communicate with me. It's a step." She expected him to be pleased, but his stern expression never changed.

Hannah shuffled a few steps and looked over her shoulder. For a second, her eyes connected with Lindie's, then she looked up at the treetops.

Lindie's heart grew heavy at the dull cast in Hannah's eyes.

"She didn't bring her pad of paper," Josiah said, as if he felt the need to reprimand Lindie for Hannah's leaving the house. He grimaced. "You need to start studying that sign language book. You spent too much time rearranging the kitchen. Have you studied today?"

Lindie shook her head.

"It's important that you're able to communicate with her."

Lindie swallowed hard, but it didn't relieve the scratchiness in her throat.

"And why didn't you stay put back there as I told you?"

"I was afraid," she said. She studied the snowy path. She didn't want him to ask why the woods frightened her.

He hung back a few steps as Hannah marched onward. "I am sorry for sounding insensitive," he said to Lindie. "Hunting season makes me nervous. Hunters don't always pay attention to private property signs."

"What did he say to you?"

"He shot the doe on state land but was caught up tracking it and wasn't aware he'd crossed onto private property. It's just not safe to be in the woods during rifle season, especially if you are not wearing a bright-orange vest."

A shudder reached her core. Hannah's running off could have been so much worse. "I'm sorry. I wanted to help you find her . . . but I ended up slowing you down."

His expression softened. "You didn't know." He scratched his beard. "So what were you afraid of, bears?"

"Bears!"

"Shh. You might wake them." He held a straight face for several seconds before a grin erupted. "*Kumm* on. Stay close and I'll try *nett* to go so fast."

"Don't worry." Lindie scanned the area. "I plan to stick to you like sap," she mumbled under her breath.

He coughed into his hand.

"Are you getting sick?"

"Hope *nett*." He coughed again.

"You sound croaky."

Without breaking his stride, he peered at her over his shoulder. "That's probably *nett* a compliment, is it?"

"Are there really bears in these woods?"

"*Jah*." He searched the ground. "So watch out for *mei* traps. The iron teeth will jerk your foot clean off and leave a stump for a leg."

She gulped and looked at Hannah up ahead. "You better get up there with her so you can watch where Hannah steps."

A wide smile broke across his face. "You're gullible. I like that." He continued walking.

At least he liked something about her. Lindie did her best to stay in his tracks.

The three of them walked back to the house in silence. Although it took longer, Lindie was grateful that Josiah routed them around the pasture so she didn't have to crawl through or over the wooden fence.

Once at the house, he opened the door and Hannah slipped in under his arm.

Lindie waited. "I think I'll stay out here a few minutes." Her stomach was threatening to erupt and she didn't want to go inside only to bolt back out the door. She crossed the porch and leaned over the railing. Dry heaves racked her sides.

He came up beside her. "I didn't mean to snap at you. Right *nau*, I'm very frustrated with Hannah."

She shouldn't have interfered. She had crossed him in front of his daughter.

Josiah sighed. "Hannah hasn't been right since her *mamm* died." He looked away a moment. "She and Caroline had come out to the woods where Simon and I were cutting trees to bring us lunch. Hannah raced ahead." He paused and picked at a loose paint chip on the banister. "The tree we were cutting . . . fell against another tree, which then snapped. The trunk crushed Caroline, who had run after Hannah. One of the smaller limbs struck Hannah and knocked her out."

How tragic for a young child to have gone through so much. Lindie knew firsthand what it was like to lose a parent.

"Hannah spent several weeks in a coma. A subdural hematoma, the doctors called it. When I brought her home . . ." He blinked a few times and tilted his face toward the sky. "Hannah was devastated to discover Caroline had died."

"I'm sorry." Her words choked and her eyes burned. Why hadn't Josiah told her this when she first arrived?

"She hasn't been the same since. Most of the time she's in this daze. In a world where I can't reach her. She wanders off alone." He rubbed his bearded jaw. "I suppose none of us have been the same. We closed the sawmill—at least the timbering portion. I avoided the woods altogether. Until Hannah's wandering off forced me back . . ."

"I'll watch her more carefully. I'll learn sign language." He should at least be able to depend on her to keep his child safe. The idea of stray bullets or strangers lurking in the woods terrified her. "Have you considered locking the door so she doesn't get out?"

"*Jah*. But after a member's *haus* caught on fire, I couldn't risk that."

"I'll do better," she said.

The deep-rooted lines across Josiah's forehead eased. He held her gaze a long moment, then smiled. "Aren't you *kalt*?"

She was beyond cold. Yet she wasn't ready to go inside. She needed a few more minutes for her stomach to settle.

"Icicles are going to form on your eyebrows if you don't *kumm* inside."

She swept the back of her hand across her face and forced a smile. "I'll be in shortly." His life was in chaos and yet he was worried about her. She should feel blessed to be his wife.

"Well, don't stay out here long." Josiah leaned closer. "It isn't *gut* for the *boppli*." He turned and went inside.

She rested her head against the banister post and closed her eyes. This was her childhood dream. She was married, pregnant, and had a husband who worried about what was good for the baby. She massaged her forehead. If only things were different.

These were the times she missed her mother the most. Her mother would know how to gain Hannah's heart. How to be a *gut fraa*. And her mother wouldn't struggle to bond with an innocent *boppli*—*a miracle growing in her womb, a gift from God*—her mother would've proclaimed.

Lindie looked up at the sky. If her mother were still alive, she would be disappointed in her daughter too.

Chapter Eight

L indie stays out on that porch a lot, doesn't she?" Simon moved away from the window, shaking his head. "The woman doesn't have much sense if she doesn't know to *kumm* in from the *kalt*."

"She's *nett* adjusting very well." Josiah opened the cupboard expecting to find coffee mugs and found plates. She wasn't the only one having trouble adjusting. Having a woman in the house again was difficult. In the next cabinet, he found the mugs. Josiah removed three and filled them with coffee.

Simon pulled a chair out and sat. "Where did you find Hannah?"

"Sitting under a tree a few feet from where the timbering trail stops." Josiah set the cups on the table, then returned to the stove and stirred the leftover chili. "Have you seen any of her drawings?"

"I've seen some of her scribbling. Why?"

Josiah shrugged. "Anything that looked like a deer or trees?"

"*Nay.* They don't look like anything." The lines across Simon's forehead deepened. "Is something wrong?"

Josiah shook his head. "It's nothing." As he filled the bowls with chili, Lindie entered his peripheral vision.

"Your husband finished preparing the meal," Simon snipped. He eyed the chair where she usually sat. "You might as well sit while he serves you."

Lindie sat down but immediately bounced back up. "Where is Hannah?"

"In her room." Josiah carried the bowls to the table. One he gave to Simon, the other he set down at Lindie's place.

"I'll let Hannah know it's time to eat," Lindie said.

Simon cleared his throat.

"I sent her to her room." Josiah motioned to the chair. "Have a seat."

Lindie glimpsed Simon's scowl and eased back into the seat.

Josiah closed his eyes, said a quick grace, then began eating. He was halfway through his meal before he noticed Lindie's bowl sat untouched. "You're *nett* hungry?"

She shook her head, but as he continued to look at her, she picked up the spoon and took a few bites.

Her big blue eyes stole his breath. It was hard to recall the same freckle-faced redhead whom he met visiting Eli's district so many years ago. Her *kapp* was still askew on her head. She hadn't adjusted it after getting it caught on the fence. Her shiny, coiled locks spilling out captivated his attention. His mind wandered with thoughts of combing his fingers through her hair and unraveling the rest of those soft curls. His thoughts would be normal had they enjoyed a normal marriage.

Josiah pushed back in his chair and stood. "Anyone need their *kaffi* warmed?"

Simon and Lindie shook their heads as Josiah grabbed his cup. He dumped the perfectly fine coffee into the sink and took a long, calming breath while refilling his cup. Returning to the table, he arched his brows at Lindie and used his free hand to brush up the back of his neck.

She cocked her head and shrugged, failing to understand that a good portion of her hair had come undone.

How could she not feel her hair spilling over her neck? Caroline would have known. His *fraa* would've—his *fraa*. He bit his lip. How long would it be before he recognized Lindie as his wife?

Josiah waited for Simon to look away, then tried to get Lindie's attention. Once more he shoved his hand up the back of his neck.

She reached to the back of her head and ran her fingers down a long red strand. Crimson-faced, she tucked it back under the *kapp*. Her eyes pleaded with Josiah's, as if seeking his approval.

Josiah nodded slightly. He probably could have let it go. Simon hadn't lifted his head from his bowl since he was served. Josiah shifted on his chair. Many times a woman's hair came loose during the day, especially after working in the garden or scrubbing floors. Now he'd led Lindie to believe *she* had done something inappropriate. His mind wandered again into restricted areas, imagining her soft curls between his fingers. No! He wouldn't let these wayward thoughts interfere with the pledge of never-ending love he'd made to Caroline.

Simon ate quickly, then used the first opportunity to leave, stating he had some things in the barn that required his attention.

Josiah understood. This new family structure was difficult on all of them. He, too, planned to find a reason to go into town later just to get away from the house for a few hours. That is, if he could trust Lindie to keep an eye on Hannah. He still needed to talk with his daughter about running off, but first he wanted to see the picture of the deer—if there really was such a picture. He hoped Lindie hadn't made it up as a way to stop him from punishing Hannah. If so, he would put an end to such nonsense straightaway. He needed a helpmate, not more problems.

꩜

Lindie had eaten all she could of the chili. The next time she made chili, she would limit the amount of seasoning. At least while she was pregnant. Her stomach would remain active the rest of the day.

She stood and reached for Josiah's empty bowl. "Would you like more?"

"*Nay, denki*," he mumbled, too preoccupied with examining his finger to look up.

She looked over his shoulder. "Is it a sliver?"

"*Jah.*" He twisted his finger sideways and tried to pinch the area with his other fingers.

Lindie set the dishes in the sink and turned on the tap. "*Kumm* wash your hand. Do you have any rubbing alcohol?"

"Under the sink." He chewed the edge of his finger.

"You won't get it out that way either." She grabbed the alcohol, then tapped the sink basin. "*Kumm* on. Let me take a look."

He hesitated.

She had her hands washed before he'd budged from the chair. Josiah crossed the room and met her at the sink.

She handed him the bar of lye. "Soap it *gut*."

She'd never seen someone so slow to lather his hands. Hadn't he had a sliver removed before? When he finally finished, she handed him a clean dish towel from the drawer and waited for him to dry them off.

"Okay, let's take a look." She reached for his hand and examined the reddened area on his finger. It was difficult to concentrate with him standing so close. She squeezed his finger on both sides of the splinter. Too deep. It didn't move. She released his hand.

"*Denki* anyway," he said.

"I'm *nett* done." She reached to the front of her dress and removed one of the straight pins she used to secure the opening.

His eyes widened.

Lindie searched the front of her dress. Removing the pin had not left a large gap. She would replace it once she took care of his finger.

She doused the pin with rubbing alcohol, then grabbed his hand once more.

He inched closer, his warm breath caressing her face.

She twisted his finger to get a better grip, causing him to flinch. "I'm sorry."

"That's okay." He changed positions, and moving closer still, he rested his uninjured hand on her waist.

Her hands trembled as they stood nose to nose in this intimate position.

"Tell me if I hurt you," she said.

"You won't."

Her knees weakened as his breath brushed her ear. She jabbed the pin under his skin. The muscles in his forearm tightened and she withdrew the pin.

He tapped her hip, but his smile turned into a frown.

"What's wrong?"

"Your bony hip isn't much to grab hold of."

She ignored his comment. "You better hold on to something. This is deep." Concentrating on her effort, she quickly finished the task. "Okay, I think I got it all."

He looked over his injured finger while his other hand remained on her hip.

The floor creaked behind them.

Lindie turned to see Hannah standing there, her mouth agape, her narrow eyes darting from her father to Lindie. The girl spun and ran down the hall.

Josiah shook his head slowly. "I told her she wasn't allowed to leave her room."

"The child's hungry."

His brows rutted. "The child is disobedient."

"Denying her food isn't right either. You worry about me eating enough for this unborn *boppli* and you don't worry about your own *dochder*." His face turned red and the veins in his neck protruded, but she continued anyway. "Your punishment is either too hard or too lax."

He crossed his arms. "Are you done?"

His expression warned her to stop, but she couldn't. "The only way Hannah will learn responsibility is if she's assigned chores, but you keep sending her to her room. Does she know how to set the table? Has she ever made her own bed? You hire out the laundry—"

"Enough, Lindie," he said sharply. He paused, and when he continued, he lowered his voice. "I'm doing the best I can." He inhaled and slowly released his breath. "But I can't allow her to be disobedient any longer." He strode from the room and his heavy footsteps echoed down the hall.

"Jesus, we need you," Lindie whispered. "This isn't how you intended family to be."

A few minutes later Josiah returned. "I looked around her room, but I couldn't find her drawing pad. If you think that's why she ran off to the woods, I have half a notion to take it away from her."

"*Nay*—" Lindie clamped her mouth closed. She'd already said more than most wives would dare. Any minute he would remind her of her place.

But he didn't. Instead, he turned, took a few steps, then circled back around. She thought he was about to say something, but he swiped the other woman's clean casserole dish off the counter and strode out of the room.

If Lindie hadn't been an outsider in his eyes before this, she was now. She squeezed her eyes closed, but prayers wouldn't come. How could she pray that this marriage would work after she'd practically chased him out the door? She craned her neck to look out the window and watched him place the woman's dish into his buggy. Running between two women wasn't part of their arrangement and was something she was not willing to accept. No Amish district, no matter where it was located, would accept that type of behavior from its members.

She moved away from the window after he disappeared into the barn. She scanned the room, from the sink piled with dirty dishes, to the counter scattered with crumbs where the bread had been sliced. The spots of chili splattered on the wall behind the stove were almost artistic. The kitchen was a mess. Even the floor under the table had puddles of water from the snow melting off Josiah's and Simon's boots. Perhaps if she hinted at having to mop multiple times a day to keep the floor clean they might leave their boots at the door.

She would get everything in order, but first Hannah had to eat. She placed the pot of chili back on the stove to heat, sliced a piece of bread, and pulled a bowl down from the cabinet. Once everything was ready, she brought the dish into Hannah's room.

Hannah looked into Lindie's eyes. The contempt was gone.

Lindie pointed to the food. "Eat," she said, making an eating motion with her hands.

The girl dipped the spoon into the chili, blew on it, then took a bite.

Lindie left the room. Josiah might be upset with her once he found out, but she wouldn't let the girl go hungry.

⌁

Josiah scribbled a note to Ellen and shoved it into his pocket. He figured she would be gone to one of the women's get-togethers and this would be a perfect time to leave the dish on her doorstep with the note about Lindie. By now, Rebecca would have spread the news of his marriage to the other women, but he figured he owed Ellen a personal explanation since she had more than once suggested they merge their families.

Josiah set the buggy brake and climbed off the bench. He carried the dish up the porch steps, set it down next to the door, then dug his hand into his pocket for the note.

The door opened and Ellen stood in the threshold smiling. "Josiah." She opened the door wider. "Please, *kumm* in."

He picked up the dish and stood. "I was driving by and I thought I would return this." He handed her the dish and shoved the note into his pocket. "I thought you would be at a women's get-together."

"Little Ted woke up with a fever. I decided he shouldn't be around the other children." She motioned for him to enter.

"*Kumm* inside so the *haus* doesn't fill with cold air, or do you need to get your laundry basket?"

"*Nay*, I didn't bring any clothes." He stomped the snow from his boots and entered. Her late husband was a true woodcraftsman. Her house was filled with the fine furniture he'd made over the years.

"Take your coat off and I'll make some *kaffi*."

"I can't stay." He cleared his throat. "Have you talked with Rebecca lately?"

"*Nay*. Is something wrong?"

He looked down at the braided rug. "I thought maybe she told you I got married last week." When he looked up, her eyes were wide. "Lindie is from Ohio. We didn't want a big wedding with a lot of fuss."

"I see." Ellen set the dish on the kitchen counter, then wiped her hands on her apron. "I suppose that would make sense *nett* to wish for a big fuss. After all, second marriages are never the same as . . . well, we both know it isn't the same as when two people are young and starting out together."

He didn't consider himself old, but he understood what Ellen meant. "I should be heading back home."

"So what did Simon think of you remarrying?"

Josiah shrugged. Simon had seen through Ellen's advances immediately and had made his disapproval known.

"Well, I look forward to meeting her. How many children does she have?"

"None yet." He looked at the floor, hoping she noticed how uncomfortable the topic was for him.

"I made an extra apple crisp." She picked up the dish sitting next to the stove and handed it to him. "Please *wilkom* your *fraa* to our district for me and let her know I'm looking forward to meeting her."

༄

According to the battery clock on the kitchen wall, Josiah had driven his buggy out of the yard exactly one hour and twenty-three minutes ago. Lindie peeked out the window, then pulled away when she didn't see him. Rushing to the window every time she heard a noise was nonsense. She needed to busy herself in other ways. She had already entered the invoices and payments received in the logbook, and had returned all the dishes to their proper cabinets. He should be relieved by that. The kitchen stove had enough wood, but the woodstove in the sitting room needed its fire built up. She tossed a couple of logs on the hot embers as the front door opened.

A gust of cold air rushed in with Josiah. He held a glass dish, this one smaller, and not empty like the one he snatched off the counter.

"It's starting to snow," he said.

"So I see." She wasn't interested in the contents of the dish, but his hands needed to be freed so he could remove his coat and hat, both of which were covered with a fine powder of snow. She didn't want little puddles all over the floor, so she crossed the room and reached for the glass dish. She would have peeled back the foil and looked, but she didn't want to appear too curious. Whatever it was, it needed heating. "I'll take this into the kitchen. I suppose you prefer eating this instead of what I have in the oven."

"*Nay*," he said, hanging his hat on the wall hook. Josiah tipped his face up and sniffed. "Chicken?"

Lindie nodded.

He shook his arms out of the coat. "It smells *gut*."

"Denki." She turned and raised the foil slightly, but she still couldn't decipher what the woman had sent home with him.

"Where's Hannah?"

"She's still in her room." She lifted the dish a little higher as she walked to the kitchen.

"It's apple crisp." He passed her and headed toward the bedroom. A few minutes later he returned to the kitchen. He tipped the empty chili bowl in Lindie's direction and arched his brows.

"Josiah, I couldn't let her go hungry. Please don't be upset."

He gently lowered the dish into the sink. *"Denki."*

"You're *nett* angry?"

"Do you remember the other day when I told you I would try harder?"

"You asked me to have patience, but this isn't about—"

"I really do want to work harder to get along." He stepped closer, his expression somber. "I know this isn't easy for you either." He cleared his throat. "But I still need your patience."

The serenity in his voice warmed her insides. "I, ah . . . the chicken should be done cooking." She hurried to set the table. "What about Simon? Does he know it's time for supper?"

"He already ate." Josiah shrugged. "That's what he told me when I was feeding the horses and putting up the buggy."

Her mind raced with thoughts of what his buggy ride might have to do with his changed mood. But she lacked the courage to ask.

"I'll tell Hannah it's time to eat." He left the room, and when he returned, Hannah was at his side. She'd stopped scowling, but throughout the meal, she made no attempt at communicating with either Josiah or Lindie.

Once the meal ended, Lindie stood. "Do you want some apple crisp?"

"Nay." Josiah slid his chair away from the table. "I think I'll go to bed early. Church is tomorrow."

Lindie's pulse raced. Tomorrow she would finally meet the woman who had sent the food.

Chapter Nine

The buggy rattled over the wooden bridge, jostling Lindie on the bench. Hannah wiggled on the seat, smiling. It was the first time she'd seen the child smile. At least one of them was enjoying the bumpy ride. Lindie might too, if she wasn't tied in knots over meeting the church members. She didn't even know the name of the woman who was causing her such stress. Was it too much to hope they would all be friendly like Rebecca?

Lindie wrung her hands. In her former district, the families that lived close to each other tended to have a tighter-knit relationship than those who only saw each other on church Sunday. She hadn't gone anywhere except the bus station and the bishop's house since arriving. Josiah had said the district was small. It shouldn't take her long to get acquainted.

Josiah glanced at her hands. "Don't be nervous."

As if she could stop herself. Had he forgotten about yesterday? He left the house with a woman's clean dish and returned with apple crisp. Did he think they wouldn't meet today? She intertwined her fingers, trying to hold her hands still.

Even Simon hadn't offered her much more than a nod. He

ate his meals with them, but spoke only with Josiah. What was even more unsettling was how little he interacted with his granddaughter. Today Simon insisted on driving his own buggy, using the excuse that the bishop had asked to meet with him prior to the service.

"Really, you'll get along fine with everyone." Josiah smiled.

Lindie wanted to ask if that included his woman friend, but didn't dare. She studied his smile. In the week and a half since she'd arrived, she'd already learned how to tell the difference between Josiah's forced smile and his genuine one by the lines that developed—either grooving his forehead or appearing at the corners of his eyes. The trace wrinkles that she saw today should have put her at ease.

She twirled her finger around a loose thread on her cape. "Didn't you warn me about raised brows?"

"Jah." He scratched his jaw. "I suppose that's bound to happen."

Her hands trembled holding the casserole dish. Bean casserole probably wasn't a wise side dish to bring. The overcooked beans had turned mushy. She should've stuck with peanut-butter sandwiches and a simple dessert. She could have brought the uneaten apple crisp.

Molly trotted up the road's incline with ease and crowned the hill. Then Josiah turned into the bishop's driveway and stopped the buggy next to the barn.

In her district, dozens of buggies would line the host family's yard on Sunday. Today she counted only six. This looked more like a women's sewing frolic than a church service.

Josiah tethered Molly to the post as Lindie helped Hannah out of the buggy.

Lindie grasped her cape at the neck. Even though the wool

material scratched her bare skin, she found comfort and an odd sense of security wrapped in it. A crisp, clean glimmer of freshly fallen snow covered the ground. It would have been colder had the sun not taken an edge off the chill in the air.

"We should get seated. The service will be starting soon," Josiah said.

Lindie wasn't sure if he'd planned to arrive at the last minute to avoid a flood of explanations, but she was grateful. She and Hannah walked alongside Josiah to the barn. As was the same custom in her district, benches were arranged so that the men sat on one side of the barn, the women on the other.

As they entered the barn, her cheeks grew hot as all eyes turned to her. Just as Josiah had warned, brows were raised, some higher than others.

Josiah sat on the second row, aisle seat.

She spotted an empty space near the back. But on the aisle opposite Josiah, the bishop's wife slid across the bench, opening a place.

"Lindie," Rebecca whispered. "Sit here with me."

Tapping Hannah's shoulder, Lindie motioned for her to sit next to Rebecca, then once the girl was seated, Lindie sat on the end, directly across from Josiah.

It wasn't long before the singing started. Josiah's baritone voice soothed her frayed nerves. The three-hour service wasn't much different from those in her district and this comforted her.

Simon stood to read the Scriptures. Now it made sense why Josiah's father-in-law was asked to meet with the bishop prior to service. Simon was one of the district ministers. She hoped the meeting pertained to the service and not to her. Simon eyed her and Josiah during his short sermon. Lindie reached for Hannah's hand, which helped disguise the shakiness in hers. At the house,

Simon hadn't attempted to cover his disapproval, and the same held true during the service. He read verses from Hebrews and afterward posed the question, "Are you provoking one another in ways pleasing to the Lord?"

Lindie glanced sideways at Josiah, but his attention was locked on Simon. She prayed silently for Jesus to forgive her for upsetting Josiah yesterday.

The bishop gave the final message, then prayed. But before he dismissed everyone, he asked the congregation to remain seated while he made an announcement.

The bishop cleared his throat. "Will Brother Josiah and Lindie please stand."

She froze. This wasn't something her bishop would do in their district, unless he was calling someone to make a public confession. She rose from the bench, her knees wobbling under her dress.

Josiah stood. His broad shoulder touched hers.

"Let us welcome Brother Josiah's new *fraa*, Lindie. They wedded a week last Monday."

Had Josiah known the bishop would call them to stand? A deep-pink shade spread up his neck and across his face. He wiped his hands along his pant legs.

She heard murmuring behind them. This was much more than a few raised brows.

"She's so young. She hardly looks marrying age," someone whispered.

Lindie silently recited James 4:10. *Humble yourselves in the sight of the Lord, and he shall lift you up. Humble yourselves—*

The dismissed congregation stood. Several patted her on the shoulder and welcomed her to their district.

Josiah disappeared into the crowd of men.

"Where is your home district?" one woman asked.

"Middlefield, Ohio."

"You're a long ways from home. How do you like it here?" the woman on Lindie's right asked.

She opened her mouth to respond, but a blond-haired woman chimed in first. "How do you think she likes it? She's married to Josiah."

The women laughed. Except one. A dark-haired woman, Lindie guessed to be in her midthirties, who stared with narrow, dissecting eyes. The laundry-folding baker, she presumed.

Hannah tugged Lindie's dress sleeve. Although Lindie welcomed the distraction, she couldn't follow Hannah's quick hand movements.

Lindie craned her neck to where she'd last seen Josiah, but the men had disappeared from the barn. She smiled at Hannah and reached for her hand, then faced the women. "Excuse us, please." She guided Hannah to the door. If she had to guess what Hannah was saying, she wanted to do so in private.

Once they were outside, she didn't have to guess. Hannah pointed to the outhouse. Lindie released the girl's hand and let her run ahead.

Lindie strolled over and waited beside the door. Faint voices drifted from the shed area. She scanned the crowd of milling men and spotted Josiah. The barn door rattled closed and the women walked in a group toward the house. Lindie wished she could hide in the outhouse.

A man's cough drew her attention. Josiah had turned away from the crowd, his hands covering his mouth. A head taller than all the others, he was handsome. Had he lived in her district, plenty of women would have offered to do his laundry, cook his meals, and be his wife. Women who were more suitable than herself. A woman he deserved.

Josiah captured her with his grin, but then looked down at the ground right away. When he looked her way again, the man standing beside Josiah elbowed him and caused his face to redden. His sheepishness took her by surprise. She stifled a giggle.

He cleared himself of the men and approached her. "Are you getting sick?"

She lowered her hand. "*Nay*. I was laughing at how cute—I mean red—" Now her face was heating.

Josiah smiled.

"I'm waiting for Hannah." She motioned to the outhouse door.

He touched his face, then looked down at the snow and shuffled his feet.

"*Denki*, Josiah."

He lifted his head. "For what?"

"I appreciate the kindness you've shown me," she said softly. "I know I upset you yesterday when I spoke up about Hannah."

He reached for her arm and gently gave it a squeeze. "I haven't treated you like I should. Like . . . *mei fraa*." He stepped closer. "It's going to take some time before everything works out."

The door opened and slammed against Lindie's backside, pushing her forward into Josiah. Inches apart, they stared at one another. Lindie's mind swirled with his last comment.

Josiah stepped back. "Maybe you should take Hannah inside with the others." He eyed his daughter, who was searching the clouds with a blank expression.

"*Gut* idea." During the service, she'd noticed other children about Hannah's age. They could all play together. First, though, Lindie needed to get the bean casserole from the back of the buggy. She didn't want to go into the house empty-handed. She reached for Hannah's hand, gave it a gentle squeeze, then pointed toward the buggies. "Let's go——" The girl turned her eyes away without giving Lindie a chance to finish. Hannah's shoulders slumped as she plodded alongside. Lindie debated if she should try to explain that they weren't leaving, but until she could sign fluently, it would just frustrate Hannah.

At the buggy, Lindie grabbed the dish of beans. Pork fat skimmed the surface. The beans would need reheating, although more cooking would make them mushier. Maybe she could shove the dish off to the side so it wasn't as noticeable.

Lindie knocked on the front door. While waiting for someone to answer, she smiled at Hannah, who stood beside her, then looked toward the gathering of men. Lindie silently beckoned Josiah. The first time attending a service was more difficult than she thought. Waiting for someone to answer the front door reminded her that she hadn't instantly blended in with the new settlement. In her district, there was an unspoken invitation. No one stood on the stoop waiting for the door to open. She hadn't yet established that level of familiarity. She looked over her shoulder again for Josiah. This time he must have realized something was wrong because he stepped away from the group, then stopped when he saw the front door open.

"*Ach*, dear," said the stick-thin woman. She opened the door wider for Hannah and Lindie. "I hope you weren't standing on the stoop long. With all the commotion in here, it's a wonder any of us heard the door."

The woman was right about the level of noise. A mixture of chatter and clanging dishes echoed from the kitchen.

"I'm Sarah." She reached for Lindie's hand. "*Kumm*, everyone will want to meet you."

Hannah stood close to Lindie. For someone who grew up in this community, the girl appeared as out of place as Lindie.

The sitting room where Josiah and she were married now had large tables placed end to end and benches that took up the length of the room. When the time came for her and Josiah to host the meal, she hoped the weather would permit eating outdoors. Seating would be cramped in their small space.

A child, perhaps a year or two older than Hannah, stood at the top of the stairs and waved at Hannah to join her.

Busy watching the youngsters' interactions, Lindie flinched when someone touched her arm.

"I'm sorry. I didn't mean to startle you." The young woman, heavy with child, introduced herself as Ada Fisher. She placed a handful of utensils on the table, then extended her hand. "*Wilkom* to Cedar Ridge."

"*Denki.*"

Sarah tapped Lindie's shoulder. "This here is Josiah Plank's Lindie."

Ada nodded. "*Jah,* I heard the bishop introduce them before service let out." She smiled at Lindie. "It's nice to meet you. I'll show you where to set your dish in the kitchen." She looped her arm with Lindie's and guided her toward the kitchen. "It'll be nice to have someone else here close to my age," she said. "Our district is small, as you probably figured out during service." She patted her belly. "I'm doing my part to increase the settlement. This one is number four."

"Congratulations," Lindie said as they entered the noisy kitchen. She touched her forehead. Moist. Meeting new people had never been easy for her. So many names to remember at once, she hoped she didn't mix them up.

Ada rattled off the names and ages of her children. ". . . and this one, William if a boy and Susan if a girl, is due next month."

Another woman joined them. "Just in time for cabin fever too."

Ada rolled her eyes. "Don't start that discussion *nau*, Naomi."

But Naomi paid no attention and turned to Lindie. "Anyone tell you about cabin fever?"

"Naomi!" Ada elbowed the other woman.

"She's married."

"Cabin fever." Ada giggled, her face blushing. "It's a joke amongst us womenfolk."

Lindie wiped her forehead.

Naomi jumped in. "Let's just say it tends to be a productive season . . ." She paused as though expecting some response from Lindie.

Lindie wasn't about to speak. Especially seeing the shade of pink Ada had turned. The idea that Josiah had already brought up the subject frayed her nerves. Only he described cabin fever as loneliness, and that sure didn't match the women's definition.

Not far from them, a small group of unmarried girls chatted about an upcoming wedding. Listening to them talk about the dress color surprised Lindie. Traditionally, at least in her home district, brides wore royal blue. Except Lindie, of course. Her dress was brown . . . and crumpled.

The dark-haired woman Lindie suspected had made the apple crisp approached the group. "What are you all giggling about?"

"Just explaining the cabin fever phenomenon," Naomi replied.

The woman's expression soured.

"Hello." Lindie switched the bean dish to her other arm and extended her hand to the woman. "I'm Lindie Wy—Plank." The first time she'd used her married name, it felt odd.

"*Jah*, I know who you are." The woman shook hands, then introduced herself as Ellen Yoder. "So you're from Ohio?"

Lindie nodded. "Geauga County."

Ada nudged her arm. "*Kumm*, I'll show you where to set your dish."

Relieved to have a reason to walk away, Lindie followed Ada as she eased around a few other women. They stopped near the stove. "I'm sorry if Naomi embarrassed you. She shouldn't have said anything, you being newly married. Around Ellen either, since she lost her husband not long ago." She leaned closer. "Although Ellen knows all about cabin fever—she has four boys with birthdays in the fall."

That explained Ellen's sour expression. A widow with four boys. No wonder her eye was set on Josiah. Lindie lifted the dish. "I probably should warm these beans." Not that she planned to eat any. Her stomach had turned queasy.

"I have other dishes to heat. I can add yours," an elderly woman said.

"*Denki.*" Lindie handed the casserole to the woman who then slipped it on the rack beside the others.

"I'm Lois. We haven't met, but I've heard about you."

Lindie dropped her smile even though Lois was jovial as she said it.

"*Gut* things." Lois chuckled. "Are you going to take your cape off and stay for a while?"

The crowded room was warm. She removed the covering as someone took hold of her arm.

"I see you've met *mei mamm*," Rebecca said, giving Lindie's arm a squeeze. Without waiting for Lindie to answer, she continued, "We are so thrilled that you've moved to our district. So many times our young men move away when they fall in love. Have you and Josiah corresponded long?"

It would raise too many questions for Lindie to admit she'd only received one letter. Indirectly at that since Josiah had mailed the letter to Eli. Thankfully, before she could think of a response, the door opened and the men filed inside.

"I better get the *kaffi* ready." Rebecca turned to the stove.

Lindie inched toward the door. She needed air. The different food scents had upset her stomach. While Hannah was distracted with the other children, Lindie slipped outside.

She rubbed her arms, wishing she had thought to grab her cape.

The door opened and Ellen stepped outside. "It gets noisy in there, ain't so?"

"*Jah*," Lindie agreed. Though it was more than noise that drove her out.

"Hannah seems to have taken to you. I suppose she thinks of you as a playmate."

She must've been the one whispering in the service. Lindie forced a smile, then scurried toward the outhouse.

Ellen followed. "So how long have you and Josiah known each other?"

Behind them, the screen door snapped and Josiah tramped down the porch steps. He took a few strides and was at Lindie's side before she blinked.

"We've known each other for several years. Our districts in Ohio were only fifteen miles apart, and her *bruder* and I worked on the same construction crew."

Ellen eyed Lindie as if trying to calculate the age difference between them.

"Ellen was the one who sent over the apple crisp," Josiah said.

"*Denki*. Excuse me." Lindie shot inside the outhouse. Not a place she wanted to loiter, but if it meant waiting until everyone went back indoors, she would. As she was busy ridding her stomach of its contents, Josiah and Ellen's conversation became a muffled background.

After a few minutes, Josiah knocked on the door. "Is everything all right? You've been in there awhile."

Lindie unlatched the door and stepped out. She must have looked squeamish because he placed his hands on her shoulders and turned her toward the buggies.

"I'll take you home."

"What will everyone think?"

"That I want to be alone with *mei fraa*."

Her muscles stiffened.

He capped her shoulder with his hand and gave it a gentle squeeze. "We're newly married. What else would they think?" He waited for her to climb into the buggy. "I have to run back inside to get your cloak and to ask Simon to bring Hannah home with him." He winked. "That way we can have some time alone."

Chapter Ten

J osiah shook his head at Lindie practically hugging the farthest
side of the buggy bench. "You look more nervous *nau* than on
our way *to* church. What's wrong?"

She shrugged without making eye contact.

He reached across the bench and clasped his hand over hers.
If she kept wringing them, her chapped hands would turn raw.
"You're *nett* feeling well, are you?"

She shook her head.

His stomach growled, a sharp reminder it was past mealtime.

"I'm sorry we left before you had a chance to eat," she
whispered.

"That's okay. Besides, I wanted to be alone with you." He
winked. "With Simon and Hannah always around, we haven't
had much opportunity."

She shifted farther away on the seat and began fidgeting with
the hem of her apron.

"Does that bother you?" He couldn't figure her out. He
would have stayed for the meal if she hadn't been hiding in
the outhouse. Now she acted frightened to be alone with him.

"Lindie," he said when she didn't answer. "Don't you want to get to know each other better?"

She sucked in a raspy breath. "Sure. If . . . if that's what you want." Her words sounded forced. She tilted her head up.

At first it looked as though she was studying the rooftop of the buggy, but then she blinked. Obviously trying not to cry.

Josiah led Molly off the main road toward home. Neither said anything until he stopped the mare next to the porch.

"I'll take care of Molly and be in shortly. Maybe you could make us some sandwiches."

"I thought—never mind." She opened the buggy door and lowered one leg.

Josiah leaned across the bench to reach for her arm. "I meant for us to get acquainted by *talking*. Over lunch." She hadn't looked this frightened since the day he brought her home. His face heated. He shouldn't have teased her about going home to be alone. He cleared his throat. "I'll be in after I take care of Molly." And after he prayed about what they'd talk about.

This time when she scurried to get out of the buggy, he didn't stop her. She needed some time alone. And so did he.

Josiah clicked his tongue and Molly lurched forward.

He spent longer than usual removing the harness, filling the water and oat buckets, and wiping off the lather buildup on Molly. He didn't believe it was right to stable a horse without towel drying her first. He also covered Molly with a blanket during the heart of the winter, when the temperatures dipped below zero, and rubbed liniment on her legs to save the mare's joints.

He already owned one horse that limped when it got cold. Josiah grabbed the ointment jar from a shelf and opened Moose's stall. He dug his hand into the gooey substance and crouched next to the horse. Each night he rubbed the gelding's joints with this special compound. Josiah's eyes watered from the pungent scent. Moose was old. Josiah retired him from dragging logs out of the woods after Caroline's death. Josiah moved to the other side and slathered the oily substance down the horse's legs. It wouldn't be long before Hannah would want to go for a sleigh ride. Another thing they hadn't done much of since Caroline died. After he'd built a flatbed with ski runners for hauling lumber out of the woods, he'd built Caroline a sleigh. On wintry nights, they bundled up and took a family ride. Hannah loved it. She would motion for him to go faster and throw her head back, laughing.

He had hoped marrying Lindie would somehow bring back Hannah's smile. A girl needed a mother. Maybe not yet, but it wouldn't be long before Hannah would need to learn cooking and sewing skills. A father could only teach a daughter so much. Boys were different. They needed to learn how to work a field, develop a trade that would enable them to support a wife and family. Josiah's chest caved with heaviness. His role wasn't just to support his wife. He was also to love his wife as Christ loved the church. He loved Caroline that way. Could he let go of Caroline in order to love Lindie?

He wiped his greasy hands on a rag and hung it on a nearby nail. His stomach growled, but he took a few more moments to load his arms with kindling for the cookstove. After lunch, he would bring in a supply for the woodstove. Those pieces were rather large and cumbersome and often meant several trips out to the shed. His arms loaded, he plodded across the yard, then stomped the snow from his boots before going inside.

Lindie was standing at the counter when he came in and tossed the handful of wood in the box next to the stove. "That should be enough for today and most of tomorrow."

"Denki." Lindie's nose twitched like she might sneeze, but she tilted her head up slightly and sniffed again.

"Liniment." Josiah held his hand next to her nose.

"Camphor, *jah?*" Her eyes watered.

"Mostly." Though the alum and oil of turpentine produced pungent odors, her excessive blinking was probably due to the high concentration of camphor. He pulled his hankie from his pocket. "Want me to wipe those teary eyes?"

She shook her head and lifted her dress sleeve to cover her nose.

Probably just as well. He hadn't thought about his hands soiling the hankie when he reached into his pocket. She might get sick. He would feel awful if she vomited because of his teasing.

"I'll wash *mei* hands." He hurried to the sink and scrubbed extra hard to remove the rancid scent. As he lathered his hands, he looked over his shoulder. Her teary blue eyes glimmered as she dabbed them with the hem of her dress sleeve. She was beautiful. He pulled his hands out from under the water and shook them. "You still bothered by the scent?"

"*Mei* eyes are watering, but at least the chemicals aren't upsetting *mei* stomach."

"That's *gut*." Too bad it wasn't the opposite. If she were sensitive to chemicals instead of food scents, she wouldn't have to battle so much to keep a meal down. He wondered if she was keeping enough down to stay healthy. He'd waited too long to insist Caroline see a doctor. Had she not convinced him the sickness was normal, she might not have miscarried. The muscles in the back of his neck tensed. He didn't want Lindie living with those same regrets.

Lindie cut the peanut-butter sandwiches in half and stacked them all on one plate. "I wasn't sure how many you would eat."

"I hope you plan to eat a couple of them too." He decided not to wait for her to reply and divvied the portions.

She shuddered.

"You need to eat for the *boppli*." Any pregnant woman should understand the importance of eating for two. At least he had always believed women developed some sort of innate protectiveness once they became pregnant.

After a moment of silence to say grace, she picked up the sandwich, took a small bite, then set it down.

"Were you able to get to know the womenfolk?"

She shrugged. "I think some believe I'm too young for you."

He had hoped she hadn't heard the whispers. He wasn't concerned about their ten-year age difference. "Do you think I'm too old for you?"

"*Nay*," she whispered.

"Then don't worry about it. They probably feel some loyalty to Caroline."

"Like you still do."

"*Jah*. She was *mei fraa*. I loved her with all *mei* heart."

The vibrancy dimmed in Lindie's eyes.

He hadn't meant to stir up sadness. "What about you? You must have some thoughts about the *boppli's* father?" A blunt question he had withheld long enough.

She picked up her plate and stood.

How could she not have feelings for the man? Even short-lived romances, which sometimes happened during *rumschpringe*, required a certain amount of commitment for her to have become pregnant. He'd known of couples who had to rush into marriage because the unthinkable happened during their *rumschpringe*.

He followed her to the sink. "Lindie, you're *nett* the only girl who has fallen into"—he eyed her abdomen—"trouble during her *rumschpringe*. Although, when they return to the faith, most—"

"Get married? Have the kind of relationship that you and Caroline shared?" Her shoulders sagged and she lowered her head. "I wasn't on *rumschpringe*."

"Lindie, I—"

"I knelt in confession once. Do you want me to do it again in your church?"

"*Nay*. But I don't understand how you could give yourself to someone and *nett*—"

She lifted one hand. "That's right, you don't understand. And you're quick to cast judgment too."

Her glare warned him not to probe further. He would respect her wishes. But he couldn't let her dispose of the uneaten sandwiches without saying something. "Why aren't you eating? Do you not care about that *boppli* you're carrying?"

Chapter Eleven

U nder the flickering shadows of the oil lamp, Lindie stared at the blank sheet of paper. The promised letter to her brother and sister-in-law was overdue. She should have jotted a quick note before now. She thumped the eraser end of the pencil on the pad of paper, unsure where to begin.

It wouldn't be fitting to tell them how Josiah had avoided her this past week or how their lunch together last Sunday had escalated into him walking out of the room. He had used the excuse of work in the barn, but she sensed it was something more. At times, his bewilderment morphed into disdain when he brought up her lack of appetite. Apparently he'd lost sleep over the situation, because the shadows under his eyes had darkened.

No, she couldn't tell Eli that his friend must feel duped into this marriage. She couldn't blame Josiah. She was probably the only Amish woman who wasn't excited to become a mother, though she prayed constantly for God to help her overcome her misgivings and change the condition of her heart.

Nor could she admit that Hannah still refused to communicate with her. The sign language book Josiah had given her to study clearly stated it took ongoing practice before one became proficient. She'd tried multiple times to correspond with Hannah and the girl only stared. Not wanting to disturb Josiah, Lindie didn't ask for his help. So she worked on it alone, settled for limited skills, and wondered why she was doing it at all if Hannah had no interest in communicating.

Lindie sipped her coffee. She would have told Eli and Margaret how Hannah had laid her hand on a wounded deer and how it had miraculously recovered, but even Josiah had dismissed the idea. Not much could be put in this letter that wouldn't cause alarm. She asked if it was normal to be sick all the time, then erased the question. Eli and Margaret would worry. She wished she had someone in this settlement to ask. The womenfolk were pleasant enough, but so far, none of them knew about the pregnancy. Still, she thought the sickness should have passed after the first trimester.

Lindie's gaze drifted out the kitchen window at the falling snow. The snow hadn't let up in four days. Even the branches of the pines near the barn drooped with snowcaps. It was a beautiful sight from inside the house. Since Josiah's avoidance, she'd stopped worrying about cabin fever. A blessing she hadn't considered, though she dare not write about it either.

She scratched out a few sentences about the record number of inches for the first part of December, asked how everyone was doing, and implied she was adapting to the north.

She signed it, *Lindie*. Adding *Plank* to her signature just didn't feel natural. She folded the paper and slipped it into an envelope. Hopefully the brief note was convincing and wouldn't inadvertently leak how homesick she was. Perhaps in the next letter she'd have good news to share. If not, she'd give them another weather update.

The door creaked open as she wrote the address on the

envelope. She paused. Josiah usually stomped the snow off his boots before he entered, but if he had, she hadn't heard him. The kettle was steaming on the stove. This time she was prepared. Almost. She should have the coffee poured and waiting for him. He came into the house for a cup of coffee this time every day. Lindie set the letter aside and went to the kitchen. Later she would ask him for one of the stamps she'd seen in the desk when she was catching up on the bookkeeping.

She filled the cup and set it on the table where he always sat. When he didn't enter the kitchen, she checked the sitting room, but didn't find him warming himself by the woodstove. She must have been mistaken about hearing the door.

She gasped. *Hannah.* Lindie dashed down the hall to the girl's bedroom and flung the door open. The room was empty.

Consumed with having Josiah's coffee ready when he came inside, she hadn't thought about the child. Lindie hurried to the door. There wasn't enough time to lace her boots so she shoved her feet into her shoes. She grabbed her cape and winter bonnet from the hook and tore out of the house, putting the garments on as she ran. Her feet slipped over a patch of ice and she teetered for balance.

Lindie trudged over a pile of banked snow and pushed through the drifts in the field until she became winded. Stopping to catch her breath, she searched for tracks, but the freshly fallen snow made it difficult to see. Not wanting to waste any time, she continued toward the woods. She made it a few feet before a piercing sharpness stopped her, buckling her at the waist. She clutched her side, panted a few quick breaths, and bit back a screech. Moments later the pain hadn't eased completely, but it had lessened enough to continue. She couldn't leave Hannah alone in the woods.

Lindie reached the edge of the woods and stopped. This time it wasn't her side that ached, but her heart was racing and she couldn't will her feet to move forward. She froze, paralyzed by memories of sticks cracking under heavy footsteps and the overwhelming scent of dead leaves. She resented her inability to cast aside the terrifying recollections.

She hated the woods—the heavy breathing—scratchy leaves grinding into her bare skin.

Being cold.

Left for dead.

"Nay!" Lindie squeezed her eyes shut, fell to her knees, and buried her face in her hands. Every fiber in her body seized.

Breathe . . .

Frigid air entered her lungs. She blew it out, gasped another lungful, and held it until her ears rang. She couldn't think. Couldn't focus.

Push through this. Hannah's alone.

Unable to bear the thought of the woods swallowing Hannah, she closed her eyes. *Jesus, keep her safe. Help me put the wicked past behind me so I can find her.*

A burst of renewed strength filled her. She pushed off the ground, shoved the low-hanging branch out of her way, and pressed forward down the trail. She reached the tree where she and Josiah found her last time, but the girl wasn't there.

Lindie scanned the area. The dense thicket made the surroundings difficult to search. She needed to choose a direction, but if she wandered aimlessly, she would get twisted around. Lost.

Branches snapped. This time it wasn't her imagination.

Lindie's back stiffened. Her knees locked in place and her hands fisted. The sound was louder than a branch falling under the weight of snow. An animal? She hoped. Just not a bear.

More twigs crunched.

She turned a circle, trees blurred. She changed directions, paced a short distance, and retraced her steps. She squeezed her eyes closed and shook while a suffocating constriction crawled up her throat.

Someone cleared his throat behind her.

Lindie spun, arms swinging. She batted Josiah's chest and shoulders multiple times before he wrapped her in a tight embrace.

"It's me." Josiah pressed her harder against his chest, whispered "Shh" over and over until she lost her fight and surrendered. Once he released his grip, she pushed off his chest.

"We have to find Hannah."

"She's in the barn with Simon." He smiled.

Hannah was safe. Not alone. Or lost in the woods. Tension drained from her body as his words registered. Then fresh anger rose. "Hannah needs to tell me when she's leaving the *haus*. Why doesn't she understand that? She can't just wander off."

"I know."

"What am I supposed to do? Tether her to my hip? I was sitting at the table. She could've told me." Her whole body racked with tremors. "I can't do this. I'm no good for her—for you."

"*Jah*, you are." He cupped her face in his hands and looked her in the eye. "Please don't say that."

"You've avoided me since Sunday. I know you're *nett* happy."

"I'm sorry." Josiah ran his thumb over her face, drying the wetness. He dropped his hands and reached into his pocket. "Here." He handed her his hankie, then looked down at her feet and frowned. "Your feet must be frozen solid. *Kumm* on, let's go home before you catch pneumonia."

She hadn't noticed how wet her shoes were. She wasn't

dressed in layers either. She was surprised he hadn't said something about that too.

He draped his arm around her shoulders and rotated her toward the path. "Let's get out of the woods. You could pass for a deer wearing all this brown."

"Didn't hunting season end in November?"

"Rifle. But *nau* it's black powder season." He looked off to the side. "You could always sing."

"Sing?"

"Jah." He chuckled. "That would keep the hunters from mistaking you for a deer. Unless you know deer that sing."

Lindie narrowed her eyes a moment. Was he serious? She drew a deep breath, readied her voice, then belted out a hymn. It wasn't easy to sing as loud as possible with her teeth chattering. She screeched out the tune anyway.

Following the footpath through the snow, he chuckled. "You might be tone deaf."

"Sing with me, Josiah." She sang a few more notes and paused. "Do you want to get shot?"

"Someone might take a shot at you just to shut you up," he said.

She clamped her mouth closed and stopped walking. Given his distance toward her lately, she wasn't sure if his comment was meant to be playful or rude. Then again, he had teased her about bear traps the last time they were in the woods together. Maybe his humor only came out in the woods. Probably his way of masking the memories of Caroline's accident. A few cut stumps poked up through the snow. For all she knew this could be the very spot of the accident. And while Josiah avoided this place, Hannah seemed to have found solace here. Why else would she return to this spot?

"Why did you stop? I was beginning to like that squawking," Josiah said.

"Squawking!" She buried her cold hands under her armpits, but couldn't stop shivering.

"You better *nett* stand in one place too long." He motioned forward with his head. "Don't get frostbitten because you're being vain about your singing."

"Vain, I'm *nett*."

"It's too *kalt* out here to sulk." He snatched her off her feet and into his arms.

"What are you doing?" The warmth of his body made her insides surge with sensations she wasn't prepared for. "Put me down."

"Nope." He marched forward. "I don't want to leave you in the woods and I'm too *kalt* to wait for you."

"Put me down or I'll start singing again."

He chuckled and kept walking.

Cradled in his arms gave her a perfect view of him. A thick, chestnut-colored beard, rosy cheeks from the cold, and dark lashes that contrasted with his royal-blue eyes. She watched him so long that he winked. She squirmed in his arms. "Okay, put me down and I'll promise *nett* to sing."

A smile lingered on his face as if he was mulling over the idea.

"You're *nett* thinking about carrying me all the way back to the *haus*, are you?"

"I might." Approaching a low-hanging branch in their path, he shielded her face with his hand and ducked his head, bringing him nose to nose with her as he passed under the covering.

"What will Simon and Hannah think?"

"I guess we'll find out in a few minutes." He readjusted her in his arms. "You need to eat more. You don't weigh much more than a goat."

"A goat?"

"A pregnant one."

"*Denki* for clarifying that." She huffed. "A goat, just what a woman wants to be compared to."

They reached the edge of the woods and he lowered her to her feet. He turned and coughed, causing his shoulders to shake and the veins in his neck to protrude.

"Are you taking anything for that cough?"

"*Nay*, but I'll be all right." His expression didn't match his words. He resumed walking, cutting a trail through the snow.

She followed behind him. "How did you know I went into the woods?"

"I was emptying a wheelbarrow of manure behind the barn and I heard what I thought was a scream."

She didn't recall screaming. A chill went down her spine. "I was afraid."

"*Jah*, remind me never to sneak up on you again. You have a solid punch." He rubbed his arm.

She smiled.

"I've known of a few goats with a mean strike, but no women."

"I have a *gut* kick too."

He unlatched the fence gate and swung it open. "I suppose I need to work on finding your soft side." He chuckled. "You do have a soft side, *jah*?"

"Maybe."

"Then I'll enjoy finding it."

Chapter Twelve

Josiah examined the bruises on his upper arms. He'd teased Lindie about having a solid punch, but she hadn't hit him hard enough to bruise. These looked more like he'd been thrown off a horse. They didn't hurt as much as they were ugly. He could only imagine what the back of his shoulders looked like. It was bad enough that a rash covered his chest. Now he had dark-blue blotches everywhere. The different signs and symptoms were all pointing to something he didn't want to face. Panic sped through him like a ball of fire. No, this wasn't happening. Not again. He fastened the hook and eyes on his shirt and pulled up his suspenders.

Breakfast smelled good. Scrambled eggs, potatoes, and a thick slice of sourdough bread. He was getting used to having someone cook for him again. He wished Hannah would participate more in preparing the food. She didn't do much besides set the table.

"It smells *gut*." He looked over Lindie's shoulder as she dished up potatoes from the skillet.

"Hungry?"

"Jah." He took his place at the table and winked at Hannah seated on his left. The door opened and Simon entered the house.

"Another *kalt* day," Simon said, pulling out a chair.

Hannah tapped Josiah's shoulder and signed, asking if she could brush Moose after breakfast.

"Maybe later I'll have time," Josiah said. He liked that his daughter was interested in spending time with the old draft horse, but he didn't have much time to watch her. He expected Hal to arrive with more lumber and he still needed to deliver the Christmas wreaths in town.

Simon huffed. "I thought it was your *fraa's* duty to watch her."

Josiah's attention snapped to Lindie, who stood at the stove. Her spine stiffened, but she kept her back to them. He leaned toward Simon. "Please don't bring up the wandering off," he said under his breath.

"Shouldn't she know what this is doing to you?"

Josiah narrowed his eyes.

Lindie set the platter of eggs on the table, took her place, and spent a long time praying.

Everyone ate in silence. Josiah's mind mulled over Simon's jab. He wished his father-in-law would accept her. After all, this wasn't a temporary arrangement.

An engine rumbled outside. Josiah leaned back in his chair. "That's Hal." He took one last sip of coffee and slid his chair back.

۵

Hannah rose to follow her father, but Simon stopped her. "You must stay," he told his granddaughter. He eyed Lindie. "It's too dangerous for her."

"I'll make sure she stays inside." She wished Josiah wasn't the only one who'd rushed outside.

Simon shoved his hands into his gloves. "Maybe you don't understand how difficult the changes have been. It isn't *gut* for Josiah's health to be under so much stress. He needs someone to watch his *dochder* and to know when she leaves the *haus*."

"*Jah*, I will." Lindie gathered the dirty dishes. The added stress had been hard on everyone. She wondered if Simon noticed the dark circles under Josiah's eyes and blamed them on her arrival. What would he say if he knew she was pregnant? He made it clear that she wasn't much of a *mamm* for Hannah. Nor was she a *gut fraa* for Josiah.

Simon left the kitchen, melted snow from his boots puddled under the table where he'd sat.

Lindie prepared a bucket of mop water and scrubbed the floor. Once the kitchen floors were cleaned, she reached for the sign language book in the center of the table and flipped it open to the place where she'd stopped the night before. She went over the new information a few times, practiced making the hand gestures, but had no idea if she was doing it right.

Discouraged over her lack of progress, Lindie scooped up the book. The key to developing the correct movements was to practice with someone who could communicate in return. Hannah hadn't been receptive yet, but Lindie was determined to at least make the effort. The girl couldn't avoid her forever. Lindie eased the girl's bedroom door open.

Hannah sat on the floor with her back against the wall, a small drawing tablet on her lap. As she squatted beside Hannah, a burning sensation speared Lindie's right side. She winced. Was this normal?

After a moment, the intensity subsided and she took a spot on the floor.

If the girl noticed, she made no indication. Her concentration remained fixed on the sketch she was working on.

Lindie leaned against the wall. Fear had doubled her over in the woods. But this pain was different. It hit her hard and felt like fire.

Hannah lifted her pencil. Her vacant gaze reached Lindie's soul. Hannah's vision dropped to Lindie's belly, then without warning, the girl stretched out her hand and rested it on Lindie's abdomen—in the exact spot of her pain.

An odd sensation worked its way to Lindie's core as Hannah's expression saddened. She lifted her hand and, without changing her expression, signed something Lindie couldn't decipher. She opened the sign language book, flipped through several pages, but could only find "sorry" as one of the hand gestures Hannah used.

Hannah shifted on the floor as if she was going to stand.

Lindie motioned to the girl's drawing pad, now clutched against her chest.

The girl's face crinkled.

Lindie signed the letters *P-L-E-A-S-E*. A long moment passed. Had she used the wrong letters? Reconfiguring her hand, she formed a *P*, then an *L*.

Hannah relinquished her prized possession. She pressed her hand over the crumpled page and smoothed out the crease, then turned it so Lindie could see her work.

Lindie smiled. She recognized the cardinal by the spiked feathers on top of its head and under its bill. Even without the use of any color. She handed the drawing back to Hannah. At the same time she signed, she spoke the words aloud. "I love it."

Hannah cracked a thin smile. It didn't last, but it was a start.

"You are . . ." Lindie struggled for the proper way to sign

talented or *gifted*. "Very good." That wasn't what she wanted to say. She wanted Hannah to understand that her talent was a gift from God.

Hannah clutched the picture to her chest.

Before the child closed her off again, Lindie rose to her feet. Hannah needed space and Lindie had cleaning to finish. She left the child's room feeling like they'd made progress.

"I poured you some *kaffi*," Josiah said as she entered the kitchen.

"I didn't hear you *kumm* in." She wasn't sure she wanted caffeine after having the sudden cramps only a few minutes ago. She set the sign language book on the table and sat. "I was practicing."

"I know. When I came inside and didn't see you, I checked Hannah's room." He smiled. "I was glad to see that."

"It's a start." Lindie sat down at the table.

He slid a paper across the table to her. "That's the invoice for the delivery."

"Okay, I'll be sure to log it in the book." She circled the rim of the cup with her finger.

"It's going to be off. Badger Creek didn't have an elm to send."

"Oh." She'd been preoccupied with thoughts of what Simon had said earlier and hadn't been listening very well.

"I promised Eli I could fill his order . . . I'll have to use some of our trees." His voice drifted off as he stared into his cup.

"What does that mean?"

The chair scraped across the wooden floor as he pushed away from the table and stood. "Timbering," he said and turned to leave.

༉

The moment Josiah stepped inside the workshop, a mild coughing fit overtook him.

Simon looked up from hammering. "You said you were going to have that cough looked at."

Josiah shot him a glare. "It happens this time every year." He flipped his thumb over his shoulder to the corner of the barn where the stove sat. "It's this dry heat." He scratched his chest over his shirt. After today, the cedar bough wreaths would be finished. Maybe the rash would disappear.

"I still think you need to see a *doktah*. With all the new stress you've been under . . ."

"Simon, please don't start in about Lindie. She's *mei fraa*. She deserves respect."

"I'm just saying, maybe the temperature change isn't the cause."

Jah, stress probably had run down his immune system. It was a combination of many things. Most were out of his control. Hannah hadn't made any progress. She remained emotionally stunted. His hopes that her behavior would change when Lindie arrived were disintegrating. Perhaps his marriage to Lindie had even compounded the issue. *Lord, let it not be so.*

Josiah picked up the hammer from the workbench. There was nothing like pounding out one's frustrations.

"Hannah hasn't seemed too interested in accepting your marriage."

Josiah drove the nail into the soft pine. "She's a child. Besides, I don't know if she really understood. You know as well as I do that since the accident she hasn't . . . progressed." He lined up another nail and struck it. "I don't want to admit it, but she's regressed more. Sometimes she acts like a three-year-old, sometimes like she's five—but *nett* eight. She's even sucking her thumb again."

"I don't know what to tell you, other than to pray," Simon said.

He had been praying, night and day. Josiah hoped Simon didn't try to involve Bishop Troyer. Lindie was into her second trimester. He didn't want to bring attention to their marriage problems or that Hannah wasn't adjusting. As it was, it wouldn't be long before the church members found out about her pregnancy. He would like to have his house in order before that happened.

He finished nailing the last wreath and set it aside. He only had a few boughs to tie before taking them into town.

"I need to speak with the bishop later. Do you want me to drop these off in town?"

"Sure." Josiah stopped himself from asking what they'd be meeting about. "It's *kalt* in here." Josiah set the hammer on the workbench and crossed the sawdust-covered floor to the other side of the barn where the potbelly stove sat. It needed more wood. He liked to keep a steady fire going so he didn't have to be bogged down in layers of clothes as he worked. Without putting on his coat, he rushed outside to the woodpile. Busy filling his arms with wood, a horse neighed before he noticed the buggy entering the driveway.

Ellen Yoder's horse.

Josiah groaned under his breath. He nearly dropped the armload of wood when the buggy stopped near the house and three women climbed out. Ada Fisher and Rebecca Troyer weren't as much a concern as Ellen. He hoped Lindie was ready for visitors.

❧

Lindie sloshed the rag mop over the sitting room floor. She hadn't realized how much soot had collected from the woodstove until she wrung black water from the mop. It didn't even look like she damp-mopped them daily. Once the soot penetrated the wood grain, it was next to impossible to restore the original shine. It didn't help that they had been neglected for so long. Josiah had more pressing matters than cleaning.

She leaned the mop against the wall and grabbed the bucket of dirty water. This was the third time she had tossed the old water and refilled the bucket. And she'd only done half the floor.

As she reached for the doorknob, someone knocked. She lowered the bucket to the floor, wiped her hands on the front of her apron, and opened the door.

"I hope we didn't catch you at a bad time." Rebecca Troyer smiled and lifted a square pan, which Lindie recognized as the one she'd taken the bean casserole in for church Sunday. "I wanted to return your dish."

"*Denki.*" Lindie opened the door wider. "Please, *kumm* in." She stepped aside so the women could pass. It wasn't the most opportune time with the floors wet and only partly mopped, but she'd so longed for fellowship and was grateful for the visit.

"*Ach*, dear," Rebecca said. "We did catch you at a bad time."

"*Nay*, believe me, I can use a break." She nudged the mop bucket out of the way with her foot. "I think it's going to take multiple cleanings before I'm able to get all the layers of soot off the floor."

Lindie started to chuckle, but suppressed it when Ellen snorted. Lindie should've suspected Ellen did more than Josiah's laundry. She must have done his housecleaning too.

"I didn't mean to sound as though Josiah lived in a pigsty. It's just that . . . there's been so much snow lately. The floors get muddy."

Rebecca laughed. "You think it's bad *nau*, wait until spring when everything starts to melt."

"Would you like some *kaffi* or tea?"

"*Nett* for me." Ada tapped her belly. "The *boppli* kicks more when I have caffeine. But a glass of water would be nice."

"I'd love a cup of tea." Rebecca elbowed Ellen, who was still eyeing the room. "You want a cup too, *jah*?"

Lindie followed Ellen's gaze to the rolled-up rug wedged against the bench. The place did look out of order with the furniture bunched together on one side of the room.

"*Jah*, sure. A cup sounds *gut*," Ellen said, bringing her full attention back to Lindie. "You didn't bring many belongings with you from Ohio, did you?"

"I arrived by bus." Lindie didn't want to discuss that this was still very much Caroline's home. The household items from her hope chest remained in the boxes. She hadn't wanted to upset Josiah by making any more changes.

"I almost forgot," Ada said, extending a small basket. "We brought you some cookies and two loaves of zucchini bread."

"That's very thoughtful, *denki*." Lindie smiled. "Why don't we go into the kitchen and I'll put the kettle on."

At least the kitchen wasn't askew. She'd mopped the floor earlier and the table and chairs were back in their proper places. Lindie led the way, although she was certain they were familiar with the layout of Josiah's house.

"Please, have a seat." She slid the lid off the cast-iron kettle and peeked inside at the water level. Not enough. That would have been disastrous had she put a dry kettle on the stove. She was trying hard to make a good impression on her first visitors.

Lindie filled the kettle to the brim with tap water. Her hands shook under the weight of the full kettle. It clanged against the stove when she set it down.

"Is there something you need us to do?" Rebecca started to stand.

"*Nay*, please don't get up." Lindie didn't want anyone to think she was incapable of preparing tea. Though it did seem like she was forgetting something. The stovetop gave off plenty of heat and before she'd mopped earlier she'd loaded the stove with wood, but she decided to check the fire anyway. When she opened the side of the firebox, a blast of heat warmed her face. Extra kindling wasn't necessary; the bed of embers glowed.

"This shouldn't take too long to heat." Lindie wiped her hands on her apron. What else? Cups. She opened the cupboard but found plates. Who moved the dishes this time?

"Let me help," Ellen said. "I know how Caroline arranged her kitchen." But she didn't. Ellen opened the next cabinet and found bowls.

Lindie searched for tea bags. Since her arrival, she hadn't drunk anything but coffee. And come to think of it, Josiah only drank coffee.

"We're having a sewing frolic on Saturday at *mei haus*. I hope you'll join us," Ada said. "We're going to sew some *boppli* clothes."

Gladness spread through Lindie. "I'd love to *kumm*. What time?"

"From ten to two. I can pick you up," Rebecca said.

"*Denki*." Lindie moved a few items around on the pantry shelf, but still didn't find the tea.

"The *boppli* is pushing hard against *mei* bladder. Do you mind if I use your bathroom?"

"Of course." Lindie walked Ada to the hallway. "It's the first door on the left."

Rebecca spoke the moment Lindie reentered the room. "I looked for you on Sunday so we could visit, but heard that you and Josiah had already gone home. Perhaps the two of you will *kumm* for supper one evening."

Lindie smiled. "I'd like that." In her district, families would often visit with one another during the week.

Ellen set the cups on the counter. "Are you sure Josiah has tea bags? I ask because he doesn't drink tea. Caroline didn't either."

Lindie closed the pantry door and stifled a smart response. Boiling water erupted from the kettle spout and sizzled on the stove's surface. As she removed the kettle from the hot spot and placed it on the back of the stove, Lindie caught sight of the dish Josiah had brought home with apple crisp. She picked up the clean glassware and faced Ellen. "I think this is your dish."

Ada entered the kitchen. "How's Hannah doing? I poked *mei* head in her bedroom to say hello and she wasn't there."

"She wasn't?" Lindie gasped. "I, uh . . . I—"

The women stood. "We understand."

Nay, she doubted they understood how upset Josiah would be. She rushed out of the room, the women following. But before she reached the door, it opened.

Josiah and Hannah entered, his hand resting on her slumped shoulder.

Lindie froze. Aware the women had flanked her, she silently prayed he wouldn't reprimand her in front of them. She searched his face. No sign of tension. He didn't appear upset. Still, he was probably waiting for the company to leave before mentioning anything. She hadn't done her job—again.

Hannah squatted down and removed her shoes, then padded down the hall toward the bedrooms.

"It was *gut* visiting with you." Ada made her way out the door.

Lindie smiled. "*Jah*, I hope we can do it again. Next time I'll make sure we have some tea."

While the others walked toward the buggy, Rebecca paused. "Josiah, I was telling Lindie that Gideon and I would like to have you two over for supper one *nacht* next week."

He smiled. "Sure. We would like that."

"*Gut.*" Rebecca gave Lindie's hand a squeeze. "It was *gut* talking with you. I'll plan to pick you and Hannah up for the sewing frolic."

Lindie shouldn't have committed herself to attend the get-together until she had spoken with Josiah. She briefly glanced his way.

"I think you'll have a *gut* time," Josiah said. "What day is it?"

"Saturday," Rebecca answered. "We're sewing clothes for the *boppli.*"

Josiah's jaw dropped.

Chapter Thirteen

Josiah's heart pounded at an irregular rhythm and his insides knotted. He followed Lindie into the kitchen. "They're planning a sewing frolic for the *boppli?*"

"*Jah*, the women planned a get-together." Lindie grabbed a pot holder from the drawer and removed the kettle from the stove. She motioned to the basket on the table without looking at him. "They brought cookies and zucchini bread."

Her vagueness upped his blood pressure. "Rebecca said it was for the *boppli*. You told them about *your boppli?*"

"It's for Ada's *boppli*."

"*Ach.*" He didn't think people fussed over a second, or in Ada's case, a fourth child. Usually the family already had enough baby clothes from their other children.

Coffee cups clanged together as Lindie scooped them from the counter.

"Why are you putting those away?"

"They're clean." Her voice was barely above a whisper.

"Did you offer them *kaffi?*" He crossed his arms and leaned against the counter, facing her. Something was wrong. "They changed their minds?"

She shrugged.

"You wouldn't have put the kettle on unless you'd offered and they'd accepted." Had Ellen said something to upset her? Caroline never had any issues with the others. They were all friends. Still, the families had all arrived at the same time to start this district; they might have formed a tighter bond than usual. Surely they would eventually accept Lindie.

Everyone wanted this district to grow. It had been several days since he returned Ellen's dish, but she had given him the impression she wanted to get to know his new wife. Then again, she had practically chased Lindie to the outhouse with questions last Sunday.

"I'll have supper ready shortly." She removed a frying pan from the bottom cabinet.

The downturned corners of her mouth tugged at his heart. "Will you tell me why you're upset?"

Lindie scooped a spoonful of lard from the tin container and chunked it into the pan. She pushed the melting lard around with the spatula, coating the bottom of the skillet.

How could he help her if she refused to talk? He sidled up beside her. "What can I do?"

"I have everything under control." The cracker-coated pork chops sizzled as she lowered them into the grease.

He should have come into the house sooner. He might have been able to defuse Ellen. "What can I do to make you happy?"

"You can get out of the kitchen. Go read the paper." She made a shooing motion with her hand. "I'll call you when it's time to eat."

"Rebecca's offer to pick you up for the sewing frolic was nice. You'll have more time to get acquainted, don't you think?"

She mumbled something under her breath, indecipherable over the snap of hot grease.

He grabbed the lid from under the cabinet and covered the frying pan.

"You can't put a lid on everything," she muttered.

He looked at her, then the pork chops, and then back to her. "What are you talking about?"

"That doesn't stop the pork chops from burning." She pulled off the lid, jammed a fork into the pork, and flipped it over.

Her being upset had nothing to do with the meal. Then again, Caroline had never wanted him underfoot while she was trying to cook either. "If you need something . . ."

"I'll call you if I do." She opened the upper cabinet, removed a plate, and set it on the counter.

He leaned against the door frame and watched her slice the loaf of bread.

She furrowed her brows at him. "Am I making the slices too thin?"

"*Nay.*"

"Too thick?"

He shook his head.

"Why are you still staring at me, then?" She finished the final slice and set the bread on the plate.

"When you reached for the plate, I guess I expected you to say something about me moving the dishes."

She faced him, knife in hand. "I looked like a fool *nett* knowing where anything was."

"I'm sorry." He watched the tip of the knife blade wag and

knew enough not to step any closer. "I shouldn't have told you to move the dishes back. This is your kitchen."

"I felt like it was Ellen's. She pointed out how you don't drink tea—*after* I searched the pantry. I looked foolish offering them a cup of tea, and more so when I had to hunt for where you kept your cups."

He'd been the foolish one not realizing how important a kitchen was to a woman. He never should have objected to her reorganizing things. "What else are you upset about?"

She tossed the knife on the counter and planted her fisted hands on her hips. "I saw your expression when you thought the women had found out about the *boppli*."

"I'm sorry. I panicked." Josiah crossed the distance between them. "Forgive me." He'd never meant to hurt her. He only wished to save her some heartache from people questioning the circumstances prior to their marriage.

She forced a smile. "I returned Ellen's apple crisp dish. I hope you don't mind."

"Why should I mind?"

She shrugged. Her mouth quivered and she turned toward the sink. "You made a point to return her last one," she said calmly.

"I did so I could tell her I no longer needed her to do laundry or clean. She sent that apple crisp over to *wilkom* you. I guess I forgot to tell you." He eased closer to Lindie. "Ellen helped me after Caroline died. I paid her to do the laundry and clean the *haus*. I couldn't keep a business running if I had to do everything. Did you think there was something between Ellen and me?"

She half shrugged with one shoulder and bowed her head.

"There wasn't. Nor would there have ever been." Nothing

he said changed Lindie's expression. "Did Ellen say something that indicated otherwise?"

She didn't respond.

His hands turned clammy and he wiped them along the seam of his pants. "Ellen has made some comments in the past about us both losing our spouses and that maybe we should think about . . . Well, she more or less hinted about marriage." He looked down at the floor. "I never considered it. I told her I—"

"Could give her your name, but not your heart?" Her sharp tone tore at his heart.

"*Nay*," he said. "I told her I didn't want to remarry. That was the truth."

Her jaw twitched as she concentrated on putting the butter and a jar of chutney on the table. "*Mei bruder* convinced you to marry me."

"Partly."

She paused and turned a careful eye on him.

He shrugged. "There was something about your answer the day at the bus station when I asked you if you wanted to go home. You sounded . . . hopeless." She opened her mouth to speak, but he lifted his finger to stop her. "I was too."

He might never become the same husband he was to Caroline. But how could he make things up to Lindie? Talking about Ellen or their marriage agreement wasn't going to help matters.

He cleared his throat. "I found Hannah's drawing pad. You were right. Her picture looked identical to the birch trees out back."

Lindie's eyes brightened a little. "I think the deer in the drawing was the injured one she laid her hand on."

Lindie had mentioned Hannah healing the deer before, but he hadn't wanted to talk about it. He also wasn't sure how useful artwork was to an Amish girl's future. Even so, he would rather talk about art than marriage.

"You asked what would make me happy, *jah*?"

"*Jah*," he said cautiously. He'd seen that twinkle in Caroline's eyes the time when she wanted a wringer washer.

"I want to buy her some colored pencils, if they aren't too expensive."

"Why? She has crayons." He had wanted to give Lindie something that would make *her* feel special. Hannah already spent so much time drawing that she had practically withdrawn from everything else.

Her shoulders slumped.

"Okay." He smiled. "If it'll make the pretty *maydel* happy."

Her eyes lit up and drew him like a magnet. Beautiful. He liked how a few strands of her copper-colored hair had sneaked out from under her *kapp* and framed her face.

"*Denki*. Hannah will be happy."

He leaned closer, his lips nearly brushing the side of her cheek. "I was talking about you."

A soft pink glow spread over her face. Even her earlobe was dusted in blush. Who would've thought colored pencils would make her this happy? He would drive to the store tonight if it were open.

The back door opened and a moment later Simon poked his head into the kitchen.

She sidestepped Josiah. "I better check the meat."

"I, uh . . ." He swiped the newspaper off the counter. "Simon and I will get out of *your* kitchen and go read the paper." He hoped he could find something to read that would take his mind off her.

☙

Lindie gathered her sewing bag and the dessert she made for the frolic when Rebecca's buggy pulled into the yard. Not wanting to keep her waiting, she motioned to the cape on the wall, but Hannah only stared. Without Josiah close by, Lindie wasn't sure if Hannah would mind her today, and for a second, she considered canceling. But Hannah needed to get out of the house and be with other children, and Lindie was desperate to form new friendships. She set the dish and sewing bag down, grabbed the cape, and helped Hannah into it. Climbing into Rebecca's buggy, Lindie whispered a prayer that things would go well.

"I'm so happy you could join us today," Rebecca said.

"*Jah*, I am too." She motioned to the dish. "I made a pumpkin spice cake."

"Oh, I can't wait to try it." Rebecca turned the horse out of the driveway. "Ada doesn't live too far." She elbowed Hannah seated between them. "Lucy will be there."

Hannah smiled.

"Lucy is *mei* youngest niece," she told Lindie. "She's just getting over the chicken pox. That's why she and *mei* little sister, Martha, were *nett* able to make the service last Sunday."

"That's *gut* she will have someone to play with."

"There will be more children, but Hannah and Lucy are especially close since they are near the same age." Rebecca spoke to Hannah. "You and Lucy have fun together, isn't that right?"

Hannah nodded.

Lindie was pleased since she rarely received anything but a blank stare when she spoke to Hannah. Obviously, the girl had no problems reading lips.

It wasn't long before they pulled up to a two-story farmhouse. The white clapboard house had dark-green shutters and empty flower boxes under the windows. Lindie pictured how beautiful the house would look in the summertime with flowers in bloom. She looked forward to spring and putting in a garden. Maybe she would plant pansies along the walkway. Lindie had always liked the deep violet ones that Margaret had planted in her own flower bed.

"Lindie, so *gut* to see you," Ada said, ushering them into her house.

Lindie set the cake on the kitchen counter with the other goodies as the children welcomed Hannah and coaxed her into another room to play. Although the gathering was small compared to the ones in Middlefield, maybe fifteen including the children, it looked as though all the women in the district were in attendance.

Ada led Rebecca and Lindie into the sitting room where several other women were already busy with their hoops and needles. Lindie found a chair and pulled out her sewing supplies.

For most of the afternoon, the conversation centered on the pending snowstorm headed their way. Lindie learned to have extra water ready just in case the pipes froze. She was certain that Josiah would know these things, but she took mental notes. As the day continued, the talk shifted to food.

"We like to make homemade ice cream this time of year," one woman said. "The fact that it doesn't melt immediately is the only thing I like about winter."

"I leave mine out on the porch," another woman said.

"I leave my meat in the pan on the back porch long enough for the fat to float to the top and harden so I can scrape it off," Martha said. "Of course I don't do that unless the bears are hibernating."

A few of the women shared their experiences with bears. They all laughed, but Lindie found nothing funny about the possibility of a bear on her front porch. "You've made me hungry *nau*," Ada said, setting her sewing hoop aside. "I think it's time we eat." She motioned to Lindie. "Would you like to help me get things ready?"

"I'd be happy to." Lindie hooked her needle into the material and stood.

"I hope you're having fun," Ada said as they walked into the kitchen. "We don't always have the chance to get together in the winter. But *kumm* spring, we will have more frolics."

"I'm having a *wunderbaar* time." Lindie opened the different containers as Ada poured the coffee. She hadn't felt sick all day, but the combination of egg salad and tuna dishes had her stomach unsettled. She placed her hand on her belly.

"Are you feeling okay?" Ada asked.

Lindie jerked her hand away. "*Jah*, I'm fine." Josiah had underestimated women if he thought they wouldn't figure out she was pregnant. Her dress was large enough to camouflage her condition for several more months, but she wouldn't be able to hide giving birth or having a newborn in the house.

"Who isn't feeling *gut*?" Ellen asked, entering the kitchen. Her eyes stopped on Lindie. "You're probably *nett* used to this *kalt* weather."

"Or maybe it's more." Ada giggled and patted her own pregnant belly. "Certain foods bothered me too in the beginning."

Lindie's face heated. If they asked directly, she wouldn't lie. But what would Josiah say about them finding out?

The children rushed into the kitchen along with several more women. Lindie concentrated on preparing a plate for Hannah.

Ada nudged Lindie's side. "How do you think Hannah will respond to a *bruder* or sister?"

Lindie gasped. Had Ada forgotten that Hannah could read

lips? She placed a spoonful of potato salad on the plate and guided Hannah away from the others. "Please be careful not to spill anything."

Hannah took the plate.

Lindie breathed a sigh of relief. The last thing she wanted was for Hannah to relay the news to Josiah and then ask him about it.

ॐ

Josiah couldn't concentrate on building pallets with Lindie and Hannah gone. He hoped everything was going well and that Hannah wasn't disobeying. If he received a bad report, he wouldn't let Lindie talk him out of punishing the child.

Josiah set the hammer on the worktable. "It's already past noon. What do you say we go inside and find us something to eat?"

"Sounds *gut* to me." Simon pounded the nail into place and stood the pallet on end.

As they plodded to the house, the postman pulled up to the mailbox.

"I'll get the mail and meet you inside," Josiah said, tugging his coat tighter around his neck and continuing past the porch. The air was brisk for such a sunny day. He skimmed through the mail, which consisted mostly of advertisements. Simon had a letter and Lindie received one postmarked from Ohio.

Once he shed his coat and hat at the door, he handed Simon his envelope. He dropped the other mail on the table. He assembled a couple of cheese sandwiches and placed them on the table.

"*Mei bruder* isn't doing well." Simon set the letter down. "He's had a stroke."

"I'm sorry to hear that."

"Abraham is *mei* last sibling." Simon's eyes closed for several moments. "His *fraa* said I should *kumm* soon before he passes."

"Then you should," Josiah said. "Do you think your hip will be okay to travel? The bus ride to Centerville will take several hours."

"I'm more concerned about the pallet orders. I don't think I'll go until the shipment is ready."

Josiah shook his head. "Don't worry about that. I can always ask Jakob Troyer to help me. But do you think I should go with you?"

Simon shook his head. "*Nay*, your place is here."

Josiah was relieved. He didn't want to leave Lindie and Hannah alone. Hannah could run off again and Lindie shouldn't be left alone in her condition, especially since Hannah wasn't aware of the pregnancy.

Neither seemed eager to talk, so they ate their sandwiches in silence.

"I suppose we should see how many more pallets we can build," Simon said, pushing his empty plate away.

Josiah gulped the last of his coffee and stood. He picked up the dirty dishes and placed them in the sink.

Rebecca's buggy pulled into the drive as Josiah was leaving the house. He met Lindie as she and Hannah were getting out. "Did you have fun?"

"*Jah.*" Lindie smiled.

He wasn't expecting the warmth of Lindie's smile to course through his veins. She had an effect on him that he wished he could deny. Hannah was smiling too, and that warmed his heart even more.

"Tomorrow is visiting Sunday," Rebecca said. "I want you to *kumm* for supper."

Josiah couldn't refuse when he saw the excitement on Lindie's face. "Sure, we'll be there." He motioned to the workshop. "I'll leave you two to decide the time. I need to get back to work." He snuck one last peek at Lindie before he turned. The day with the womenfolk had done both Hannah and Lindie good.

~

Lindie's hands trembled as she spooned potatoes onto her plate. She gave Hannah some, then passed the bowl to Rebecca, seated on her other side. Sitting across from Lindie was Josiah, whose watchful eyes took in everything she put on her plate.

Lindie tried not to notice his glare. She was nervous enough having supper at the bishop's house.

The men carried the table conversation. Mostly about the weather and the escalating price of livestock feed.

Lindie complimented Rebecca on the tender pork roast. She loved the subtle hint of rosemary.

"When do you plan on leaving, Simon?" the bishop asked.

"In a few days." Simon motioned to Josiah. "I told *mei sohn-in-law* I would stay until the pallet order is ready for shipment."

Lindie hadn't heard any of this news. Simon was leaving?

"I thought I would ask Jakob if he was interested in helping me. That way Simon can leave sooner," Josiah said.

The bishop's son sat straighter in his chair. "Sure. Just tell me when." The young man glanced at Betsy seated across the table from him and smiled.

Lindie recognized the couple's furtive exchange even before Rebecca mentioned their upcoming wedding. In Lindie's district, most of the weddings took place after harvest season, but here it made sense to have them in the winter when much of the work was at a standstill.

"We'll have most of the pallets done," Simon said.

Josiah took a sip of his coffee. "I have some trees to bring down."

Lindie couldn't help but notice Josiah's hand tremble as he lowered his cup to the table.

Simon's jaw twitched, but he said nothing.

The bishop quickly changed the subject.

Lindie couldn't eat. Her stomach was tied up. What made Josiah decide to start timbering again?

The meal ended and Rebecca tapped Lindie's shoulder. "Would you help me serve dessert?"

"I'd be happy to." Lindie pushed her chair back and stood. She was anxious to leave the table so she could pull her thoughts together.

"Did you know Simon was leaving?" Rebecca asked once they were out of earshot.

"*Nay*," Lindie whispered.

"He *kumm* by last evening and spoke with Gideon. They kept their conversation private, but I gathered it wasn't just about his *bruder* being ill."

Rebecca sliced the pound cake and placed it on the plates.

Betsy stepped into the room. "Do you need more help?"

Rebecca handed her future daughter-in-law the drum of homemade ice cream and a large wooden spoon. "I only want a small scoop on mine, but I'm sure all the men will want a large serving." Rebecca slid a jar of apricot preserves closer to Lindie. "Would you mind adding the topping?"

Lindie licked her lips. "This looks delicious. I'd love to get the recipe."

"Remind me to write it down later." Rebecca handed a couple of the topped desserts to Betsy with instructions to serve the guests first, then leaned toward Lindie. "It's a *gut* way to sweeten Josiah." Rebecca chuckled. Probably at Lindie's widened eyes. "Don't worry, dear, you don't have anything to worry about. I saw the way Josiah looks at you. He's already sweet on you."

"You did?"

"Like a man who is in love. It's obvious."

Lindie's cheeks warmed.

"You don't have to be embarrassed," Rebecca said. "You're newly married folks."

In love . . . Rebecca's words swirled in Lindie's mind. But she quickly reminded herself of the day they'd met. He'd made it clear that he couldn't love her. *Wouldn't ever*—his words.

She'd accepted those conditions. The same as he accepted her pregnancy. Truth be told, for someone incapable of falling in love again, he treated her well. He was a good father. And despite Simon being upset now, Josiah was a good son-in-law. He was . . . everything she'd ever wanted. Yet this marriage wasn't anything like she'd dreamed marriage would be. Not without love. The realization stabbed her heart. She had the perfect husband—in name only.

ॐ

The tension between Josiah and Simon spilled over on the ride home. Neither spoke. Lindie didn't dare say anything either.

Once they arrived, Simon offered to take care of Molly.

Hannah signed something to Josiah. The girl's hands moved

too fast for Lindie to follow, but whatever it was, she dashed toward the barn after Josiah responded. Lindie wanted to be part of the conversation—part of the family.

Josiah reached for Lindie's elbow. "The steps might be slippery."

They weren't, but Lindie liked his attentiveness.

"You hardly ate," he said.

"*Jah*, I did."

He shook his head. "*Nett* enough for two."

She waited for him to open the door, then stepped inside. "You never said anything about Simon leaving."

"His *bruder* had a stroke. He wants to see him before the *gut* Lord takes him." Josiah went to the woodstove and checked the fire.

"When did you decide to start cutting trees again? I thought you shut down the timbering."

"I told you I couldn't get any elm trees from Badger Creek." He must have realized his tone was sharp because he took a moment before continuing. "I need elm lumber to fill Eli's order."

"Surely he would understand."

"I gave him *mei* word." He jabbed the poker into the fire and sparks flew.

"But if Eli knows it means you have to cut—"

"Let it be, Lindie." Without adding more wood to the stove, he headed to the door. "I told Hannah she could feed Moose and I need to check on her."

Lindie stepped into the kitchen and stopped. On the table was a note propped against a box of tea bags. It merely said *I hope this is the kind you drink*. But she focused on how he signed it: *Love, Josiah*.

She loaded the stove with kindling and filled the kettle with water. She was rereading the note when the door snapped open.

Hannah stopped at the kitchen threshold, a puddle forming at her feet. Her teeth chattered as she pulled her wet dress at the seams to keep it from clinging to her body.

"Ach!" Lindie dropped the note and crossed the room. "You must be freezing," she said, not expecting Hannah to reply. Lindie held up her index finger. "Wait here." She grabbed a towel from the bathroom closet, then wrapped it around Hannah's small form. Even the girl's *kapp* was wet. Where had she been? Josiah said he'd sent her to the barn. Hannah was shivering and too cold to answer questions now.

Lindie guided Hannah toward the woodstove in the sitting room. That was the warmest place for her to stand until Lindie could fill the bathtub.

She returned to the kitchen, grabbed the kettle from the stove, and took it to the bathroom where she dumped the hot water into the tub. Eli's house had a gas-generated hot water heater. Here she had to use heated water from the stove, then adjust the temperature with cold tap water. Once she had the bath prepared, she helped Hannah out of her clothes and into the tub. Surprisingly, the child didn't resist.

While Hannah soaked in the tub, Lindie stepped out long enough to stoke the fire and add more logs to the woodstove. Heat drifted from the sitting room, down the hall, and into the bathroom. Still, the door needed to stay open in order for the heat to reach them.

Lindie squatted next to the tub and soaped a washrag. Hannah didn't resist her attentions. Lindie unfastened the pins holding the girl's *kapp* and unwound her hair from the bun. She was busy washing her hair when the floor creaked behind her.

Josiah stood in the doorway. "Sorry for sending her inside without any notice." He rolled his eyes. "Hannah created a little water problem out in the barn. It might take me awhile to clean out the stall and lay fresh hay."

Lindie shielded Hannah's eyes as she poured warm water over her hair.

"I always seemed to get soap in her eyes when I used to do that." Josiah turned away. "I better take care of the mess in the barn."

Lindie emptied another pan full of water over the girl's head, rinsing the suds away.

Hannah blinked a few times and looked at Lindie, smiling.

Lindie sighed. That little smile might just brighten her whole winter.

॰৲

Josiah couldn't pull himself away from the bathroom doorway despite the layer of ice forming on the calf pen floor. Watching Lindie wash Hannah's hair reminded him of the countless nights he'd walked by the bathroom and seen Caroline bathing their daughter. Maybe Hannah was finally starting to bond with Lindie. The realization sheathed his heart with a mixture of warmth and heaviness. This was what he'd wanted. He married Lindie to give Hannah a mother.

Josiah shoveled the wet straw from the stall floor and tossed it into the wheelbarrow. He wished Hannah had paid attention and not overfilled the trough. He didn't want to dwell on his daughter's shortcomings. She was in tears when he'd found her trying to turn the water off.

The shovel scraped the cement slab as he loaded the last

of the soggy straw. He climbed out of the fenced enclosure and grabbed the pitchfork leaning against the wall. Once he had the new bedding spread over the floor, he called the calves, then fed and watered the rest of the livestock.

He debated if he should talk with Simon before he went back to the house, but decided he would wait until tomorrow. Simon didn't take the news well about cutting trees again and Josiah understood why. The decision hadn't been easy to make. He still had nightmares about Caroline crushed under the tree.

He trotted back to the house. He wouldn't be surprised if it snowed another foot by morning. The tracks he'd made earlier, walking out to the barn, had already disappeared under snow cover.

Josiah stomped his boots on the porch before entering the house. He peeked in the kitchen, then, not finding anyone, continued down the hall, following the dim lantern light that glowed from the bathroom doorway.

But it wasn't Hannah soaking in the tub.

He caught himself before a gasp escaped. Stunned by the sight of her back, he froze. Red spiral tresses touched her shoulders. He shifted his weight and the board under his foot creaked.

Lindie shot a glance over her shoulder. Her eyes connected with his and widened. "Josiah!" Water splashed over the side of the tub as she scrambled to cover herself.

If he had a shred of decency, he would turn away and give her some privacy. But she'd drawn her knees to her chest and had wrapped her arms around her legs. She was covered.

"How long have you been standing there?"

He leaned against the door frame. "You left the door open."

"To get heat from the woodstove!"

Now probably wasn't the right time to talk about how emaciated she looked. He would deworm her if she were a horse. Every bone protruded: the shoulder blades, the individual vertebrae of her spine, even her ribs had no meat on them. Malnourished.

She looked over her shoulder at him again and cringed. "Please don't tell me you plan to stand there all *nacht*."

He still couldn't get over how well her dress had disguised her skinniness. It wasn't likely that she could carry a baby to term.

"Josiah," she growled through clenched teeth. She rested her cheek against her bent knees and squeezed her eyes closed.

"Ah . . ." What was he doing gawking at her? She was naked. He pushed off the door frame. "Do you want this door open or closed?" His words ran together.

"You have to ask?"

No sense reminding her that she'd left the door open to get heat from the woodstove. He chuckled, trying to lighten the situation, but it came out sounding as if something was stuck in his throat. Lindie probably wished he'd swallowed his barn boot.

Chapter Fourteen

Last evening's humiliation in the bathtub burned in Lindie's mind the moment she awoke. She snuggled deeper into the bed. Her mind reeled with how to avoid Josiah across the breakfast table. There wasn't a way.

She flung back the covers and crawled out of bed. She scanned the dresses in her closet and selected the gray one. It seemed appropriate considering how gloomy she anticipated this day would be. She pulled on the dress and fastened it closed with straight pins. Adjusting her black apron as she left her room, she bumped into Josiah in the hallway. Her line of vision shot up from his chest, but he kept his eyes on the floor.

"I, ah . . . I thought you would be out in the barn," she finally sputtered.

"I'm heading there *nau*," he said, not lifting his gaze.

Good. He had the decency to be embarrassed over last night. Despite the tension she had anticipated, her stomach was calm. Probably the first morning since she'd found out about the pregnancy. Perhaps her body had stopped waging war against itself.

"I better get breakfast started." She pointed to the kitchen but dropped her arm. This was his house; she didn't have to explain where the kitchen was.

"*Jah*, I have stuff to do in the barn." He took a step and stopped. "Did you see the letter that came for you yesterday?"

Lindie smiled. "It was from Margaret. Eli sends his hello."

"Tell them I said hello the next time you write."

She nodded, then padded to the kitchen, the hardwood floors chilly against her feet even wearing wool stockings. Looking out the frosted window, Lindie spotted Josiah trudging across the snow-covered path. She rubbed her hands over her arms and shivered. No wonder the house seemed drafty. Multiple inches of snow had fallen during the night. The morning-pink glow reflecting off the snowcapped barn roof was breathtaking. So were the icicles that dangled from the porch roof. Days like today made her wish she were a child again and could spend a lazy afternoon after the chores were completed traipsing through the snowdrifts.

Lindie sighed.

She was a grown woman now with responsibilities, and breakfast wouldn't cook itself. Maybe after they ate, she could take Hannah outside and the two of them could play in the snow.

Margaret had said they were having a mild winter so far. Her sister-in-law said she'd been busy baking for Christmas. Lindie hoped to do the same. But she wasn't sure what staples Josiah had in the pantry for doing the amount of baking she and Margaret used to do.

Lindie opened the pantry and scanned the contents. So many jars of jam. Why? Lindie pulled the mason jars off the shelves and set them on the table. According to the labels, Ellen specialized in jam. Blackberry, strawberry, raspberry, even blueberry. What did the woman do with her time—just pick berries?

Lindie lifted a jar of strawberry-rhubarb jam and squinted at the date. More than two years ago. The date of the jam wasn't important, she merely wanted to see how long Ellen had been supplying his pantry.

Hannah entered the room, poked Lindie's back to get her attention, then closed her hand into the form of a *C* and moved it down the middle of her chest.

Thirsty? Hungry? Lindie forgot what the book said the gesture meant. Whichever it was, she needed to adjust her priorities and make breakfast. Inventorying the pantry could wait. She smiled at Hannah and pointed to the chair. "Sit and I'll make you something to eat."

Hannah crinkled her nose and repeated her hand movements. This time she emphasized the motion by touching her chest.

It had to mean hungry. Lindie pushed the jars to one side and pulled the chair out from the table. "Sit," she said, tapping the seat.

She sliced a few potatoes thinner than normal so they would cook faster and tossed them in a fry pan. She'd washed the eggs earlier and had the coffee kettle heating on the stove.

Hannah sat perched on the chair, eyeing Lindie as she worked. The girl needed something to do.

Lindie motioned for Hannah to come to the counter. She handed the girl a bowl and a long-handled wooden spoon, then added the ingredients. "Stir them together." She made a stirring gesture. Hannah mixed the concoction as Lindie checked out the window for Josiah and Simon. Like clockwork, they were plodding toward the house. Lindie hurried to butter the pan, and at the same time, the men clambered into the house. More concerned about Simon's reaction than Josiah's that the meal wasn't ready, she motioned for Hannah to stir faster.

Josiah stepped into the kitchen. He scanned the table. "What's all this?"

"The pantry," Lindie said, flipping the potatoes in the pan. "I'll put it back after breakfast."

Josiah shifted his attention to Hannah and smiled. "I see you have a helper today."

Lindie eyed her young assistant. Flour powdered Hannah's nose, but she smiled, apparently pleased with her duty. "The pancakes might take a few minutes yet," Lindie told Josiah.

He winked at his daughter. "I don't want to rush the cook. Take your time."

Lindie wasn't so sure Simon shared the same sentiment. He stood beside Josiah, running his hand down the length of his beard. She set the spatula aside. The kettle was hot, so she could at least pour them some coffee while they waited.

It wasn't long before they had the meal prepared. Hannah beamed ear to ear over the golden fried cakes.

Lindie felt like she had finally done something right. Until she set her fork down and noticed Josiah's raised brows. She ignored his subtle hint about the uneaten food and sipped her coffee.

Simon pushed his chair back and stood, holding on to the corner of the table for support. "I'm going to start on the pallets."

Josiah stood to assist Simon. "Would you mind if Hannah tags along for a little while?"

"That's fine with me."

Josiah signed something, and based on Hannah's smile, he must have told her how much he liked the meal. But by the end of the message, her smile had faded.

Lindie's heart tugged. Why was he sending the child away? She was hoping they could play in the snow after the kitchen was cleaned.

Hannah rose from her chair and followed Simon from the kitchen.

Josiah pushed Lindie's plate closer to her. "Eat." He rested his elbows on the table, planted his chin on his folded hands, and stared at her.

Now it made sense. He must have expected a scene about not eating enough for two. But she felt as stuffed as a Thanksgiving turkey. "I'm *nett* sure I can eat any more."

"You're pregnant. You have to eat."

"Josiah, I'm full."

He slid his chair away from the table and stood. "I can't sit by and do nothing anymore. Get ready to go into town. I'm going to hitch the buggy."

~

Josiah pulled the buggy up to the porch and jumped out. What was taking her so long? He had work to do when they got back.

Inside the house, he noticed Lindie's cape still hanging on the hook beside the door. He continued into the kitchen and stopped, spotting her standing at the sink doing the dishes. "I thought you were getting ready."

"*Jah*, I *redd-up* the kitchen." She crinkled her brows and looked down at her dress. "Did you want me to change?" The dress she had on wasn't her Sunday best, but it wasn't worn thin like some of her others.

"You look fine." He bobbed his head toward the door. "*Kumm* on. Get your boots and cape on so we can go."

She rinsed the suds off her hands, then dried them on the dish towel. "I didn't realize you were in such a hurry." She tossed the towel on the counter and adjusted her apron on the way to the door.

He trailed her. "Sometimes *Doktah* Ethridge's office gets really busy. He's usually *gut* about squeezing new patients in, but—"

"*Doktah?*" She spun around and plowed into his chest. "I thought we were going after colored pencils for Hannah."

"I'm sure we'll have time for that too." He placed his hand around her back and guided her toward the door. "If we can get on the road."

"Really, Josiah, I don't need to see a *doktah*."

"*Jah*, you do. You've been sick too much."

"*Nay*." She shook her head. "The queasiness will pass."

He pulled her cape off the hook and wrapped it around her shoulders. "Maybe so, but I'm still taking you." He gave her shoulder a nudge, but she'd planted her feet. "Lindie, don't give me a hard time. You're losing weight when you should be gaining. Your belly is no bigger today and neither are—"

She gasped and quickly folded her arms across her chest.

"Your ankles. What did you think I meant?"

"*Ach!*"

"Don't get yourself into a tizzy." Maybe he should have refrained from stating his observations so bluntly. Still, Caroline's belly had swelled early on and continued to balloon until Hannah arrived. He didn't want to frighten Lindie, but not gaining weight had to indicate something was wrong.

Her eyes narrowed and her face turned crimson. "If you didn't like what you saw last *nacht*, why did you loiter so long?"

He smiled. "Oh, I liked everything I saw." Too much. Thoughts of her kept him awake half the night. Wrestling not only with his attraction but with how ghastly underweight she looked for a pregnant woman.

Her eyes widened. "You should have been decent and *nett* looked."

"Probably." He leaned closer. "Tell me the next time you want to bathe and I'll stay out in the barn longer." He reached around her and opened the door. "*Kumm* on, *mei* bathing beauty. Let's go into town."

She mumbled something he couldn't hear.

When he stepped outside, a blast of wind lifted his hat. He caught it from flying off and pressed it down hard.

Lindie sat on the bench and rubbed her hands over her legs. "What do you think the temperature is?"

"Near zero." He reached for the quilt behind the bench. "Here, this should help."

Her teeth chattered as she unfolded the blanket and draped it over her legs. "*Denki*, this is much better."

"You need to start dressing in layers." This weather was mild compared to January, February, and March. Some of those days could be so cold that he wasn't able to feed the woodstove fast enough.

"I hope Hannah doesn't catch a cold from last *nacht*. I can't believe she got all wet."

"She does a lot of strange things . . . since Caroline died. But she seemed happy to be cooking with you." He remembered the time Hannah and Caroline had picked mushrooms in the woods and how proud Hannah had been showing him her basket. She had more twigs than mushrooms, but he'd made a big fuss over what she'd collected. Hannah had helped Caroline make homemade noodles, then they'd sautéed the mushrooms in butter and served them in a rich cream sauce.

Lindie cleared her throat, pulling him back to the present. "I think you'll be surprised at how much Hannah will like the pencils."

"She sure spends a lot of time drawing."

Lindie frowned. He hadn't meant to sound negative.

The traffic picked up as they approached town, so he kept Molly near the shoulder. His thoughts drifted to Caroline. What would she think of their daughter spending so much time drawing? He had to shake this guilt over seeing Lindie in the tub. Last night thoughts of Lindie nearly drove him mad. He had to admit he missed having a real marriage. But when thoughts crept in about becoming Lindie's husband in the biblical sense, memories of Caroline pulled him away.

He reined Molly onto Cedar Street.

Lindie leaned forward, taking in the scenery. "The wreaths on the lampposts are nice. This town really decorates for Christmas, ain't so?"

"Simon and I made those wreaths."

"You did?"

"The Chamber of Commerce buys fifty every year to hang in town and around the courthouse. This year several of the businesses ordered them for their storefronts. I delivered the last of the orders the other day."

"I didn't know that was what you were doing in the barn."

"It's extra income during the holidays. The hardest part is clipping and dragging the cedar boughs out of the woods. Attaching them to the chicken wire isn't difficult." He turned the corner onto Elm Street and stopped Molly outside of the doctor's office.

"I'm feeling much better," Lindie said amid a flurry of cold air. "I'll be able to eat—for two. Promise."

It wasn't that simple. No baby could survive her emaciated state.

Chapter Fifteen

Josiah sat in the lobby of the doctor's office, his elbows resting on his knees and his head in his hands. At least he picked a good time of day to bring Lindie; the office lobby was empty. From the corner of his eye, he caught a glimpse of a white lab coat and looked up.

"Your wife will be out shortly," Doctor Ethridge said. "Perhaps we could all talk in my office?"

"Sure." Josiah rose from the chair. The last time the doctor suggested a talk in his office, the news was devastating. A deep, racking cough overtook Josiah and he had to pause until it passed.

"Coughing a lot, Josiah?"

"Some." Lately he coughed more than he cared to admit.

"Any blood?"

"No." Up until now, the cough was mostly dry and nagging, not productive. He had an idea of what the doctor was getting at, but Lindie was the patient, not him.

Doctor Ethridge stopped at the end of the hall and faced Josiah. He leaned closer and eyed Josiah over his wire-rimmed glasses.

Too close. He didn't like being under this form of scrutiny.

"Your color doesn't look too bad. Any night sweats?"

Josiah shrugged. Yes, he had night sweats. He married a woman he didn't know. He scanned the area. He didn't want Lindie to overhear these questions.

"Josiah, I think we need to do a blood workup."

"I'm healed." He lowered his voice. "You said so yourself six years ago."

"We should check to be sure that's still the case." Doctor Ethridge opened the door to his office and motioned to one of the chairs positioned in front of his desk. "Please, have a seat."

Josiah sank onto the chair's overstuffed cushion. This room hadn't changed. The same framed documents adorned the wall behind the mahogany desk. Matching bookcases flanked the windows. He'd crafted the office furniture in lieu of payment for his and Caroline's medical services. He scanned the room, wondering what the doctor would take in exchange for delivering Lindie's baby. The office didn't appear to need more furniture. Perhaps crown molding, but even that wouldn't be much in trade. They would work out something. Doctor Ethridge was known for fairness and his willingness to barter services.

"When did we last do a full panel of blood work on you?"

"I don't know, but my blood is checked a couple times a year." He wasn't sure what type of tests they did, or if a full panel had something to do with how many tubes of blood they took. Sometimes they sent the blood to a specialty lab. It cost him three hundred dollars when they did. Unfortunately, the doctor had no bargaining ability for the outsourced lab work.

Doctor Ethridge picked up the phone and pressed a button. "Monica, will you pull Josiah Plank's chart and bring it to me? Thanks." He lowered the phone.

Josiah shifted on the chair. The back of his neck was moist.

He tugged on the collarless hem of his shirt. The office was too warm. If he weren't under such scrutiny, he would ask for a glass of water. He cleared his throat. "Did you say Lindie was going to meet us in here?"

"I ordered blood work on her as well, so it might take a few more minutes. The nurse will bring your wife in when she's finished."

"How's the baby?"

"I'm concerned. The baby isn't developing according to the charts." The doctor folded his hands on his desk. "Until the blood work comes back and I can do an ultrasound, it's difficult to determine the gestational age of the fetus. Based on the date your wife provided, she should be in her eighteenth week." He flipped open the folder before him, skimmed the page with his finger, then repositioned the chart so that Josiah could look at the graph. "If the date is correct, this is what she should measure." He moved his finger down the scale. "But this is her measurement. I'm afraid she isn't developing as she should, which places her in a high-risk category."

Josiah recalled how Caroline's last two pregnancies were termed high risk. "Is that because she's sick all the time?"

"That could play a part in the underdevelopment, but morning sickness is common. Even into the second trimester."

"But Lindie is sick multiple times a day. It isn't just in the morning. I think she's losing weight instead of gaining it."

"That is a problem." He studied the paperwork in the chart a moment, mumbling something about a BMI, and ended with saying, "She's underweight even if she wasn't pregnant."

"That's what I thought."

"How would you rate her stress level?"

Sky-high. "She's under quite a bit of stress."

Doctor Ethridge jotted a note on the paper. "Interesting. I didn't find her high-strung. If anything, she appeared somewhat despondent. But some people internalize stress."

Josiah swallowed hard. "Do you think she will . . . be all right?"

"We'll have to keep a close watch on her and monitor the development of the baby. Is this her first prenatal checkup?"

Josiah nodded.

"I understand Amish women prefer to have their children at home, but I would strongly advise a hospital delivery."

He and Lindie hadn't discussed anything about the delivery. Caroline labored fifteen hours before giving birth to Hannah. The only exposure he'd had to a difficult delivery was when he aided a heifer birthing her first calf.

"The hospital is equipped to handle any complications that might present themselves during the delivery."

Josiah wiped his hand over his perspiring brow.

The doctor leaned forward. "She mentioned having sharp pains the other day. If she has any more, or if she starts to bleed, you'll need to bring her in immediately." A light tap on the office door pulled the doctor's attention. "Come in."

"Here is the chart you asked for."

"Thank you. Please send Mrs. Plank in when she's ready."

"Oh, she left."

Josiah bolted up from the chair. "When?"

"A few minutes ago." The woman shrugged. "I set her next appointment for a month from now."

Doctor Ethridge rose from his chair. "I need to see her before then. Didn't you read my notation in her chart?" He turned to Josiah. "I wanted to talk with you about doing an ultrasound tomorrow."

"I'll bring her. What time?"

"What does the schedule look like tomorrow?" he asked the nurse.

"First patient is at ten."

"Let's add Lindie in before that." He turned to Josiah. "Can you bring her in at nine?"

Josiah nodded, his mind still swirling about Lindie having sharp pains that he hadn't known about. Perhaps they occurred during the night and she hadn't wanted to wake him.

The nurse led the way down the hall. "I'll give you the papers explaining the test and how she needs to prepare for it."

"Josiah," Doctor Ethridge said. "I'll take your blood samples when you come in tomorrow."

"Okay." He hurried toward the door. Over the years he'd given blood routinely and it always came back fine. Even when he had a cold last winter and coughed so much he barely slept or kept food down. He couldn't concern himself with the tests now. His mind was on why Lindie had left the office. He hoped she hadn't panicked when she didn't find him waiting in the lobby.

～

Lindie shivered in the corner of the buggy bench. She hadn't stopped shaking since the nurse instructed her to shed her clothing and put on a paper gown for the exam. Mortified, she pulled her cape tighter, wishing she could disappear under the covering completely.

The buggy door opened and Josiah poked his head inside. "Why did you leave without me?" His smile faded and he climbed inside. Only instead of grabbing the reins and releasing the brake, he slid across the bench closer to her. He cocked his head sideways. "You weren't worried about *nett* finding me in the lobby, were you?"

"*Nay*," was all Lindie managed before she choked. She blinked to clear her blurry vision.

He pulled her into his arms and pressed her hard against his chest. "Please try *nett* to worry about the *boppli*."

His woodsy cedar scent washed over her, and her heart rate ratcheted into a gallop. Images of that night swirled in her head. Pinned down by the man, her screams suffocated. Lindie panted and pressed her forearms against his chest, struggling to break the circle of his embrace.

"Lindie?" he whispered against her ear before pulling away from her. "I know this has all been very stressful. You've had so many changes to adjust to—pregnancy, marriage—I guess what I'm trying to say is: we're in this together. You and me . . . and Hannah. And the new *boppli*. We're a family."

She stared at him skeptically. There wasn't a kinder man than Josiah Plank, but they were far from the traditional Amish family. He had wanted their marriage to be in name only, and she wasn't complaining. Although hesitant at first, she'd begun to trust the boundaries of their arrangement, a miracle since she'd vowed never to trust any man.

Josiah scooted to the driver's side of the bench. "Do you feel up to going into the general store? They sell art supplies and we could pick up a set of those colored pencils that you wanted to give to Hannah."

She cracked a smile. "*Jah*, I would like that."

He released the buggy brake. "The store is only a few blocks down." He clicked his tongue, and Molly perked her ears and lurched forward.

The steady, almost musical clip-clopping of the mare's hooves against the pavement eased Lindie's frayed nerves. Things could be much worse. Josiah could be overbearing, even demanding, with his authority over her. He certainly was better to Hannah than Lindie's own father had been. Her father had forbidden her to spend time drawing foolish pictures, whereas Josiah was making the effort to encourage his daughter to develop her God-given gift.

↭

Josiah parked the buggy behind the building. Buying special pencils was a waste of time and money. Girls needed to learn to cook and sew, not create fancy artwork. But this was for Lindie as much as Hannah. She seemed to think his daughter had a special gift. Why hadn't he recognized it?

He opened the shop's door, then followed Lindie inside.

She scanned the room, eyes wide and mouth agape. "Don't you just love that smell?"

He sniffed. "Turpentine?"

"*Jah.*" She tilted her head up, a smile stretched wide across her face.

"Don't inhale too much. It can't be *gut* for the *boppli.*"

She drifted down the aisle and stopped in front of a large selection of paintbrushes. Certainly not meant for painting barns, these brushes had fine bristles. He tried not to stare at Lindie, but he couldn't get over how large her eyes grew when she inspected the different types.

He reached for one and ran his finger over what felt like a tuft of hair. "What do you use this one for?"

"That's a filbert. It's probably the most popular." She picked up one shaped like a fan. "This one is nice for painting grasses

164

or brush in a landscape. The round brushes are *gut* too, and so are the flat and angled ones." She returned the brush to the shelf.

Lindie left the paint section and strolled down a few rows before stopping in front of some sketch pads and pencils. She looked at several sets before selecting one. "I think Hannah will like this set."

"Does she need any special paper?"

Her eyes brightened. "*Jah*, if it isn't too much."

He would pay a high premium to keep the smile on Lindie's face. "Pick out what you think she would like."

Lindie surveyed the selection and handed him a pad. "She's going to be thrilled."

He picked up another pad and set of pencils. "I think you need your own supplies."

She blushed. "It isn't necessary to—"

"*Jah*, it is." He turned toward the front of the store. "*Nau* let's pay for these so we can eat lunch." He expected her to say she wasn't hungry, but she didn't. Josiah paid the cashier, then stole a sidelong glance at Lindie while he waited for his change. Focused on her rosy complexion, he barely heard the cashier count back his money. He thanked the cashier and grabbed the bagful of art supplies. "*Nau* let's eat."

Lindie paused on the threshold and pointed to the silver bell that dangled by a string over the door. "We need a bell like that at home to warn us when Hannah leaves the house."

"That's a *gut* idea. We can stop at the hardware store on the way home." He studied the way the bell was mounted, then followed Lindie outside. The temperature had dropped several degrees as cloud cover now blocked the sun. It would snow before nightfall. She shivered beside him, and without thinking he placed his arm around her shoulder.

"Do you feel like walking? The restaurant is only a couple of blocks down."

"I feel fine." She faced him and smiled. "*Denki* again for the art supplies."

Anything for you, he caught himself from saying. Her eyes danced with joy. He lowered his arm from around her shoulders and cleared his throat. "I'm looking forward to seeing your drawings."

"I haven't drawn anything in years." Her smile faded.

"Why?"

She shrugged one shoulder. "I didn't have much time to pursue it, I suppose. I spent all my free time sewing to stock *mei* hope chest."

He wasn't sure which was causing her sudden sadness, the lack of time to draw or something about her hope chest preparations. This time alone with her was too wonderful to spoil by asking.

He motioned to the diner ahead. "I don't see many cars. It must *nett* be too busy." Once they entered the restaurant, he let her pick the table.

Lindie fiddled with her paper place mat as they sat in a corner booth.

Something about her childlike fidgeting stirred him. Was she nervous?

When the drinks arrived, she swirled the ice cubes in her glass. "We lived so far out of town, I can only remember going to a restaurant once," she said as though needing to explain her behavior.

"The food here is pretty *gut*. I hope you like it." She hadn't ordered much. A cup of potato soup and half of a BLT sandwich wouldn't have been enough to satisfy his hunger. He decided on the open-faced beef sandwich platter with extra mashed potatoes.

She sipped her soda, then set the glass on the table. "Margaret and I made homemade root beer for Eli's birthday last year." She trailed a drip of condensation down the glass.

"Maybe you could make some for us."

She nodded. "I'll write home for the list of ingredients."

Home. Would she ever feel Michigan was her home? He pushed the thought aside.

"I want you to give Hannah the art supplies as a gift from you."

"Don't you think it would mean more from her father?"

He shook his head. "I think it might help the two of you bond."

"I hope you're right. I don't sign many words correctly. And I'm slow." She shrugged. "Hannah tends to brush me off."

"I'll talk with her about that."

"Nay." She reached across the table and grabbed his hand. "Please don't." She looked down and her eyes widened as she jerked her hand free. "I . . . uh . . . I'm trying to improve my speed without messing up the words," she said in one long breath.

"You can practice with me."

"Okay." Her blue eyes twinkled as she searched briefly out the window. She turned back to him and signed.

He grinned.

"I did it wrong, didn't I?"

"Nett if you need to shower and shave."

She frowned. "I meant to say the snow needs to be shoveled."

Josiah signed it correctly, then repeated it more slowly so she could study the hand movements. "That's *gut*," he said when she followed all the right gestures. They continued signing. He used hand movements with every response. Then he signed, "You are the most beautiful creature God has created," working his hands as quickly as he could.

She crinkled her eyebrows. "What did you say?"

"I'm *nett* telling." He grinned.

"That's *nett* fair. Do it again."

He repeated the statement, only faster.

"You're going too fast."

He shook his head. "You'll have to figure it out."

She was in the middle of objecting when the server arrived with their meals. Without prodding, she finished all her food. Maybe it helped that in between bites they practiced more words. He shared silly stories of when he first started signing, and watching her laugh, he didn't want the meal to end.

"We'll have to do this again on our next . . . outing." *Date.* There probably wasn't another man whose hands turned clammy on a date with his wife. Josiah shoved his gloves on as they walked to the front door.

Once outside, Lindie tilted her face to the sky and stuck her tongue out to catch the falling snowflakes. She whirled about playfully. "It feels a little disorienting, catching snowflakes, *jah*?"

He'd become disoriented all right, but it had nothing to do with snow.

Chapter Sixteen

Lindie struggled to restrain her smile. She didn't want the buggy ride home to end. Her insides fluttered when his leg brushed against hers under the blanket they shared.

"Are you warm enough?" he asked.

"*Jah*, are you?"

He nodded. "I had a very nice time today. We need to go into town together more often."

Lindie smiled. "I did too."

She peered out the window. In the short time they had been driving, about an inch of snow had collected on the ground. Even Molly's brown fur looked sprinkled with flour. "It's snowing hard."

"This is just the start."

"We don't always have a white Christmas in Ohio." She remembered when the temperature was in the sixties one year. Of course, that was unusual.

"That's a couple weeks away. We'll probably be snowed in by then."

"I thought I would make a list of baking supplies." She had wanted to do it earlier but he'd rushed her off after breakfast.

"What supplies do you need?"

"I thought I would make a couple pies and I usually bake several types of cookies during Christmastime."

"Sounds *gut*. *Mei* stomach is already growling."

She nudged his side. "You just ate."

"*Nett* cookies or pie." He smiled. "We can get whatever you need tomorrow."

"*Denki*. And *denki* for the tea. I meant to tell you last *nacht*, but I got . . . sidetracked."

He grinned. "I would have made you a cup to drink in the tub, but I didn't think you would appreciate the effort."

Her breath caught in her throat. "Josiah!"

He chuckled.

Lindie enjoyed hearing him laugh. Simon had indicated Josiah's stress was from marrying her and she didn't want to be the cause any longer.

Josiah veered Molly into the drive and stopped next to the house.

"Is there anything in particular you want me to cook for supper?"

"*Yummasetti* sounds *gut*. It's one of Simon's favorite dishes too." He climbed off the bench and walked around to her side of the buggy.

"Then that's what I'll make." Lindie accepted his hand.

"It looks like I need to put some salt on these steps." He placed his arm around her waist and helped her to the door. Returning to the buggy, he asked, "If Hannah is out in the barn, do you want me to send her inside?"

"*Jah*." Lindie couldn't wait to see Hannah's reaction to her gift. Perhaps if she hurried with supper, she and Hannah would have time to sketch.

Lindie stomped the snow off her shoes before entering the house. Once inside, she set the art supplies on the floor, then kicked off her wet shoes. Her stockings were drenched and her toes tingled. She considered soaking her feet in a pan of warm water. Instead, she changed her stockings and put on a pair of wool socks. Afterward, she added a few logs to the stove, then took the art supplies into the kitchen.

The door opened and closed a few minutes later. Hannah stepped around the corner. She eyed the bag on the table, then looked at Lindie and signed, "Is that for me?"

"Yes." Lindie pulled the chair out from the table, motioned for Hannah to sit, then sat beside her and reached into the bag.

Hannah stared at the box of colored pencils. Finally, she lifted her eyes to Lindie. "Thank you," she signed with exaggerated hand signals.

"From your *daed* too." She wished Josiah wasn't out in the barn. He would be pleased with his daughter's reaction. Her hands were even trembling as she opened the box.

⁓

Josiah unhitched the horse from the buggy and then led the mare inside the barn.

Simon ambled across the straw-covered wooden floor. He stopped in front of the half wall separating the stalls. "Is this a *gut* time to talk?"

"Sure." Josiah wondered when his father-in-law would bring up Josiah's plan to start timbering again.

Simon leaned against the gate. "Hannah helping with breakfast this morning was a big step forward, *jah*?"

"I hope it's a start," Josiah said, loosening the girth strap.

"*Sohn*, there's something else I've been meaning to talk with you about . . ."

Josiah stopped fussing with the equipment as he noticed Simon kicking at some loose hay on the floor. "What is it?"

"Just because you've *kumm* to an agreement, it doesn't make an arranged marriage easy. In many ways they are a *gut* bit tougher."

Josiah hadn't told a soul and never planned to do so either. He faced Simon. "Our agreement is that obvious?"

"I've seen it before."

Josiah teetered between relief and embarrassment that his father-in-law had figured it out. Either way, he didn't want to discuss this. He worked his way around to the backside of the mare and over to her other side.

"You'll have several obstacles to overcome . . . but you can make it work."

Detecting sadness in Simon's tone, Josiah leaned his forehead against Molly's neck. He had to say something.

"I want you to know . . ." Josiah's dry throat made it difficult to speak. He swallowed. "I'll always love Caroline. I won't let anyone take your *dochder's* place in *mei* heart."

His brows lifted. "And you've told Lindie that?"

"*Jah*. I was truthful. She knew right from the start that what I needed was someone to care for Hannah." His feelings toward Lindie had betrayed him lately, but he could rein them in if he worked harder on it.

Simon's forehead creased. "Then you've misunderstood what God commands. You should've spoken with the bishop before entering into the marriage covenant."

Josiah's stomach wrenched as if he'd been kicked. What he

thought would please his father-in-law had produced the opposite effect.

"Lindie is a young woman. She will want to have children."

"But how do I love—"

Simon's hand shot up. "In the Bible, Jacob didn't love Leah.
She was older and considered undesirable for a wife. But he didn't
mistreat her and he gave her offspring."

Something rose up in Josiah to defend Lindie. None of this
had anything to do with her not being desirable. That was far from
the truth. But children? Simon knew nothing of her pregnancy.
Otherwise he would realize it was enough for Josiah to accept her
unborn child as his own.

Simon clapped his shoulder. "I had to pray about how I was
treating Lindie. I realized it wasn't God's will for me to *nett* accept
your *fraa*. You need to pray also. Your marriage isn't too hard for
God, but it does require you taking your place of authority as
head of the *haus*."

Josiah's mind reeled.

"I think you've already made that decision, though."

"What do you mean?" Josiah's voice quivered.

"I know the decision to cut down trees again wasn't easy to
make. But you're ready to move forward. I see that."

This wasn't about moving forward. Was it?

"Simon." Josiah pushed the lump forming in his throat down
with a hard swallow. "I only plan on taking down an elm tree or
two. I wasn't going to reopen the sawmill."

Simon rubbed his beard. "*Sohn*, moving forward is something Caroline would want you to do."

Josiah wasn't sure how to respond. When he first recognized
his growing feelings toward Lindie, he purposely reminded

himself of his love and devotion to Caroline. Now Simon was giving his blessing to move on.

ॐ

The sun was setting by the time the men came inside. "It's snowing hard," Josiah said as he entered the kitchen.

Lindie smiled at the way his hair was matted down from his hat. "I'll have the table set in a minute. Did you see Hannah's drawing?"

Josiah leaned over his daughter's shoulder. "Wow." He looked up at Lindie. "She's really *gut*, isn't she?"

Simon peered longer at the picture. "Did you know she could draw?" he asked Josiah.

"*Nett* that *gut*."

Lindie pulled a stack of plates out of the cabinet. She had just set them on the counter when Hannah rushed over and wrapped her arms around Lindie's waist. Lindie paused a moment and then put her hand on the girl's shoulder. A child's love felt so pure.

During the meal, Lindie sensed a new atmosphere in the room. Even Simon talked more and made a point to marvel at Hannah's ability to capture a true depiction of nature. When the meal ended, Simon retreated to the *grossdaadi haus*.

Josiah excused Hannah. She went to her bedroom with her art supplies, while he loitered around the kitchen.

Lindie stacked the dishes. "You know what we forgot?"

"What?" Josiah took the dishes from her hands and carried them to the sink.

"The bell for the door." She placed the stopper in the sink, then turned the tap water on and added soap.

"We can stop in the morning after your *doktah's* appointment."

She froze. "What appointment?"

"He wants to do a . . . I forgot what he called the procedure, but you're scheduled for one at nine o'clock." He grabbed a dish-cloth and dried his hands.

"I'm *nett* going back. I want a midwife to deliver the *boppli*." Certainly he would respect her decision. She was the one having the baby.

He stared at her.

"Josiah, that's how it's done in *mei* district."

"Didn't the *doktah* tell you? You're at high risk."

She chewed the inside of her lip.

He locked eyes with her. "Did you hear me? High risk," he repeated.

"I still want a midwife."

He shook his head. "*Doktah* Ethridge is *gut*. He delivered Hannah. Besides, our district is so small we don't have any mid-wives. Even if we did, she would refer you to a *doktah*."

"A lot of women have their *boppli* alone. Without anyone. I can deliver—"

"*Nay!* You can't possibly think of having the *boppli* without a medical person's help. It's *nett* safe."

She stared at the floor.

"You seem uninterested in the *boppli*. I don't know what hap-pened between you and the *boppli's* father. Any decent man would have married you," he mumbled under his breath as he crossed the room. "That's what you're upset about, isn't it? You can't get over the fact that the father didn't marry you."

That was furthest from the truth, but she held her tongue. She recalled how Eli had jumped to conclusions and stormed over to Moses's parents' home to confront him. Had Moses not already left town to go work for his uncle, her brother would have put him on the spot to marry her.

"I knew it," he said. "Pretending the *boppli* doesn't exist won't make it so." He continued, "Just because some man rejected you, you can't reject this innocent—"

"That's *nett* why." She ground the words through clenched teeth. A sharp pain struck her side and she gasped.

"Wha—what's wrong?" Josiah wrapped his arm around her waist and guided her to a chair. He knelt beside her. "Lindie, are you having pains?"

She clutched her side. "I'll be all right," she said through guarded breaths.

"I shouldn't have said anything. I didn't mean to upset you." Josiah spread his hand over her belly. He closed his eyes.

She should be praying too, but she couldn't focus on anything but the shards of pain coursing through her. Unable to hold it in, she whimpered.

Josiah opened his eyes. "It's *nett* any better?"

She shook her head.

"You're sweating." He hurried to the sink and returned with a wet dishrag. Kneeling beside her, he dabbed the cool cloth against her forehead, uttering another prayer under his breath.

A moment passed. "The pain is easing *nau*."

"*Ach gut*," he said, blowing out a breath. "Will you tell me if it happens again?"

Before she formed her response, another driving sharpness stole her breath. This time the intensity passed quickly. Even so, the pain had left her weak. What else could it be but her body rejecting the baby?

"Do you want to check yourself?"

A dull hum filled her ears. "What?"

"You know. Go in the bathroom and see if you're bleeding?"

"*Jah*, I suppose I should." She stood too fast and swayed. His arm came around her waist and she leaned against him, thankful for his support. Taking small steps, they ambled to the bathroom.

He opened the door and entered the room with her.

She cleared her throat. She might be dizzy, but she wasn't about to invite him to stay.

"Are you going to be all right?"

"*Jah*."

"Let me light the lamp." He struck a match and lit the wick. "I'll be in the hall." He reached for the knob and hesitated. "Call me if you need me."

She nodded.

Lindie waited until the door clicked. She then made her inspection. Nothing. Relief washed over her. *Lord, please forgive me. I don't know why I'm still struggling to accept all that's happened. Help me, Jesus, to see this pregnancy through your eyes.*

Lindie sank to her knees and cried.

He knocked. "Are you okay?"

She wasn't ready to leave the sanctuary of the bathroom.

"Lindie?" He knocked again.

She drew in a hitched breath. She wasn't okay. This was all too much.

"Cover yourself if you need to. I'm *kumming* in." Josiah opened the door. He knelt beside her and pulled her into his arms. "I'm sorry. I shouldn't have upset you." He brushed the stray hairs away from her face and kissed her cheek.

His tenderness soothed her.

"Are you . . . ?" His focus dropped to her abdomen.

"I didn't lose the *boppli*," she whispered.

"Praise God." He wrapped her in a tighter hug.

She silently thanked God for a concerned husband. He was a good man. Any woman would be singing praises to be married to him.

"Can you get up?" He rose, reached for her elbow, and helped her off the floor.

"*Denki*," she squeaked as he ushered her into his arms. Lindie buried her face in the crook of his neck and closed her eyes as he rubbed her back.

"For what?"

"For *nett* despising me."

He pulled back. When she lowered her head, he tipped her chin up so that she had no choice but to look at him. "I wish you would tell me about your past."

She flinched. "I—I'm *nett* ready yet."

"I'm trying to understand, and I'll wait . . . but I want you to know, no matter what, I'll always be your husband."

Tears blurred her vision. She didn't deserve him.

"*Kumm* on. I'm taking you to bed."

"I have to *redd-up* the kitchen. The dishes aren't even done."

"Tomorrow is another day." He guided her down the hall and into the bedroom. Once she was seated on the bed, he lit the lamp and went to her dresser. He pulled out a nightdress and handed it to her. "Are you going to be okay changing alone?"

"*Jah. Denki*, though."

He strolled to the door and paused. "Don't stay up too late. You need rest for your *doktah's* appointment in the morning." He left the room.

Lindie eased into her nightdress. She would pray for a blizzard, if she thought God would listen.

⌒

Josiah whispered another prayer thanking God that Lindie's pain had subsided. He nearly gasped when he felt her abdomen. She was small—the baby no more than a bump. And this was her second trimester. After leaving Lindie's room, he poked his head into his daughter's room. "Don't burn your lamp wick down. It's time to go to sleep," he signed.

Hannah set her pencil down and stretched out her arms toward him.

Josiah hugged her, then took a moment to study her picture. "Very good." Lindie had been right about his daughter's talent. The bird looked real. He waited until she packed her supplies, then he pulled the covers up and kissed her forehead. *"Gut nacht."*

His daughter hadn't been this happy since before Caroline died.

Neither had he.

Josiah glanced at Lindie's closed door. He still didn't understand why she would want to risk delivering the baby without a doctor. Maybe the intense pain she had experienced was God's way of helping her see she could not do this alone. Her stubborn determination to hide her past didn't help.

Josiah entered the kitchen. He didn't want Lindie waking up to a sink full of dirty dishes. Besides, if he tried to go to bed now, he would only wrestle with his thoughts. Had she turned and faced him after he kissed her cheek in the bathroom, he would have kissed her the way he wanted. And that might have led him to break his own rules of the marital arrangement.

Chapter Seventeen

M r. Plank?" The nurse stood at the end of the office lobby. His stomach pitted as he rose from his chair. It hadn't been more than a few minutes since they took Lindie to the exam room. "Is something wrong?"

The nurse smiled. "I thought you might like to see your baby on the ultrasound screen."

"Ah . . ." He exhaled louder than he intended.

"Fathers." She rolled her eyes. "You men are always so nervous." Chuckling, the nurse turned. "Follow me. I'll show you to the room."

He trailed the nurse to the first door on the left, then entered. A half second later his eyes adjusted to the darkened room. The dim light from the monitor illuminated Lindie's unwelcoming stare.

The nurse nudged him forward. Josiah cracked a smile at Lindie and inched closer. The black-and-white image on the screen sure didn't look like a *boppli* until the woman doing the test pointed out the *boppli's* positioning. He reached for Lindie's hand and squeezed it. "It's an amazing sight, *jah?*"

The tiny, shadowy mass moved on the display. Her eyes welled and she nodded.

Josiah looked off to his side at the small-framed woman who was busy adding more ointment to Lindie's abdomen. Even to him her belly looked too small to be holding a baby. "Everything is all right, isn't it?"

"Once I'm finished getting the measurements, Doctor Ethridge will discuss everything with you." The woman glided the wand over the gooey substance, then stopped. The screen faded to black. "I think I have all the measurements needed, but before you empty your bladder, I'd like the doctor to come in and take a look." She disappeared from the room.

Lindie stared at the ceiling.

"I'm sure that's standard," he said.

Doctor Ethridge entered the room. "Sorry to keep you waiting," he said, washing his hands at the sink. He took the seat before the monitor and added gel to the wand. "This will probably feel cold." He circled the wand around Lindie's belly.

"Did Lindie tell you about the pains she had last night?"

This time she reached for his hand and squeezed it. Hard.

Doctor Ethridge lifted the wand from her belly. "How would you describe the pain?"

"Sharp . . . hot, like a fire poker was jabbing me."

"Can you show me where you felt the pain?"

Lindie hesitated.

Josiah took that as his clue to leave. "I'll wait for you in the lobby." He winked at Lindie and slipped out of the room.

Stepping into the hallway, the nurse stopped him. "Doctor Ethridge wants me to draw your blood."

If only he had smothered his coughing yesterday while the

doctor was around. Josiah followed her down the hallway and into the lab room.

"Have a seat while I get things ready." She motioned to the only chair.

He sat. The posters on the wall showing the network of arteries and veins hadn't changed. The refrigerator still hummed like a fan blade was bent.

He didn't need more lab work. Most people caught a cold in the winter. At least that was what he told himself.

"You know the routine," she said without looking up from arranging the supplies.

Too well. Over the years he'd been poked so many times, he complained that his blood could leak just by squeezing his arm. But despite believing it was a waste of time, money, and good blood, Josiah pushed up his sleeve.

She tied the rubber strap around his arm and tapped his veins until they gorged. She studied his arm. "Make a fist. I need to find a good vein. Doc wants the works."

The works meant anywhere from five to seven tubes. Six years ago when he gave that much blood, he nearly fell out. Not that the sight of blood brought on the willies. His veins had shut down. Collapsed, the nurse had told him. Bottom line, what he learned was that most of his blood was depleted of oxygen, which had caused the dizziness. He had a vivid memory of the foul scent of ammonia that had brought him back to consciousness.

"You're going to feel a little poke." She drove the needle into his vein and blood pooled into the glass tube.

Josiah closed his eyes and reviewed the last few weeks in his mind. The night sweats started after Eli had approached him about marrying Lindie. Those were stress induced. The coughing was the start of a cold. Nothing to worry about. The other routine questions that Doctor Ethridge had asked during his yearly exam weren't as easy to dismiss: unexplained bleeding, bruising, lumps, rash, fever, and fatigue. He pushed the negative thoughts aside. Lindie needed him now. He would worry about his own health later.

Josiah opened his eyes as the nurse filled the last tube and released the rubber strap.

She pressed a piece of gauze where the needle had been and secured a Band-Aid over it. "How do you feel? Do you need a glass of orange juice?"

"I'm fine." He pushed his sleeve down. He would be even better once he could check on Lindie.

✑

Doctor Ethridge peered over his wire-rimmed glasses at Lindie. "No caffeine. No lifting. Limit your household chores. Do you have a powered washing machine?"

She shook her head. "It's a manual wringer."

He looked back at the paper and continued jotting notes. "No laundry."

"That's *nett* possible." Seated in front of the doctor's desk, Lindie leaned forward to catch a glimpse of what he was writing. What did he want her to do all day, lie in bed? That wasn't what Josiah had bargained for in a wife.

Lindie pointed her finger at his paper. "You're rendering me useless."

The door opened and the nurse led Josiah into the room. He sat in the empty chair beside her.

"I was just reviewing a list of restrictions for Lindie to follow."

She sensed Josiah watching her, but couldn't bring herself to look his way. He must already regret her presence in his life, and now he had reason to resent the arrangement. He hadn't asked much of her. Some of the husbands of friends back home expected their wives to work out in the barn and field, on top of keeping up with the household duties. She had yet to see the inside of Josiah's barns.

"Basically, I want her on light duty as much as possible."

"I told him that wasn't doable," she said to Josiah.

"*Jah*, it is." Josiah's tone was stern, his words final.

She shifted in her seat.

"When do you want to see her again?"

"You can make the appointment for two weeks, but if she cramps again, I'll need to see her immediately."

"Okay." Josiah leaned closer to her. "So if you get those pains again—"

"I didn't just *kumm* into the room. I heard what he said," she snapped.

She lowered her head and studied the cotton fabric of her dress. Josiah was a lot like her brother. Eli had treated her as though she were incapable of making decisions. Wise ones anyway. Josiah thought she was irresponsible for not eating more, and Eli had accused her of lacking sound judgment after she didn't come home that night. Privately, she condemned herself. Part of her didn't care if the baby lived. God certainly couldn't be pleased with such selfish thoughts. Perhaps she should have taken the drug Moses tried to get her to take to end the pregnancy. At the time, she couldn't imagine the morning after pill being part of God's plan.

"Lindie?"

She lifted her head.

Josiah and the doctor were standing.

She rose and followed them into the hallway, then down the short corridor to the waiting room where she saw Ada and her husband sitting.

"Lindie, what a surprise." Ada crossed the room, a knowing grin on her face. "I didn't expect to see you here." She patted her extended belly. "I'm due at the first of the year."

Josiah winked at Lindie and motioned to the office window. "I'll take care of the paperwork." He made it as far as the magazine rack before Ada's husband stopped him.

Lindie was torn between listening to Ada talk about her pregnancy and trying to observe Josiah. She couldn't decide how he felt at having run into the other couple.

"*Doktah* Ethridge is a *gut boppli* doctor," Ada said. "I think you'll like him. Was this your first visit?"

"Ah . . ."

"I shouldn't jump to conclusions. *Doktah* Ethridge is a general country *doktah*. He set *mei sohn's* cast when he slipped on the ice last winter." Her eyes twinkled with mischief. "But I know a pregnant woman when I see one," she whispered.

Lindie looked at Josiah for support, but he was too far away to be of any help. The men seemed engrossed in their own conversation. Judging by Josiah's relaxed stance, they were probably talking about livestock.

Ada nudged her. "So tell me, how are you and Hannah getting along?"

"*Gut.*"

The nurse entered the lobby. "Ada, if you'll come with me, I'll get your weight and vitals."

"We'll talk more on Sunday." Ada waved at her husband, then pointed at the nurse.

Her husband left Josiah and the couple disappeared down the hall.

Lindie met Josiah in front of the office window.

"The doctor wants to see you in two weeks. Do you want a morning or afternoon appointment?"

Lindie shrugged.

"Afternoon, please," Josiah said to the receptionist.

"I'll put you down for two o'clock." She jotted the time on a slip of paper and handed it to Lindie. "We'll see you in two weeks."

Her next appointment was two days before Christmas, traditionally one of the busiest cooking days of the year. She recalled how much she loved *Mamm's* butter pecan cookies. She pictured herself as a young girl standing in front of the oven as they baked. The kitchen would be abuzz with laughter. Even the very young children would have participated in mixing the sugar-cookie dough. But if the doctor didn't take her off bed rest, she would not be sharing this experience with Hannah.

Cold air blasted her face.

They walked with their heads down into the snowy gust of wind.

He bunched the collar of his coat under his chin and drew his shoulders up. "If you don't mind, I'd like your help picking out some paint and brushes. But I want to keep it a Christmas surprise."

"Sure." She'd never known a child who received a store-bought gift for Christmas, unless it was a new pair of shoes. Even that was rare. Most shoes were handed down from older siblings or cousins. But never something worldly like paints.

He opened the buggy door and she climbed inside. Her teeth chattered as she pulled the quilt over her legs.

Molly's winter coat was wet from the snow. Josiah untied the mare from the post, then jumped inside the buggy. White clouds escaped his mouth as he blew into his fisted hands.

"It's freezing out there," he said with a shiver.

Lindie pulled the quilt from around her neck and offered it to him. She hadn't expected him to wrap his arm around her and pull her closer.

"Ach!" Her stomach fluttered and she winced when he tucked the blanket between her backside and the bench.

"Sorry," Josiah said as he finished draping the quilt over her shoulder. He tucked it under her chin, then encased himself with her. "We need to warm up a minute."

Her internal heater ignited the moment he cocooned them. His warm breath on her cheek caused her to shudder uncontrollably.

"Are you having pains again?"

"I'm *nett*—" His hand blindly crawled under the cover, under her cape, and rested on her belly. She sucked in a breath. Now the flutter moved directly under his hand.

"Have you felt the *boppli* move yet?"

She shrugged. Tingles rippled. *Jah*, something was happening—because he had breached her personal space.

"It might be too early. I don't remember when Hannah started kicking." His chest expanded and fell. Then his eyes widened and he jerked his hand away. *"Ach* . . . I'm sorry. I got carried away. We better go." He grabbed the reins.

Silence fell between them. He turned the buggy in the opposite direction as the art store.

"I thought you wanted to stop at the store for paint."

"I forgot you need bed rest."

That was something she wanted to forget. She couldn't take care of Hannah lying in bed all day. What would people think of her? What would Simon think?

He crinkled his face. "What's wrong?"

"Ada knows about the *boppli*." She cringed. "I didn't tell her. She guessed."

"Don't concern yourself about it."

How could she not? Just the other day he panicked when he thought the women knew.

"It's fine, Lindie. Really, it is." He sounded sincere. "I overreacted the other day. I was wrong." He reached for her hand and squeezed it. "We've been married a month, let them draw their own conclusions."

"And when the *boppli* arrives three months earlier than everyone expects?"

"We will still be the proud parents of a new addition to the family."

She dared not remind him that Simon would find out too. He hadn't shown any sign of accepting her yet. This pregnancy would compound the matter.

Lindie cleared her throat. "There's something I've been meaning to bring up. Why isn't Hannah in s*chul*?" Without giving him a chance to respond, she continued, "The child is in the *haus* too much. She's isolated and . . . and probably lonely. She needs to be around other children more."

"She was in *schul* . . . for a while." He shrugged. "The more she fell behind in her learning, the more she acted out. Someone even told me that I didn't discipline her enough. I was embarrassed and angry. It doesn't look *gut* for a man to *nett* have control of his *haushold*."

Lindie understood. Even at her age, Eli thought protecting her meant sending her away—marrying her off.

"Will you please give the matter some thought? She could return after Christmas break."

He cringed.

"She needs to move forward. I would offer to homeschool her, but I think it would help her to be in a learning environment with other children."

"*Jah*, I agree."

The snow continued to fall the entire ride home.

Josiah pulled up to the house and climbed out. "It's icy," he said, extending his hand. He walked with her up the steps and into the house. "I'll be leaving shortly to pick up the bishop's son, Jakob. He's going to start helping in the workshop. Do you mind making up a list of brushes and any other painting supplies that come to mind?"

A smile rested on her lips. "I think I saw a beginner's kit. It would have everything that she needs."

"Hmm . . . a beginner's set? Will it have all those fancy brushes?"

"Probably *nett*." She shrugged her shoulders out of the cape, then hung it on the hook.

"I want the very best for *mei maydel*."

"Be careful, Josiah." Lindie wanted to add that it wasn't good to spoil a child. She untied her winter bonnet and removed it. Snow fluttered to the floor. "Maybe you should consider starting off small. She could build her supplies as she learns."

"So you think I'm spoiling her?"

She lifted one foot to remove her boot and wobbled.

Josiah steadied her while she finished taking them off. "Well?" He waited.

"You said yourself that you wanted the *very best* for your *maydel*." She pushed the wet boots out of the way. "Sounds like spoiling to me."

"So it does." He smiled. "There should be paper inside the

top drawer of the desk. Will you jot me a list of the names of those fancy brushes?"

"Sure." She sat down at the desk, pulled out a piece of paper from the drawer, and wrote down the names. She also made a list of ingredients she needed for baking.

The door opened and Simon and Hannah entered. Hannah shucked her coat at the door.

Simon craned his head toward the desk. "Did you find the package that came for you, Lindie? I left it on the kitchen table."

"A package? For me?" Lindie shot out of the desk chair.

She scooted past them and rushed into the kitchen. The return label on the box was Eli's address. She grabbed a knife from the drawer and cut open the package. Yarn. She stopped herself from squealing with delight. Margaret knew how much she loved to knit. Lindie pulled out several different colored balls. At the bottom of the box, she found material—enough yards to make several outfits for the baby. Perhaps even a new dress for Hannah and herself. She opened the note.

Lindie,

I wanted to send you some material.

I wish we could spend the day sewing together like old times.

The yarn is left over from knitting, but you should be able to make plenty of potholders out of it.

I miss you. Write when you can.

Margaret

Lindie smiled. "I miss you too," she whispered.

"*Nau* you'll have something to do while you're on bed rest," Josiah said, coming up beside her.

"Shh." Lindie didn't want Simon to overhear and ask if she was ill. She reached for cups from the cupboard and set them on the counter.

"*Nay* caffeine," Josiah said as she lifted the coffeepot.

"Half a cup."

He shook his head. "The *doktah* said none."

Footsteps stopped behind them. Simon cleared his throat. "While you're going after Jakob, I'd like to talk with Lindie."

Chapter Eighteen

Lindie tried to recall the last time Simon had spoken directly to her. She wiggled the kettle. "Can I pour you a cup of *kaffi?*"

"*Nay denki.*" He pulled a chair away from the table and sat. "Will you join me?"

Lindie returned the kettle to the stovetop. She swept her hand over the front of her dress and drew in a steady breath. She took the seat opposite him at the table.

Simon cleared his throat. "I know things were rough for you at the start given the . . . unusual circumstances."

He hadn't indicated he was aware of her pregnancy before, but she couldn't imagine what else he could be referring to.

"You seem to have adjusted."

"I think so."

"Hannah has too. And Josiah . . ." His voice drifted off.

Lindie swallowed hard. "Is something wrong?" She didn't know Simon well enough to decipher the distant look in his eyes or his sober expression. Earlier, under the quilt in the buggy, she had felt so close to Josiah. His face had lit up when he spread his hand over her belly. In that moment, she'd allowed herself to pretend it was Josiah's baby growing inside of her.

"Josiah's been under a lot of stress lately."

Lindie nodded. "That's *mei* fault." She barely mouthed the words. Simon had told her that himself not long ago.

"This cough he has . . . it's lingered for weeks. He hasn't had a cold this prolonged in six years. Has he complained of *nacht* sweats?"

She hadn't shared the night with him to know the answer. Warmth spread over her face, and she shifted on the chair and looked down at the puddle of melted snow from Simon's boots.

"I'm worried about him. I don't know that he should be taking trees down."

Lindie bowed her head. *Give me the right words of comfort, Lord.* She looked at him and spoke softly. "I know it was hard on both you and Josiah losing Caroline the way you did. I don't know why he's so adamant about timbering again. I told him *mei bruder* would understand."

"I'm worried he isn't well enough to be working in the woods."

The door opened and Hannah peeked around the corner. Josiah walked up to the kitchen table. "I left word for Jakob to *kumm* over when he can. The bishop said he was running an errand."

"I think I'll work on the pallets," Simon said as he made his way to the door.

Josiah leaned close to Lindie. "What was that all about?"

"He's worried about you."

He pulled back and pointed at his chest. "Me?"

"He thinks you've been coughing too much."

"Someone needs to tell him this is flu season." Josiah laughed, but it broke into a cough.

"Hmm. Sounds like Simon has a valid point. I think you need to stay inside where it's warm."

"Are you the *doktah nau?*" He wagged his brows. "You're on bed rest yourself. How are you going to take care of me? Because I can cough a lot more." He exaggerated a fake cough, then winked.

"In all seriousness, Josiah, I don't think you should work in the woods. Wait until spring."

His playfulness sobered. "This is something I have to do."

"I'll write Eli a letter and explain how—"

His fingers covered her mouth. "It isn't about Eli." He dropped his hand, turned, and picked up the box she'd received. "*Nau* follow me."

She trailed him to her bedroom where he set the box on the floor, then fluffed the feather pillows and pulled the covers back.

"Get in," he said.

Only two weeks to get Christmas gifts and baking done and she was stuck lying in bed all day. Lindie batted her eyes but failed to get a different response from him. She plopped down on the bed.

Josiah sat on the edge of the mattress. "In a few minutes, I'm going to send Hannah in here. I don't want her outside when I bring those trees down. Can you make sure she stays with you?"

᠄

Josiah decided not to wait for Jakob. If the trees were already down when Jakob arrived, Josiah could use him to help debark and lumber them. Besides, the more he thought about it, he couldn't risk the trees falling the wrong way. He didn't even want to bring Moose out until the trees were ready to be hauled out of the woods.

Josiah sharpened the axe against the grinding stone, his thoughts flitting. Could he really move forward? Simon seemed to think Josiah was ready. But he and Lindie had a long way to go before any real change would happen. They must build a friendship first before he would consider inviting her into his bed. A prickly sweat broke out under his clothes at the thought. He wasn't ready.

Josiah checked the blade's sharpness. It was ready. There was no sense putting this off. He'd spent three years wondering what life would be like had the tree fallen in a different direction.

The snow crunched under his boots as he made his way out to the woods. The long walk provided ample opportunity to unearth the past. Memories he'd buried in order to protect his heart now were exposed. It was time he dealt with reality. He supposed this was part of the healing process. Until recently, he never thought he would want to go forward.

Josiah scanned the area. The lumber trail, once wide enough for a wagon, was overgrown with brush. The chains would easily get tangled. He chose a standing of elm trees close to the edge so it wouldn't be too difficult for Moose to drag them out.

Josiah leaned the axe against the tree, pulled his hankie out of his pocket, and wiped the sweat from his brow. Taking the first swing was more difficult than he thought. He swept the snow off a fallen log and sat down.

Jesus, I need your strength to get beyond this moment. I believe Caroline is with you and it's time for me to go on with mei *life. Hannah, Simon . . . we all need to move forward. Jesus, will you show me how to open* mei *heart to Lindie? Love her the way you love the church?*

Josiah sat with his elbows on his knees and rested his head in his hands until the cold and wet log soaked into his pants. He stood, walked around the selected tree, and determined the best direction for it to fall. He chopped a few notches in the side he wanted to drop, then moved to the opposite side.

He readied the axe as someone cleared his throat behind him. He brought the axe back down.

"I thought you could use some help," Simon said.

"Are you sure you want to do this?"

Simon nodded.

Josiah and Simon worked in unison, both consumed with their own thoughts. When the tree hit the ground with a thunderous thud, they shared a moment of silence.

Josiah wiped his face with his coat sleeve. He cleared his throat. "I'll start removing the limbs if you want to get Moose and the chains."

"*Jah*, okay." Simon limped over to the field.

Josiah straddled the log and chiseled away at the branches with the hatchet. When Simon returned with Moose, Jakob was with him. Several hours later Josiah held his lower back and stretched. Every muscle ached. He ambled into the house exhausted.

Lindie met him at the door. She helped him out of his coat, then insisted he sit down.

She knelt down in front of him and unlaced his boots. "Are you okay? You look dog tired." She tugged hard and his sock came off with the boot. "You smell like cedar pitch. I thought you were taking down elm trees," she said, pulling off the other boot.

"I needed an extra tree."

"What for?" She set his socks aside.

He leaned down and smiled. "Can't a man have any secrets?"

"You were out there so long, you had me going crazy with worry."

He reached for her hands and pulled her up off her knees, then stood. "I think I like the sound of that," he said, leaning toward her. He caught himself about to kiss her and jerked back. He hadn't meant to embarrass her, but a crimson shade flashed over her face.

"I'm sorry," he whispered.

"I'll get you a dry pair of socks."

Chapter Nineteen

Under Josiah's mandate, Lindie had followed the doctor's orders and for four long days she'd stayed in bed. It hadn't been all bad. She'd had plenty of time to knit Josiah and Simon scarves for Christmas. She hoped they weren't too put off by the multiple colors. None of the balls of yarn were full skeins. But since Joseph in the Bible had a coat of many colors, maybe they'd be okay with it.

But now it was Sunday. Lindie tossed the covers aside, crawled out of bed, and quickly selected a forest-green dress and black apron to wear. Josiah couldn't possibly expect her to miss church service.

Standing at the stove, Josiah looked sideways at her and frowned as she entered the kitchen. Not the warm greeting she'd wanted.

"What are you doing out of bed?" He stirred the oatmeal, which smelled like cinnamon.

"This is Sunday." That should be enough reason, but she continued, "I feel fine. Great, in fact. And I'm well rested."

"Is that so?" He removed the spoon and set it aside, then

moved the pot of oatmeal over to the wire cooling rack. "You feel great?" He crossed the room.

"*Jah.*" She squared her shoulders.

"Well rested, you say?" Josiah placed his hand on her lower back and turned her toward the hall. "*Gut*, then I must be doing something right." He prodded her forward.

"Josiah." She wheeled around, bumping into his chest. He stepped back, but she closed the distance between them. "Up until *nau*, I've bitten *mei* tongue when you've hovered over me as though you were calculating every calorie I consumed."

"And you're finally gaining some weight." His eyes traveled the length of her.

"I'm *nett* spending another day in that bed. *Mei* backside will spawn bedsores."

He grinned and tugged on her elbows, drawing her closer to him. She peered up into his eyes as he towered above her.

He bent so that his cheek rested against hers and whispered next to her ear, "I can make a paste that will take care of your backside problem."

She sprung back, finger pointing. "That's *nett* funny."

Still grinning, he shrugged.

"Don't you have livestock to feed before church?"

"I already did the chores. I wanted to have enough time to sit with you while you ate breakfast."

"You mean monitor *mei* intake. Are you keeping record of what I eat?"

"*Jah*, I am." He turned her around. "And by the way," he said, nudging her toward the hallway, "you're *nett* drinking enough milk. *Nau* get back into bed and I'll bring your breakfast in."

"Jo-si-ah," she pleaded. "Don't make me miss church."

His compassionate gaze locked on hers, Then he shook his head. "You can read your Bible and pray in bed."

"I don't think God wants me isolated from the others. I think you do. You want to hide me until—"

"That's *nett* true." His brows furrowed.

"What's Simon going to say?"

He crossed his arms. "Don't you care what your husband says?"

"*Jah*, I do, but—Josiah, please. I can't stay another day in that bed."

He paused. "Okay. But promise me that you'll go to bed as soon as it's over."

"I will."

He stepped closer. "I'm warning you, Lindie. I'll crawl in bed beside you if you so much as wiggle a toe outside of the covers."

She sucked in a breath, terrified that he might be serious.

❧

Tension simmered between Josiah and Lindie at the breakfast table. She forced down the last spoonful of gummy oatmeal as if it were a dose of bitter medicine. She wouldn't give him a reason to complain about how little she ate.

Josiah stood. "Will you help Hannah with her *kapp* while I get the buggy ready?"

"Sure."

Lindie gestured to her hair and signed, asking Hannah to bring her the brush.

The girl scooted out of the room in a hurry.

Meanwhile, Lindie collected the dirty dishes and started the dishwater. A few bowls, utensils, milk glasses, and the pot Josiah cooked the oatmeal in wasn't even a sinkload, but she didn't want the kitchen untidy when they left for church. Simon left earlier, saying he needed to meet with the bishop prior to church. Josiah thought it had something to do with Simon's trip schedule. He bought his ticket to Centerville for the day after Christmas.

Hannah raced back into the room with the soft bristle brush and sat down at the table.

Leaving the dishes to soak, she unraveled Hannah's hair, setting the pins aside until she had all the tangles brushed out. She worked quickly and had the hair in place when the bell Josiah had mounted over the door jingled.

He stuck his head into the kitchen. "Are you two ready?"

"Almost," Lindie replied. She secured the last pin in place.

Hannah touched the top of her *kapp* and stood. Smiling wide, she stretched her arms around Lindie's waist and hugged her tightly.

Lindie's heart warmed. If it hadn't been time to leave for the Sunday service, she would have held the child until Hannah broke from the embrace. But Lindie didn't want to keep Josiah waiting, so she tapped the youngster's shoulder and motioned toward her father.

Josiah signed for Hannah to put on her boots and cape. Once she skipped from the room, he turned to Lindie. "She's needed a maternal hug for a while *nau*."

"I could spend more time with her if I wasn't in bed all day." She arched her brows and offered her most persuasive smile, but to no avail.

"You won't sway me by sulking either. I don't intend to change *mei* mind."

"A bit overprotective for someone with a closed mind—closed heart," she muttered, adding, "I got that message on day one." She said the last part loud enough for him to hear, but his reaction was unreadable—a blank canvas.

"We need to go." He walked away.

She grabbed the jar of peanut butter and a loaf of bread off the counter. She hadn't had time to prepare something for the meal after the service and didn't want to arrive empty-handed.

Once outside, Lindie drew in a lungful of crisp air and coughed. Having been shut in the house for several days, her lungs needed cleaning out from inhaling smoke fumes from the woodstove.

Josiah coughed too as he took his place on the buggy bench. "This cold air has a way of taking your breath away."

"I think it's from being trapped indoors."

"Trapped?"

"Inhaling woodstove smoke all day is bound to clog anyone's lungs."

Josiah focused on reining Molly onto the road.

Fresh snow blanketed both sides of the plowed road. Molly trotted, her nostrils expelling white clouds into the air.

Hannah snuggled up against Lindie's side and intertwined her arm with hers. Gratitude washed over Lindie as she looked down at the child. Lindie closed her eyes and prayed. Denki, *Father, for your unending love and grace. For giving me a glimpse of motherhood.* Lindie rested her hand on her belly and smiled. *I've struggled to understand all that's happened, but, God, I'm beginning—*

Josiah nudged Lindie. "Are you feeling okay?"

"*Jah*, why?"

His eyes flicked from her hand over her belly, up to her eyes, then back to the road. "I thought maybe you were having problems."

"*Nay*," she said. "Just enjoying the day."

He pulled into the drive of a large two-story farmhouse and parked the buggy beside the others.

Lindie stepped out of the buggy and, waiting for Hannah to slide out, scanned the yard. There were buggies, but no activity. Everyone must be in the barn, trying to stay warm. But it, too, lacked the normal bustle that occurred just before the service started. "Where is everyone? The barn looks dark."

"We meet in the *haus*." He looped the reins over the rail. "The Masts have a large basement that can hold everyone, so most of the services are held here during the winter months." He went to the back of the buggy, pulled out a ratty wool cover, and gave it a shake. Then he draped it over the mare.

Lindie reached inside the buggy for the bread and peanut butter. "I should have prepared something warm to eat."

"You should still be in bed," Josiah mumbled, coming up beside her.

"We're here *nau*. Let's go inside." She hunched her shoulders, shielding her face from the wind, and hurried along the shoveled path.

Once inside, Josiah joined the men in the basement, while Lindie took the food into the kitchen where the women were gathered. She placed the loaf of bread and jar of peanut butter on the counter just as one of the women announced the service was ready to start. She would make the sandwiches later. Lindie and Hannah followed the others down the narrow staircase and found a place on a bench.

The service seemed long, and Lindie found sitting for three hours difficult as the unforgiving bench caused her back muscles to stiffen. She shifted, then shifted again, but it seemed impossible to find a suitable position.

Once the service ended, she stood, and Josiah was at her side.

"What's wrong? You fidgeted throughout the entire service."

"I'm all right *nau*." She kept her voice low.

"I think we should go."

"We haven't even had time to eat or fellowship." She motioned to the women filing up the stairs. "I need to make some sandwiches."

"I don't want to stay long," he said.

"Okay." She joined the women in the kitchen.

The large farmhouse kitchen had plenty of working counter space. Lindie sliced the loaf of bread, stacking the pieces on a plate.

Ada came up beside her and elbowed Lindie. "You look better today than the day I saw you at *Doktah* Ethridge's office."

"*Denki*, I'm feeling better." She spread peanut butter over the bread.

"I hope you'll be feeling well enough for the Christmas visitations." Rebecca sank a spoon into the bowl of baked beans. "Since our district is so small, we have made it our second Christmas tradition to caravan to each other's homes."

"It's an entire day of fellowship," one woman said.

"And eating," another woman added.

Lindie smiled. "It sounds like fun."

"It is." Ada tapped her oversized belly. "But I'm *nett* sure how much extra baking I can get done between *nau* and Christmas."

Rebecca patted Ada's shoulder. "We'll put you on the list for hot cocoa, then."

"That I can do." Ada laughed.

"We all serve something different. Last year I made a large pot of vegetable soup," Rebecca said. "And it was *gut* that I did. It had snowed hard and by the end of the evening we were all half frozen."

Lindie spread the peanut butter over the last sandwich as she listened to the women's banter about who would serve what. She wanted to join in the festivities and hoped Josiah would agree. But that would take convincing since she was on bed rest.

Ellen leaned over Lindie's shoulder. "*Nay* jam?"

Lindie shook her head. "I forgot it. And *mei* pantry is loaded with jars dating back two years." She lifted one shoulder in a shrug. "Josiah hasn't seemed interested in eating it."

Ellen frowned. "So when is your *boppli* due?"

Ada cringed. "I'm sorry. I spilled the news about seeing you and Josiah at the *doktah's* office." She looked at Ellen. "I told you it was her first visit."

"So have you decided on names?"

Josiah cleared his throat and crossed the room. "I hope if it's a *bu* she names him after me." He smiled at Lindie as he placed his hand on her lower back. "You wouldn't mind two Josiahs, would you?"

Struck speechless, Lindie couldn't do anything but smile.

"Lindie, we should think about leaving soon." He looked around the room at the other women. "*Doktah* Ethridge is concerned about this being her first *boppli* and doesn't want her overdoing it. She should be on bed rest until her next appointment." He tapped her back. "Why don't you make us a plate to take home? I'll go get Hannah."

Lindie nodded, still consumed with the thought of two Josiahs.

Ada reached for Lindie's hand and squeezed it. "Is the *doktah* worried or is Josiah just being overly protective because of Caroline's miscarriage?"

"What?" She looked to where Josiah had been standing, but he'd disappeared into the other room.

Ada put her hand over her mouth. "You didn't know."

So that was why he was so insistent on bed rest. The doctor

had said light housework, not to stay off her feet completely. She wished Josiah had told her that Caroline had lost a baby. But then again, she wasn't ready to share her past. How could she expect more from him?

"Are you ready?" He stopped at the doorway.

"Um . . ." Lindie wiped her hands on her dress apron.

"I'll get the buggy ready." Josiah tapped Hannah's shoulder and motioned to the door.

Rebecca reached for a plate and began to fill it.

Ada heaped food onto another one.

By the time the women finished preparing the plates, Lindie had enough food for two days.

"We don't need this much." Lindie juggled the plates in her hands.

"Josiah and Simon will eat it. It won't go to waste." Rebecca walked her to the door. "I'll stop by sometime this week and check on you."

Simon. Now he would know about the baby. Maybe she should have stayed in bed today. Lindie climbed up on the bench after Hannah and waited for Josiah to untie Molly from the post. He took his place beside them and tucked the quilt around them all.

"All set?" He smiled.

"Why didn't you tell me that Caroline miscarried?"

Chapter Twenty

L indie's question blindsided Josiah. He wished she hadn't said
anything in front of Hannah, but at least his daughter didn't
seem aware of the conversation.

"This isn't the time to talk about that." He nodded toward
Hannah. Not that his daughter, seated between them, would have
a direct view of their lip movements, but he couldn't chance her
following enough of the conversation to ask her own questions.

The rest of the ride home felt strained. He pulled into the
yard, stopped the buggy next to the front door, and climbed out.
"I'm going to take care of Molly and feed the other animals." He
took hold of Lindie's hand and helped her down.

"We can't forget the food." She leaned to reach inside, but he
stopped her.

"I'll *kumm* back for the plates."

Hannah bounced off the buggy seat, whisked by them, and
nearly lost her footing on the slippery steps.

Josiah signaled Hannah to slow down, then wrapped his arm
around Lindie's waist, giving her support while they climbed the
icy porch steps together. "I need to salt these again," he said.

"I can do—"

He merely frowned and she stopped talking. He appreciated her eagerness to help, but he wouldn't let her risk slipping on the ice to spread rock salt. "You promised after church you would go straight to bed."

She frowned. "I will after I warm up the meal."

"I'll do it after I'm finished in the barn." He opened the door for her.

"You're *nett* going to let me even do that? The food is cooked. It's just a matter of warming it."

"And that's something I can do." He moved past her in the entry where she was removing her cape and went to the woodstove. After a quick check, he added another log.

"Does Simon know I'm pregnant?"

"If he doesn't hear something during the church meal, he will in a day or so after the women tell their husbands." He wiped the bark off his hands.

"What are you going to tell him?"

He shrugged.

Lindie shuffled down the hallway toward the bedrooms.

Josiah closed the firebox, then went outside and led Molly to the barn.

He jabbed a forkful of hay and tossed it over the stall's half wall. This simple task caused him to break out in a sweat. He lowered the pitchfork and leaned against it as he pulled a hankie from his pocket. Josiah wanted to believe he had overexerted himself, but that wasn't the truth. As soon as he wiped his forehead, more perspiration accumulated. The back of his shirt clung to his skin. Chills racked his body. If the doctor had not quizzed him so hard, he would guess this was the flu. Still, he refused to accept it was something more serious despite what looked obvious.

When the barn chores were completed, Josiah returned to the house. It didn't take long to warm up the meal. He set a plate for Hannah at the table, then took another into the bedroom for Lindie.

She sat with her back resting against the pillows. Her eyes followed him as he crossed the room. "Are you feeling all right?"

He handed her the plate of food. "*Jah*, why?"

Her bright-blue eyes studied his. "You look pale. Sickly."

He touched his forehead. Moist. "I'm fine." He pointed to her plate. "You need to eat."

"I'm worried you'll get run-down if you keep trying to do everything. Please, stop being so protective. I don't need to stay in bed all day. Let me help."

He shook his head.

"I know you're worried that I'll miscarry too, but I'm not Caroline."

He sat on the edge of the bed and faced her. "Caroline lost two *bopplis*. One the year after Hannah was born and the other two years later." He didn't tell her that he blamed himself. The doctor had warned them about potential infertility issues associated with his chemotherapy treatment. So when Caroline became pregnant, they were shocked and overjoyed at the same time. The stillborn births were difficult on Caroline. It tore him apart. He was haunted by the idea that she'd lost the babies because of him.

Lindie reached her hand out and touched his arm. "I'm sorry."

We'd talked about having a houseful of children.

"You should get some rest too," Lindie whispered.

Josiah agreed and stood. "Let me know if you need anything."

Perhaps a short nap would help. His muscles ached. As hard

as he tried to push it from his mind, he couldn't help but com-
pare the symptoms to those he had when his lymphoma was
first diagnosed. He had tried to convince himself otherwise but
he couldn't ignore the unexplained bruises—or the fever and
fatigue. But he hadn't found any lumps and they had been a significant factor in his diagnosis.

⁓

Hannah curled up in bed beside Lindie with her drawing pad and
pencils and began to sketch. Lindie snagged her own drawing set
from the side table next to the bed and joined her. While Hannah
worked on a picture of a horse, Lindie drew the view of the livestock barn outside the bedroom window.

Hours passed and the shadows shifted with the falling sun.
Lindie's weighted eyelids drooped closed. She wasn't sure how
much time had elapsed when she opened her eyes and stretched
her arms out from under the covers, but it was dark outside.

Hannah was gone, and her art supplies too.

Lindie kicked back the blanket and bounded out of bed. Her
heart thumped hard against her chest as she sped down the hall.
Not finding the child in her bedroom, she hurried to the kitchen.

Hannah looked up from her bowl of cereal and smiled.

Lindie sighed with relief. She signed, asking where her father
was, but Hannah shrugged. Not sure if she signed the question
correctly, she asked if Josiah was in the barn.

The girl shrugged again, then set her spoon down and said
with her hands that she hadn't seen him all day.

Lindie looked out the window, but it was too dark to see if
his buggy was parked under the lean-to. If he was working in the
barn, his lantern would give off some light through the windows.

The barn was dark. Simon wasn't around either. Although Simon often preferred to eat something simple in the *grossdaadi haus*. It wasn't like Josiah to not make supper. Especially since he was the one so adamant about her staying in bed.

Lindie tiptoed down the hallway, then eased Josiah's bedroom door open and peeked inside. A steady purring snore came from the bed. Lindie smiled. Josiah had looked exhausted earlier. She was glad to know he was catching up on his sleep.

Returning to the kitchen, Lindie grabbed a bowl from the cupboard and joined Hannah at the table. The oatmeal looked stiff. Hannah must have eaten what was left over from breakfast. At least she had taken the initiative to fix her own meal. She hoped in time Hannah would demonstrate more independence.

Hannah tapped Lindie's arm. "Did you sleep good?" she signed.

Lindie lowered her spoon. She wanted to give Hannah her full attention since this was her first time starting a conversation. She signed, "Yes," then asked Hannah if she finished her drawing.

Without responding, Hannah pushed back her chair and left the room.

Lindie's shoulders fell. Apparently her communication skills still weren't adequate.

A few moments later Hannah reappeared, toting her artwork. She lifted the paper for Lindie to see.

"Wow." She quickly held up three fingers to form *W*s and opened her mouth wide to form the *O*.

Hannah smiled.

The drawing of the horse pulling a sleigh was the best work she'd ever seen. She had even drawn an Amish family riding in the sleigh and snow falling.

Hannah flipped the page. The next drawing was of a deer drinking water from a pond. Her picture contained rich details as though the deer had literally posed for the drawing. Deer especially seemed to have an innate ability to sense when a human was close and would run away. It made Hannah's drawing even more compelling.

"I see them," Hannah signed. "Sometimes I feed them. In the woods."

"Feed them? Out of your hand?"

Hannah nodded.

"You are special." Lindie smiled.

"That's what God tells me too." She pointed to her head. "I hear him. He calls my name."

The hairs on Lindie's arm stood on end. Though Hannah hadn't always communicated with Lindie, and even Josiah at times, the girl was listening to God. Tears welled in Lindie's eyes.

Hannah shook her head. "Don't be sad."

"These are tears of joy."

Hannah's face crinkled.

"Gladness." That didn't change the girl's expression, so Lindie signed, "I'm happy," while smiling so large her face hurt. "Did God tell you to lay your hand on the deer that was shot?"

Hannah nodded. "I prayed too."

"And the doe was healed." Lindie spoke slowly so Hannah could read her lips.

"God said it was."

She had never seen such a miracle as when the deer rose, and to know that God told Hannah to lay hands on the animal warmed Lindie's core.

After finishing her oatmeal, Lindie demonstrated how the shading changed depending on what angle she held the pencil.

There really wasn't any other technique she could teach Hannah, she had such natural ability. Even so, the child seemed receptive to the attention and that thrilled Lindie.

While interacting with Hannah, Lindie lost track of the time. The wall clock indicated it was past the child's bedtime. She hated to stop their time together, but Hannah needed her sleep. Lindie also wanted a few minutes alone to sketch a doll pattern. With the material Margaret had sent, Lindie wanted to sew Hannah a doll for Christmas, which was only four days away.

After she tucked Hannah into bed, Lindie returned to the kitchen to start working on the pattern. Having made several in the past for her nieces, it didn't take long to complete the sketch. She opened the drawer and removed the scissors. She never liked to cut paper and material using the same shears, but she would have to make do with the only pair she could find.

She had most of the pieces cut when a noise startled her. Adrenaline surged. She spun around, her scissors raised defensively.

Josiah grabbed her wrist.

She exhaled her pent-up breath and unclenched her hand. "I'm sorry. You frightened me."

"I noticed." He took the scissors from her hand and placed them on the table. "What are you doing up?"

She motioned to the material. "I'm cutting out a doll pattern I want to make for Hannah."

He cocked his head to one side and grimaced. "Lindieee."

"Please don't be upset. It's a Christmas gift and I don't have much time to get it done. Besides, I got a long afternoon nap so I'm not tired yet."

He groaned and squinted at the clock, then ran his fingers through his hair as he looked out the window.

"Is something wrong?"

He looked at the clock again, then at her. "It's late."

"*Jah*. Are you okay?" He was acting disoriented. He needed to eat.

"I feel fine." He rubbed his jaw. "I guess I was really tired."

"And probably hungry." She remembered a time when one of the ministers in her district had acted similarly. The minister didn't get better until after he'd eaten something. She heard later that his bewilderment was from his blood sugar dropping too low. "There are sandwiches left over from church." She placed one on a plate and handed it to him.

"*Denki*."

Lindie filled a glass with water and brought it to the table. "What about Simon? Should I take him something to eat?"

"I spoke with him before I laid down. He was going to warm up some soup at his place." Josiah ate a few bites and washed it down with a long drink.

"Did he mention anything about me being pregnant?"

He shook his head. "I didn't bring it up either."

She picked up the scissors and resumed cutting the material. Josiah's reply, though honest, hurt. Why did she think he would be up front with Simon? She tried to concentrate on the pattern but felt his stare. "What—why are you looking at me like that?"

"You're beautiful."

She leaned back, startled by his words. He was disoriented.

Then, as if he realized what he had said, he shook his head. "Lindie, go to bed. Please." He drained the water, set the glass on the table, and stood.

"I need a flat surface to make *mei* cuts." She snipped around ment, but most likely it was a slip of the tongue.

She shifted her thoughts to what she would use for the face and hands of this doll. The navy-blue material was fine for the dress and apron, but she needed something different for the flesh tones. Tomorrow she would look through her clothes. A dishtowel would work. The off-white muslin would—

Josiah came up beside her, his arm rubbing her shoulder as he reached for her hand doing the cutting.

Their eyes locked and she released the scissors to him.

He dropped them on the table without breaking eye contact with her.

She swallowed hard.

Josiah cupped her face in his hands, lowered his lips to hers, and kissed her softly.

She trembled as his mouth moved over hers. Placing his hand on the center of her back, he drew her against him and trailed kisses along her cheek to her ear. His breath, warm against her skin, raised the hairs on her arms.

"Lindie, I never thought I could feel this way again," he whispered, then moved down her neck with kisses.

She closed her eyes to block out the horrific memory of the *Englischer* and that awful night. The man's putrid stench was embedded in her senses, forcing a mental replay of his raspy demands. *Don't fight me.*

"*Nay*. Don't touch me." She pressed her hand against Josiah's chest and shoved him hard. "You shouldn't have done that."

"I'm sorry," Josiah said quickly. "I just assumed—"

"That wasn't our arrangement," she choked out and then fled the room.

Chapter Twenty-One

Josiah lifted his head, punched the feather pillow, and plopped back down. He couldn't sleep. Every time he closed his eyes, he envisioned Lindie wrapped in his arms. He should have told her his feelings had changed and not assumed hers had too.

That wasn't our arrangement.

Her words had cut him to the core.

He entered this marriage expecting difficulties, and it had been difficult being married to someone he didn't love. But it wasn't nearly as hard as being married to someone who didn't love him in return. He should have kept his distance. They were doing fine before he . . . fell in love.

So much for following Simon's advice. She didn't want to consummate the marriage. Far from it, she had a look of terror in her eyes when he touched her.

Oh, Lord, what a mess I've made of this. I need help. How am I going to keep the agreement we made?

He closed his eyes and tried to focus his thoughts on Caroline, but Lindie's face appeared. Even when he closed his eyes tighter, her freckles and bright-blue eyes loomed before him. So did the lingering memory of her soft lips.

All this thinking and restlessness had caused him to sweat. He tossed the covers off. The woodstove didn't usually pump out this much heat. Not in December. He sat up, removed his T-shirt, and hurled it to the floor.

჻

The following day he woke before daybreak and went out to the shop. He used the jack plane to mill the rough bark and reduce the thickness. Later, to achieve a more accurate measurement, he would spend time flattening and truing the boards. Josiah worked until his arm muscles throbbed from the back-and-forth movement.

Simon limped into the workshop. "I didn't realize you wanted to start so early."

"I didn't wake you, did I?"

"*Nay*. I don't sleep much anymore. I've been up reading the Bible." He came closer and inspected the board. "Started with the cedar first? I thought you had orders for the elm."

"I do." He guided the planer over the wood, and wood shavings curled and fell on the floor. "This is a Christmas gift for Lindie. I should have started it earlier."

"It has a nice grain." Simon motioned to the *grossdaadi haus*. "I made some *kaffi*. Would you like a cup?"

Josiah nodded and set the tool on the bench. "Jakob should be here shortly. I thought we could work on rough cutting banisters out of the elm." Josiah followed Simon into his house.

"What about your cedar project?"

"I don't think that will take too long. Especially if these sleepless nights continue," he muttered under his breath.

218

Simon poured a cup of coffee and handed it to Josiah as someone called out from the shop.

"Josiah? Are you out here?"

"There's Jakob." Josiah took his cup with him and stepped into the shop.

ॐ

Not wanting to get on Josiah's bad side, Lindie stayed on bed rest. But it didn't ease the awkwardness between them. When he brought her meals into the room, he didn't stay long. Sometimes he didn't say anything other than what the meal was and that he hoped she liked it.

With so much time alone, she prayed for courage to tell him what had happened. How it wasn't his fault she panicked when he kissed her. Moses recoiled as if she were poison when he heard the truth. He blamed her and she did nothing to try to change his mind. Nothing she said would have changed the outcome. Maybe Josiah would blame her as well. She couldn't bear to live in the same house, under any arrangement, if he recoiled at the sight of her too.

Someone tapped on the door. "*Kumm* in," she said.

Josiah cracked the door open but didn't enter the room. "You didn't forget about your *doktah's* appointment, did you?"

"I guess I did. I'm sorry." She had lost track of the days spent in bed. That meant there were only two days before Christmas. She missed the flurry of baking she and Margaret used to do. It didn't feel like Christmas at all.

"We need to leave soon." He closed the door. His footsteps tromped down the hall and shortly after, the bell jingled over the door.

She crawled out of bed and chose a dress. Black. Not unlike the bleakness she felt. She pinned the front closed, then touched her *kapp*. Her hair had come undone from lying in bed all day. By the time she unraveled and brushed out the tangles, twisted it back into a bun, and secured it under the *kapp*, it was time to leave.

Josiah had the buggy waiting outside the door. A cold gust of wind swirled around them. He took her elbow and guided her down the steps and over the path blanketed in wood shavings.

Hannah sat beside Lindie and they shared the quilt. Josiah refused, saying he was warm enough.

"I made arrangements with Rebecca Troyer to watch Hannah while we are in town," he said, adding, "Simon and Jakob are busy and I didn't want her to get in their way." He turned the buggy onto the main road and they traveled the short distance in silence.

Josiah set the brake. "I'll be just a minute." He climbed out and waited for Hannah. She mitten-waved good-bye to Lindie, then hurried to the house.

Lindie readjusted the blanket to leave enough for Josiah should he change his mind. So far he'd kept his distance—both physically and emotionally. Why had he complicated things, crossing the boundaries—the boundaries he set?

Josiah pushed the blanket aside when he sat down on the bench. The silence made the trip into town seem longer than usual.

Doctor Ethridge was happy with her weight gain and that she hadn't vomited since her last visit or experienced any more sharp pains.

"Does this mean I can increase *mei* activity?"

"I don't see why not. I'm very pleased with your progress.

As long as you don't overdo it, I think it will be fine for you to resume your normal routine."

"Will you tell Josiah?" Maybe he would feel as relieved as she was to hear the news from the doctor.

"Sure." He picked up the phone and gave his receptionist instructions to send Josiah into his office.

Josiah entered the room and sat in the chair beside Lindie.

"The baby doesn't appear to be in any distress," Doctor Ethridge said. "The gestational measurements are still less than I'd like, but I'm very pleased with Lindie's weight gain. According to Lindie, she hasn't had any more pains, nor has she vomited in the last two weeks." He smiled at Lindie, then turned his attention back to Josiah. "I told her it would be all right to resume normal activities provided Lindie comes into the office if she experiences more pain or begins vomiting again."

"That's *gut* news," Josiah said to Lindie.

She smiled.

"Do either of you have any questions?"

They both answered no at the same time.

"I would like to see you in a month to make sure your weight gain is still on track." Doctor Ethridge closed her chart and stood. "I won't keep you." He walked to the door. "I'm sure you have last-minute things to do before the holidays."

Lindie's thoughts whirled with special dishes she wanted to prepare for Christmas and the house-to-house visitation the women had discussed last Sunday. Josiah hadn't mentioned anything about it, but now that she was no longer on bed rest, he would surely approve of fellowshipping within the settlement.

Josiah touched her arm. "Why don't you go up front and make your next appointment. I'll meet you in the lobby in a minute or two."

"Okay." His sober expression was difficult to interpret. She hoped he wasn't planning to convince the doctor to keep her on bed rest. She proceeded toward the corridor. It wasn't right to eavesdrop, but surely God would forgive her if the conversation was about her.

"The tests came back inconclusive. They need to be repeated." The doctor's voice was muffled, yet discernable.

Lindie looked over her shoulder as the door shut behind them. What tests? She arranged for her next appointment with the receptionist, then sat on the cushioned chair against the wall and waited for Josiah.

A few minutes passed before he came to the lobby. "Everything all set?"

"*Jah.*" Lindie stood. "I made an afternoon appointment, is that all right?"

"That's fine." This time he seemed more eager to leave the office than she did. Once outside, he guided her by the elbow down the sidewalk, then helped her into the buggy.

Josiah took his spot on the bench. White clouds of air escaped from his mouth and he shivered.

She lifted the corner of the blanket. "I'll share with you if you're *kalt.*"

He shook his head. "I'm fine." He clicked his tongue, signaling Molly, and the mare lurched forward.

They traveled out of town and over the first hill before Lindie broke the silence. "It snowed while we were at the *doktah's* office. Are the roads slippery?"

"A little."

Another long stretch of silence followed. Since her arrival, she hadn't had much of a chance to develop any close friendships. Not like those she had in Ohio. The houses were too far apart to drop in on neighbors as she had done in Ohio. Besides, she hadn't wanted to ask Josiah to take the buggy.

"I gained five pounds," she volunteered, hoping to start a conversation.

"That's *gut*."

Lindie stared at the snowy field. She blinked back tears and tried to clear her head but failed. *Oh, Lord, I feel so alone.*

Josiah slipped his hand under the cover, found hers, and squeezed it. "What are you upset about?"

She shrugged and the blanket fell off her shoulder.

He pulled his hand away from hers and gripped the reins. A car sped past, its back end sliding to the shoulder. Josiah kept both hands on the reins, his eyes fixed on the road. "These hills are getting bad."

It took longer than normal to reach the bishop's house. Anxious to talk with Rebecca, Lindie pulled the cover away.

Josiah stopped her. "Stay warm. I'll get Hannah."

"I wanted to find out more about the house-to-house visits."

Josiah rubbed his jaw. "You want us to join in with the activities, don't you?"

She lifted her brows. "I'm *nett* on restrictions anymore."

"I'll be right back." He hurried up the steps and Rebecca was quick to answer the door.

Lindie closed her eyes. *Lord, I'm still struggling to understand your way.* She paused and thought about Moses's sister, Mary. Lindie thought nothing would separate their friendship, but Mary stopped talking to her after news spread that Lindie had skipped the singing to spend the night with an *Englischer*. Mary had openly rebuked her, even said she was glad her brother changed his mind about marrying Lindie.

Voices outside drew her attention and she opened her eyes.

Rebecca waved from the doorway and Lindie returned the greeting.

The buggy door opened and Hannah slid across the bench and snuggled close to Lindie. Josiah took his place and released the buggy brake.

"I asked Rebecca if we can serve hot cocoa and cookies," he said, then added, "I don't want you overdoing it."

She shifted to see him over Hannah. "What about Ada? I thought that's what she wanted to serve."

"We'll go to Ada's at the beginning and our *haus* will be the last stop on the loop. It's a long *nacht*. It takes several hours going by sleigh through the open fields and woods."

"It sounds fun."

He shrugged.

Christmas without Caroline must have been difficult for him. Lindie wished things could change this year—for all of them.

⁓

Josiah jabbed a pitchfork into the stack of hay with all the force he could muster. He couldn't get the echo of Doctor Ethridge's voice out of his mind. *Inconclusive tests . . . possible relapse . . .* The doctor couldn't say for certain if his lymphoma had returned. He rattled off blood levels and their ranges as if Josiah could keep track of what was not within normal limits.

This news wasn't any different from what he received six years ago. The doctor's pat assurance, *I don't want to unnecessarily worry you, but . . .* was the same today as all those years ago. Josiah remembered Caroline sitting in the chair beside him as Doctor Ethridge explained how he routinely repeated any abnormal blood work. Tears ran down Caroline's face, but

Josiah was too stunned to offer her the hankie he had tucked in his pocket.

Over the last several weeks he'd denied the symptoms, but in truth, he knew. His body was responding now as it had before. A persistent cough, unexplained rash, fatigue, along with night sweats so severe they soaked his T-shirt and drenched his bedding. Josiah forked a mound of hay. Somehow he had to stay strong. At least long enough to get his house in order. He tossed the hay over the calf fence. In hindsight, had Lindie accepted his advances, things really would have gotten complicated.

Josiah fed the other livestock, but he wasn't ready to go inside. He didn't want to face Simon or take a chance that Lindie noticed his emotional state and bombarded him with questions. He dared not think of what it would mean if he were no longer in remission. Relapsed or not, he wasn't promised tomorrow. He had to make the most of today.

He leaned the pitchfork against the wall, pulled off his leather gloves, and touched the area on his neck that had swollen to the size of a goose egg six years ago. His gland didn't feel enlarged now. He unbuttoned his shirt. Sliding his hand under the fabric, he palpated his chest and under each armpit. No lumps there either. Maybe he could rest on Doctor Ethridge's admittedly thin possibility that it was an infection of some sort.

He covered his hand over his nose as a tickling sensation caused him to sneeze. When he pulled his hand away from his face, it was covered in blood.

Chapter Twenty-Two

Lindie and Hannah baked dozens of cookies Christmas Eve morning. Nowhere near the amount Lindie was accustomed to baking for the holidays, but she enjoyed teaching Hannah how to roll cookie dough. After each batch was ready to come out of the oven, Hannah would lick her lips in anticipation.

Even Josiah meandered in and out of the kitchen to sample the sweets. He favored the peanut-butter cookies and praised Hannah for her work creating the crisscross patterns with the fork. He dabbed flour on his daughter's nose and she giggled, a sound Lindie had never heard. It was beginning to feel like Christmas. Lindie wished the giddiness would last longer, but Josiah left the room, saying over his shoulder that chores needed to be done.

He spent the remainder of the day in the barn and didn't return again until suppertime. Even then, once the men ate, they disappeared back outside.

Lindie stood at the window. A faint light flickered in the barn. She couldn't imagine what chores took this long. Didn't he want to say good night to Hannah? Lindie waited a few more minutes, but when he still didn't come inside, she walked Hannah to her bed and tucked her under the covers. Then she sat at the kitchen table and resumed sewing the doll. After she sewed the apron and *kapp* and attached them to the doll, the Christmas gift would be complete.

Under the flicker of the oil lamp, she threaded the needle. She had just stitched on the apron when the bell above the door rang and something thumped near the back door. Lindie set the doll on the table and rushed from the room, but stopped at the sight of Josiah wiggling himself and a wooden cradle through the entryway.

She touched her abdomen and smiled. He probably thought she was in bed and meant it as a surprise. Even so, she couldn't just stand there when he was struggling. "Let me help." She drew closer and stopped. Simon was at the other end. The swinging part of the cradle wouldn't stay in place.

Josiah and Simon walked it farther into the room and set it down. "*Denki* for all your help."

Simon nodded. "It's late. I should get to bed."

"It's beautiful." Lindie drew closer, unable to take her eyes off the smooth wood.

"Simon helped me with it."

"I just followed your pattern." Simon turned. "*Gut nacht.*"

"*Denki*," Lindie said, stopping him. "This really means a lot to me."

He lowered his head and nodded before disappearing out the door.

Lindie looked at Josiah. "How long has he known about the *boppli*?"

He shrugged. "I came back from town the other day and he was working on it. He said he didn't think I had enough time to finish it before Christmas."

"And he wasn't upset?"

"Nope." Josiah ran his hand along the wood grain, then looked at the dust. "It needs a *gut* cleaning."

"I'm sorry if I ruined your surprise," she said, swaying with her hands interlocked behind her.

"You didn't spoil all of it." Josiah winked. "Although I did think I could sneak it inside without you seeing. Aren't you tired?"

She motioned to the kitchen. "I have some sewing to do on Hannah's doll before tomorrow or it won't have an apron or *kapp*."

The cradle started her thinking about sewing little quilts and clothing for the baby, something most women in their second trimester had already started. Maybe after the first of the year, she and Hannah could work on a quilt together. She could teach her some simple stitches.

Josiah trailed her into the kitchen. "Please don't wear yourself out."

"This won't take long." She pulled out a chair, sat, and picked up her material.

He reached inside a drawer for a dishrag, dampened it at the sink, then wrung out the excess water. He stopped next to the table and leaned over her shoulder. "She's going to like the doll."

"I hope so. I would have made her a new dress that matched her doll, but someone kept me in bed." She guided the needle through the material.

"If you overdo it, you might find yourself back in bed again."

She looked up at him and frowned. The dim lamp glow had cast dark shadows under his eyes, making him look tired and older than his thirty-two years.

He turned and coughed into his hand.

"I think you need to heed your own advice and get some rest," she said as he walked out of the room.

Lindie had the tiny pleats stitched on the *kapp* by the time

Josiah reentered the kitchen. Once he spread the cloth over the edge of the sink basin to dry, he said *gut nacht* and reminded her not to stay up late.

She would follow soon, but first she wanted to sew the strings on the apron, then wrap the gift in a brown paper bag. The scarves she made for Josiah and Simon needed to be wrapped too.

Lindie quickly tied a knot and clipped the thread with the scissors. She turned the doll over a few times, examining her work, and smiled. She wasn't much younger than Hannah when her mother had given her a doll for Christmas. Lindie remembered holding that doll like a baby and carrying it with her everywhere. She rested her hand on her belly. In a few short months, she wouldn't be carrying a doll, but a son or daughter. An odd sensation filled her with warmth. She went into the sitting room and stopped next to the cradle. *Lord, please equip me to bring up this baby in a way pleasing to you.*

⟡

As Lindie and Hannah worked to prepare the Christmas meal, Josiah leaned against the wall at the kitchen entrance. He hadn't seen his daughter this excited in a long time. She mixed the biscuit batter while Lindie washed and peeled the potatoes, then plunked them into the pot of water. The scent of roasting turkey teased his senses. He watched the two of them interact. Lindie's signing had improved, and even when she made a slight blunder, Hannah didn't correct her. He could not have found a better *fraa*. He wished she shared the same feelings about marrying him.

Lindie placed the pot of potatoes on the stove to boil. She caught a glimpse of him from the corner of her eye and smiled. "I didn't know you were standing there."

"It sure smells *gut*." He stepped farther into the kitchen.

"The turkey is almost finished cooking. What do you think is keeping Simon?"

He shrugged. "He's mentioned a few times that he wants to give us space. But don't worry, he won't miss Christmas supper."

His daughter looked his way and smiled. The kind of smile that reached his heart and reminded him there was a God. And God had given him back his daughter. His throat constricted with emotion. She signed that she was making biscuits, and he asked if he could taste one the minute they came out of the oven. Hannah nodded, then returned to dropping mounds of dough in a row on a cookie sheet.

Armed with pot holders, Lindie opened the oven, removed the lid of the roasting pan, and peered at the golden brown turkey.

He craned his neck when she stabbed it with a fork in a few places. The bird looked cooked to him. Juices bubbled on the bottom of the roaster. After a few more jabs she replaced the lid and closed the oven door. "It needs more time."

"I better get out to the barn. I'm *nett* the only one hungry today." He scooted out of the kitchen.

"Make sure you get Simon," Lindie called out as he was putting on his coat.

Out in the barn, he fed and watered the animals. His thoughts turned to Hannah. His daughter certainly seemed happy to be working in the kitchen with Lindie. He hoped this new relationship between them continued to grow. The possibility of having relapsed niggled in the back of his mind. He pushed the thoughts aside, finished the chores, and tapped on Simon's door. "Supper is ready."

A moment later Simon came out carrying three burlap bags.

"Are you hungry?"

"I've been looking forward to the meal all day," Simon said.

When they entered the house, they were met with the scent of turkey and biscuits. Josiah licked his lips. Simon set the bags down next to the cradle while Josiah went to the kitchen.

Lindie placed the bowl of potatoes on the table beside the gravy. Hannah was arranging the silverware by the place settings.

"Give me a minute to wash my hands and I'll set the turkey platter on the table." Josiah didn't want Lindie trying to carry the fourteen-pound bird.

When he returned, she was rummaging through the drawer of utensils. "I don't see a carving knife."

He set the turkey on the table and helped her search.

"I'll get one." She left the kitchen and went down the hall.

Curious whether he'd heard her right, he followed. Josiah stopped at the bedroom doorway and watched her search through one of the boxes she had brought from Ohio. He cleared his throat. "Why do you have household items boxed up in here?"

She rose from her squatted position holding the knife. "These are the things I brought from Ohio. Articles from *mei* hope chest."

"But why are they in a box?"

"I couldn't bring the wooden chest on the bus."

"Lindie, no one stores household items once they're married." He crossed the room. "You haven't unpacked anything, have you?"

She shook her head. "I didn't know if you . . ."

"What?"

She hesitated. "You were upset when I rearranged the dishes. I didn't want you upset if I added mine to yours."

He sighed and ran his hand through his hair. "I've treated

231

you like a guest when this is your home." *Why didn't I see this?* "I'm sorry. You're *mei fraa*. I don't want you to leave your things packed away. Everything in the kitchen is yours. If you want to get rid of something, that's up to you. But please, make this into your home. Okay?"

She smiled.

"You've been very patient with me. I'm a blessed man." He cupped her shoulders and turned her toward the door. "Let's go eat."

Once they were all seated, Josiah reached to his right for Lindie's hand and to his left for Hannah's. Simon joined the circle from the opposite end of the table. They gave thanks for their first Christmas meal together.

When they had eaten all they could, Lindie stood and collected an armload of dishes. "When I was growing up, *mei* father read the story of Jesus' birth after supper."

Josiah gathered the remaining dishes and joined her at the sink. "We can start that same tradition, if you want."

Her eyes brightened.

"The dishes can wait until later." Josiah turned to Simon. "If you will read the scriptures, I'll sign."

"I would like that."

They all went into the sitting room where Simon picked up the Bible and opened it to the book of Luke.

Hannah found a place on the rug in front of the woodstove, her eyes bright and attentive to her father.

Simon finished the reading and closed the book.

Josiah stood. "I'll be back in a minute." Josiah slipped down the hall and into the bedroom where he'd hidden a box filled with Christmas presents.

Hannah's eyes lit up when he returned with the box. He

handed her a package he'd covered with meat-wrapping paper and tied with twine.

"*Ach*, can you wait a minute?" Lindie rushed out of the room and returned with three packages, which she handed to Simon, Hannah, and Josiah.

Josiah gazed at the yarn-tied package. He hadn't felt sentimental about receiving a gift in a long time, but something stirred in his heart when she handed him this one.

Josiah gestured for Hannah to open her presents first.

She peeled the paper off the package that he'd given to her and smiled as she lifted the boots out of the box. Hannah set them aside and signed thank you, then lifted the present from Lindie onto her lap. Tearing into the package, her eyes widened. She carefully removed the doll as if it were made of porcelain. She cradled it in her arms, then rose to her feet and hugged Lindie.

Warmth spread through Josiah's core. Lindie offered Hannah exactly what she needed—a mother's embrace—a gift of love that couldn't be bought or made.

Hannah returned to her spot on the floor, stroking her baby doll. Then she set the doll down, picked up a brown paper bag, and handed it to Lindie.

"*Ach*, what's this?" She opened the bag and pulled out the framed picture. "It's beautiful." She held it up for Josiah to see. "Look, it's a picture of hands. All different sizes." Lindie studied the picture closer. The hands all rested on a pregnant belly.

Josiah pointed to the wall. "I thought we could hang it over the desk."

"I'd like that." Lindie pointed to the largest set of hands in the drawing. "Who is this?" she signed.

Hannah signed and Josiah answered, "God."

The second-largest hands, she pointed to her father. The next were Lindie's, then Hannah pointed to another set and then at herself. But one set of hands—a tiny set—remained.

Josiah leaned closer to get a better view of the picture. When he measured the paper to make the frame and even while he was framing it, he hadn't noticed the extra set of hands.

Hannah cradled her arms and swung them.

The baby? It made no sense. Obviously, the rounded belly in the picture meant Lindie was pregnant. It was a perfect gift none-theless. "I'll hang it." Josiah took the picture. He already had the hammer and nail waiting on the desk.

Lindie gave Hannah a hug and thanked her for the picture. She blotted the corners of her eyes with her dress sleeve.

"You do beautiful drawings," Simon told Hannah as she handed him a gift. "For me?"

Hannah nodded.

Simon opened his and showed everyone the picture of the deer. "I love it." Even his eyes turned glassy.

Josiah's gift from Hannah was a picture of the old draft horse, Moose. "I'll make a frame for it tomorrow," he said, thanking his daughter.

"He will get up," Hannah signed.

Josiah wasn't following. He asked her to repeat the hand gestures. She repeated the same message. He nodded, though still confused. Maybe she meant hang it up.

Simon handed each of them a bag. A saw for Josiah and matching dresses for Lindie and Hannah. "I had Rebecca make the dresses. She suggested the bright-blue color."

"Denki." Lindie held hers up. "I'm going to wear this to the sleigh ride tomorrow *nacht.*"

"I'm glad you like it," Simon said. Josiah's father-in-law smiled, which he didn't often do.

Hannah resumed playing with the doll.

Lindie motioned to the gifts she'd given Josiah and Simon. "Are you two going to open the ones from me?"

"Absolutely." Josiah peeled the packaging away. "When did you have time to do this?"

"Lying in bed all day."

Josiah unfolded the colorful scarf and several hankies fell out. Her thoughtfulness left him speechless. He swung the scarf around his neck. "*Denki*, I won't get *kalt* this winter."

Simon unwrapped his package and smiled. "People won't be able to tell us apart, Josiah."

They all laughed.

"I'm sorry they're not all one color," Lindie said.

"They're perfect." He would have stood and hugged her as Hannah had if Simon wasn't in the room.

Josiah reached into the box that held the presents. He pulled out another gift for Hannah and then handed one package to Lindie and one to Simon. He wasn't so interested in Hannah's response to the bag of saltwater taffy, and he assumed Simon would be pleased with his new straw hat and suspenders, but what he was really anxious to see was Lindie's reaction when she opened her paint set.

Lindie's eyes widened. She looked at him, then Hannah, then at him again. She shifted in her chair, cleared her throat, then stood. "I'm going to make some *kaffi*."

He thought for sure with the way she eyed the brushes in the art store that she would have liked the gift. Now he wasn't so certain he had bought her the right thing. "I think I'll check on the *kaffi* too," he told Hannah and Simon.

Steam hissed from the kettle spout on the stove. Lindie stood at the window, her face hidden in her hands.

"Lindie?" He moved closer. "If you don't like the paint set, you can return it."

She shook her head.

He lowered her hands, and her eyes glistened. "What's wrong?"

"You gave me the cradle. Why the paint set? You said you were buying Hannah a set. Did you change your mind because of *mei* comment about spoiling her?"

He smiled. "I said I wanted to spoil *mei maydel*—you. When we went into the store to buy colored pencils, I watched you study those brushes. I thought you liked painting."

She lowered her head. "I do, but you didn't have to buy me such an elaborate present."

He tipped her chin. "You're important to me."

Her eyes budded with fresh tears. "I shouldn't have pushed you away the other *nacht*. I'm sorry. I . . . I know a *fraa* is supposed to be—"

"It's Christmas. Let's *nett* talk about it *nau*." He hadn't intended to sound stern, but his frustration had come through. He wanted more from her than a dutiful wife. Yet falling in love was his doing, not hers. She hadn't forsaken the rules—he had.

The kettle whistled and she removed it from the stove. "Do you want *kaffi*?"

"*Nay*."

"Me either. Should I pour one for Simon?"

"Later." He reached for her hand. "There's another gift for Hannah to open from both of us." He shrugged one shoulder. "So I wanted to spoil both of *mei maydels*."

"You bought her a paint set too?"

He nodded. "I couldn't resist."

Chapter Twenty-Three

The sudden snowstorm made it treacherous to follow the other sleighs in the house-to-house caravan. Earlier in the evening a soft glow of lamplight flickered on the snow-covered landscape as the families traveled in a group across the open fields. However, the whiteout changed that. Suddenly any trace of lantern lights from the other sleighs had vanished.

Lindie scanned the area. "I don't see anyone's lights."

"*Jah*, I wish we had more moonlight to guide us." Josiah looked down at Hannah leaning against Lindie. "Is she asleep?"

"*Jah.*" Lindie marveled at how the child could sleep during a blizzard. Lindie had wrung her hands so much during the last hour that she had worn a small hole in her knitted mittens. If she had even a portion of Hannah's peace, Lindie would be grateful.

"We should all have agreed to postpone the last half of the visitation," Josiah said.

The only homes left were the Troyers' and theirs. Did he have another reason for wanting to postpone the visit? Perhaps even traveling the fields was too dangerous. It didn't lessen her disappointment.

Traveling through the woods and across the fields, she hadn't recognized the Troyers' barns until Josiah veered the buggy to the left and maneuvered Molly between the two buildings. He stopped at the hitching post next to the house where the others had parked.

Lindie nudged Hannah.

The child stirred, then yawned and stretched out her arms.

"All this fresh air should help her sleep *gut* tonight," Josiah said. "What about you, are you tired?"

"*Nay*, I'm wide-awake." Yet the moment Lindie stepped into the house, the heat from the woodstove zapped her energy. She removed her boots at the door and helped Hannah take off her cape. The child was still groggy. Hannah turned to Josiah and lifted her arms for him to pick her up.

Rebecca motioned to the dark hallway. "You can lay her down in the back bedroom if you want. Just take one of the lamps from the sitting room for light."

Lindie grabbed the lamp and led the way.

"She's really worn out," Josiah whispered as he lowered Hannah onto the queen-sized mattress. "I'm wondering *nau* if we should have skipped this and gone home."

"There's still another stop on this outing."

Hannah rolled onto her side.

Josiah guided Lindie out of the room. "I hope you won't be upset if I cancel." He eased the door closed. "No one expected it to snow this much tonight."

"I understand." She followed him down the hall to the sitting room and the sound of chatter.

The weather had delayed the caravan. Several of the women mentioned how late it was. Ada's family had cut their evening short after the second house on the loop, saying the temperature had dipped too low for the children. It made sense with Ada so close to her due date.

"I made soup and sandwiches," Rebecca announced. She waved Lindie to follow her into the kitchen. "What time did Simon's bus leave today?"

"Six this morning. Josiah said his bus should have arrived by *nau* so at least he missed the storm." Lindie ran her hand over the arm of her dress. "By the way, you did a nice job sewing *mei* dress. I was very surprised when Simon gave it to me."

"He's had a difficult time. First he lost his *dochder*, then his wife a few months later. But I think you'll find he's making an effort to accept Josiah and Hannah's new life." Rebecca nodded to the men in the other room. "Is Josiah feeling all right?"

"I think so. Why do you ask?"

"Doesn't he look a little pale to you?"

Lindie leaned to see into the other room. She caught a glimpse of him seated across the room. Either the lamplight was reflecting an unnatural shade over him, or Rebecca was right and he looked sickly. Lindie should have noticed earlier. He turned away from the men and coughed, then touched his neck. Was he checking his temperature? No wonder he suggested ending the evening.

Naomi entered the kitchen, carrying a sleeping toddler in her arms. "Lindie, I hate to disappoint you, but I don't think we're going to make it to your place tonight."

Sarah rounded the corner behind Naomi. "Us too. Abe is talking about leaving *nau* before it snows any more." She patted Lindie's arm. "I am sorry. I hope we can get together again soon."

"I hope so too." Noticing Josiah sitting quietly, it was obvious they needed to head home.

Rebecca reached out her arms toward Naomi. "I'll hold David while you put your cape on."

"I shouldn't keep Abe waiting," Sarah said, leaving the kitchen.

Lindie peeked into the sitting room half expecting to see Josiah signal that it was time to leave. He didn't.

"The ham and cheese are on the counter if you want to fix sandwiches for yourself and Josiah." Rebecca continued to rock the child in her arms.

Lindie had eaten something at each house they'd visited tonight and wasn't hungry, but she prepared a sandwich for Josiah. The bishop was asking about Simon as Lindie entered the sitting room.

"His bus should have arrived in Centerville sometime after four. It's *gut* he left before the storm or he might have been snow-bound," Josiah said.

Bishop Troyer nodded. *"Jah*, I know he wanted to see his *bruder."*

Lindie handed Josiah the plate with the sandwich.

"Denki." He smiled.

Dark shadows circled his eyes. If she could speak with him alone, she would suggest they leave. Instead, she asked if he wanted a cup of coffee.

"Maybe a glass of water." His voice sounded hoarse. "Please."

She hurried back into the kitchen, filled a glass with water, and brought it to him. The bishop and Rebecca were both distracted with good-byes.

"Are you having fun?" Josiah took a drink.

"Jah, but anytime you're ready to leave is okay with me." Guilt gnawed at her. Had he participated in the visitation only for her benefit? She wanted to visit with the women, but not at the cost of his health.

"I haven't said anything yet about canceling our stop." He took a bite of the sandwich.

"I mentioned it to the women in the kitchen. They all agreed the weather has gotten worse."

After standing by the door as the visitors left, Rebecca brushed her hands against her arms. "This might be one of our worst winters yet." She turned to her husband. "Don't you think they should stay here tonight?"

The bishop nodded.

Lindie forced a smile, waiting to hear Josiah's response.

Mischief twinkled in his eyes when his gaze connected with hers. "*Denki*," he said, turning back to the bishop. "I think we'll be all right to travel home."

She eased out a long breath.

Josiah finished the sandwich and handed Lindie the empty plate. "We shouldn't wait too much longer. I'll go get Hannah."

꒰

Lindie tucked Hannah into bed before going to the kitchen to *redd-up*. She opened the cabinet and was returning the stack of clean plates as Josiah entered.

"It should warm up soon. I loaded the woodstove." He snatched a cookie off the plate as she picked it up. "I'm sorry the get-together ended early. You went to a lot of fuss making so many cookies."

"Hannah and I had fun." She removed the lid to the cookie jar. "Did you want more before I put them away?"

He took another one. "I wouldn't want your hard work to go to waste."

"It was just as well that everyone didn't *kumm*. Hannah was exhausted." She transferred the cookies from the plate into the jar.

"She probably could have slept all *nacht* at the Troyers'." He smirked. "But I didn't think you wanted to stay."

"It would have been a little awkward . . . to keep our arrangement."

He muttered something undecipherable under his breath and took a bite of the cookie.

She continued tidying up the area, wrestling with the decision to talk to him about her past.

"We'll host a gathering soon," he said, interrupting her thoughts.

She chewed on her bottom lip. "I wanted to talk with you about the other *nacht*."

"You don't have to explain." He started to turn and she caught his arm.

"It isn't that I—" She cringed. This was harder than she expected.

He stepped closer. "Don't say anything."

"I must." Or else she might never. "I wanted you to kiss me." There, she said it. "It's just that—"

"It's all right." He cupped her face in his hands and looked her in the eye. "It's all right if you don't feel the same way about me."

She couldn't hold back the truth. Even if he rejected her as Moses had. "You asked me about the father of the *boppli*." His hands dropped from her face and he groaned, but she continued anyway. "You asked why I didn't tell him I was pregnant."

He lowered his head.

"I don't know the father."

"What?" He jerked his head up. "Eli made it sound as though—"

"*Mei bruder* doesn't know." Acid coated the back of her throat. She fumbled with a loose string on her apron, unable to look him in the eye. "Moses and I had gotten into a spat." Her voice shook. "He tried to kiss me and I wouldn't let him. We had promised each other we would wait until we were married. But he was leaving the next day for his *onkel's* and . . ."

"I don't understand." He moved in front of her. "You said you don't know who the father is—"

"I was stubborn. I refused to ride to the singing with Moses. *Mei* friend was hosting the *nacht* and we lived two farms apart, so it was a short walk. It should have only taken me a few minutes." She squeezed her eyes closed and forced herself to continue. "A car slowed. I kept walking—even faster when the man yelled out the window at me. He said some things . . . that frightened me. Then the car stopped." Her heart pounded hard, recalling the screeching sound of the brakes, the car door opening, and the footsteps thundering against the pavement. "I ran into the woods to hide. Only I tripped over a stump—and—and—" She gasped for air.

Josiah ushered her into his arms and pressed her against his chest. "I won't let anything happen to you again."

Every fiber in her body quivered. She fisted her hands against his chest but suppressed the impulse to push him away. "I couldn't fight him. He tore *mei kapp* from my head and crammed it into my mouth. I screamed—until I passed out." Anger flared. "He took what he wanted, then left me for dead."

He held her a little tighter. "You're safe *nau*."

His soothing voice relaxed her. A long stretch of silence fell between them. Her throat was dry. She stepped out of his embrace. Her hands trembled as she filled a glass with tap water and drank.

"Why didn't you tell Eli?"

She lowered the glass from her mouth. "I couldn't."

"Lindie, it wasn't your fault."

"The man threatened to burn every barn in the district if I told. I believed him. He knew where I lived, and that I ran Margaret's vegetable stand." She took another drink, then set the glass on the counter. "That's why I could agree to your terms of marriage. Love didn't matter as long as it meant leaving Ohio."

"And Moses? Surely if you had told him, he would still have married you."

Shaking her head, she said quietly, *"Nay."* He didn't press her to say more, but she did. "I confided in him. He wanted me to take a pill that he said would solve everything. When I refused to end the pregnancy, he said I wasn't what he wanted for a *fraa*. I was . . . tainted." She lifted one shoulder in a half shrug. "He wasn't wrong."

"Jah, he was."

She took another drink. "I made a kneeling confession in church that I was sorry I stayed out all *nacht* with an *Englischer*." She bowed her head. "I was accepted back into the flock, but Eli worried I would never find a man who would marry me." She shrugged. "I didn't understand why you would be willing to take me . . . but I was grateful." She lifted her head. "I couldn't stay in Ohio with that madman loose."

"You should have told the bishop what happened."

"I thought being shunned would be easier than living with guilt if the man burned down the barns. Besides, he knew where I lived—everything about me. He would have . . . violated me again." Tears welled, blurring her vision. "Can you forgive me?"

"For what? Lindie, you never sinned." He cupped her face in his hands. "You have nothing to be ashamed of. Nothing."

She blinked and warm tears cascaded down her cheeks.

He leaned down and brushed his lips against her forehead.

Tension shot through her and she stiffened. *God, will I ever get over those vile memories? I don't want to feel detached from Josiah every time he touches me.*

"I'm sorry," he said, releasing his hands. "I didn't mean to frighten you with *mei* advances."

"I'm sorry too. You deserve someone better than me."

Josiah shook his head. "Don't say that." He reached for her hand and held it. "I want to be your husband—more than just in name. But only if you want our agreement to change also."

She opened her mouth to speak, but he spoke first.

"Don't decide *nau*." He smiled. "We're in this marriage for our lifetime. I'll convince your heart eventually."

"You said you wouldn't ever change your mind."

"At the time, I believed that to be true." He shrugged. "Apparently *mei* heart didn't listen, because I'm in love with you."

Chapter Twenty-Four

Lindie kicked at the bedcovers. If she wasn't going to get any sleep, she might as well read the Scriptures. She blindly groped the side table for the matches and lit the lamp wick. Flickering shadows danced on the walls as a warm glow filled the room.

She flipped opened the Bible, stopping in the thirteenth chapter of 1 Corinthians, and began to read. "Love is patient, love is kind . . ." Josiah was both. She skipped ahead. "It always protects, always trusts, always hopes, always perseveres. Always," she repeated. "Love never fails." She aimlessly flipped more pages and resumed reading in Philippians. "Then make my joy complete by being like-minded, having the same love, being one in spirit and of one mind." All the passages she read brought Josiah to mind. In many ways, she and Josiah were like-minded. They both loved the Lord and wished to serve him above all. *The same love* . . . Could they really share the same love for each other?

She'd never experienced such tenderness as when Josiah held her, offering her a safe haven. She closed her eyes, recalling the warmth his arms provided.

Lindie eased out of the bed and onto the floor where she knelt and folded her hands. *Lord, I was so consumed with trying to avoid rejection that I closed my mind to what you had provided. You have given me a kindhearted husband. But I rejected him. Please forgive me. Help me overcome my past so that I can be the wife that you would have me be.* After a long moment, she rose with a renewed purpose and proceeded to the door.

⏣

Josiah stirred at the sound of the bedroom door opening. *Hannah?* He rubbed his eyes when they refused to focus. Looking again, moonlight streaming from the window silhouetted Lindie's form.

"Is everything okay?" He pushed back the covers and stood. The cool air reminded him that he'd stripped off his T-shirt earlier and now stood before her dressed only in a pair of long johns.

Moonlight seemed to follow her as she crossed the room.

He expanded his lungs to capacity, then released his breath in a rush. His thoughts flitted as he tried to rationalize her standing before him in her nightdress.

"If you still want to change our arrangement"—her voice quivered—"I want to be your *fraa.*"

Unable to pull his eyes away from her fingers working the hooks on her gown, he stammered, "I, ah . . . I—"

"I'm sorry," she said, tugging her garment in place. "I shouldn't have put you on the spot." She whirled around and bolted toward the door.

"Don't go." *Fool.* Why did he gawk? Josiah lunged into the hall and stopped her before she could disappear.

Backed against the wall, she lowered her head and fumbled

with the nightdress closures. She squeaked something between panic and frustration. Finally, unable to work the closures with her trembling fingers, she balled up the material in her clenched hands.

He stepped closer, yet reined in his craving to take her into his arms. "Please give me another chance."

She kept her head down.

"What did you mean when you said you were sorry for putting me on the spot?"

She shrugged.

"I admit I've never been struck speechless before." If she had an inkling of how hard his heart was beating, she wouldn't feel insecure about her decision to come into his room. He lifted her chin and brushed his fingertips over her soft cheek. "I don't want you to leave."

Her eyes searched his for reassurance.

"I love you." He leaned closer and kissed her. This time she didn't push him away.

ॐ

The brisk morning temperature woke Lindie before dawn. Had she been sleeping in her bed, she would have burrowed deeper under the blankets to conserve heat. But she wasn't in her bed— or alone.

She eased the blanket back, slipped one foot out from under the covers, then, pushing herself up, sat on the edge of the bed. Daylight would spill through the windows at any moment and wake the household. She wanted to keep things discreet, at least for the time being. She scanned the floor.

Where was her nightdress? If she thought she could slip the

top blanket off the bed without waking Josiah, she would wrap herself in it in order to walk across the hall to her room. She reached for the blanket's corner at the foot of the bed and gave it a tug. Freeing the quilt from between the mattress and footboard, she gingerly pulled it toward her. She hoped she wouldn't wake Josiah.

Josiah stirred. Then, rolling up onto one elbow, he stretched his arm around her waist and pulled her toward him. "Where are you going? It isn't even daybreak," he said in a husky, dry voice.

"I didn't mean to wake you." Her eyes caught sight of the patch of hair on his chest and heat crawled up her neck. She looked away.

"*Guder mariye.*" He scooted closer. "Did you sleep all right?"

She nodded.

Josiah lifted the corner of the blanket, kissed her shoulder, then slipped his hand under the covers.

She sucked in a breath. "Don't you . . . have barn chores?"

A sheepish grin spread over his face. "They can wait."

Without a lantern lit last night, she hadn't noticed the purple discoloration on his chest. "How did you get those bruises?"

"From you when I found you in the woods."

"*Nay.* Bruises don't last that long." She touched his skin gingerly. "Do they hurt?"

"*Nay.*" He kissed her forehead.

Her hand moved over his chest, touching a red blotchy area. "What about this rash?"

"I've been working a lot with cedar boughs." Josiah pulled away from her. "You're right. I have some chores to do in the barn."

Chapter Twenty-Five

More snow had fallen in Cedar Ridge over the past week than Ohio had seen all of last winter. The weather was normal for mid-January, according to Josiah, but Lindie couldn't get over how bone-chillingly cold it was in northern Michigan. She rose from the desk, having caught up on the bookkeeping for the recent shipment of pallets.

Hannah had waited patiently so they could paint together. But Lindie signed that first they needed to take some letters out to the mailbox. They had been stuck inside for so many days it would do them both good to get some fresh air.

Wading through the heavy drifts, Lindie wondered if they should be out in this cold at all, but Hannah jumped into the deepest snowbank and laughed out loud. Then she dropped to her knees and logrolled down the hilly yard. She reached the mailbox before Lindie and waited for her to put the letters inside. Hannah pulled up the red flag, then they went back inside.

Hannah started painting immediately. Lindie took longer to decide on a scene, but she managed to paint the sky and a wispy cloud before it was time to make lunch. Lindie dipped the brush in a small jar of turpentine, then cleaned it with a rag. Usually the two of them stopped painting at the same time to prepare the noon meal together. But today Hannah was so captivated, Lindie didn't interrupt her.

Lindie was still trying to shake the cold off from walking out to the mailbox. Though she didn't mind the bad weather, especially now that the last pallet order was shipped, because Josiah spent more time in the house. Since their night together, they had formed a tight bond. Her face flushed like a new bride. No wonder the women talked about cabin fever and the number of babies born at the end of summer.

Lindie selected a quart of canned chicken broth from the pantry, emptied it into a pot on the stove, then diced some carrots and celery. As the soup simmered, she leaned against the window casing and watched Josiah chop wood. White puffs of breath escaped his mouth as he swung the axe and split the chunk of wood in half. He tossed the pieces aside, placed another log on the block, and repeated the process.

Lindie's heart fluttered when he looked toward the window and smiled. She couldn't help but believe that fifty years from now his smile would still captivate her.

He loaded the wood in his arms and traipsed across the yard to the house. She rushed to open the door. A blast of cold air entered with him.

"Denki." He crossed the sitting room and dumped the pile into the woodbox. He swept the bark from his hands, then shook out of his coat and slung it over the back of a chair in the sitting room.

"Is that wet?"

He nodded. His teeth chattered and he tucked his hands under his armpits. "It's colder than yesterday."

"So I see." She touched his beard where ice had formed in spots. "Why don't you sit down and I'll make you a hot cup of *kaffi*."

He winked and pulled Lindie into his arms. "Is Hannah painting in her room?"

"*Nay*, she's sitting at the kitchen table." She touched his cheek. "You are *kalt*."

He brushed the back side of his icy hand against her cheek and kissed her, sending a shiver straight through her.

"Are you trying to get me *kalt*?"

He smiled. "Maybe."

With the blizzard conditions driving him indoors the past several days, they had snuck kisses and done their best to keep their charged emotions hidden.

"I have soup on the stove," she said.

He frowned.

"And I for one am hungry." She knew that would divert his attention.

"Let's eat, then." He smiled and gave her shoulder a squeeze, then gently nudged her toward the kitchen.

Once she filled the bowls with vegetable soup and placed them on the table, she offered to make sandwiches. Josiah and Hannah both turned them down. They seemed to be in a rush to finish their lunches. Lindie assumed Hannah was eager to paint more, and Josiah had something else on his mind.

Lindie breathed softly as she lay cuddled in Josiah's arms. Over the last several days, they'd fallen into a familiar routine. He coiled his finger around a lock of her red curls and studied the tiny freckles that dotted her nose. She was beautiful. When he thought about the trauma she'd gone through and how she carried the burden alone, it angered him deeply. She had suffered so much. He recalled how she had trembled in his arms even after he reassured her of his love.

Lindie opened her eyes and smiled. "How long did I sleep?"

He kissed her forehead. "An hour or so."

"And how long were you planning to let me continue?"

"I wouldn't have let you miss your doctor's appointment tomorrow."

She rolled her eyes. "Maybe it'll keep snowing."

"Maybe." But he wouldn't let snow stop them from keeping her appointment. Even though he wasn't looking forward to having his lab work repeated.

She glided her hand over his rashy area, making it difficult for him to think. He closed his eyes as the skin under her hand developed goose bumps.

Her hand stopped near his armpit and her fingertips circled the area. "Did you know you had a lump here?"

"Where?" He touched the raised area where she indicated.

"Does it hurt?"

"*Nay.*"

"Have you always had that?"

He pushed himself up and swung his legs over the side of the bed.

"Josiah?" She sat up behind him and placed her hand on his shoulder.

"It comes and goes." He didn't want to explain the circumstances surrounding the lump. The last time his lymph nodes swelled, he underwent several months of chemo. He rubbed his beard.

"Is this something serious?"

Before he could form his answer, the bell over the door sounded. He pushed off the bed. "I have to check on Hannah."

Lindie was fastening her dress with pins when he rushed out of the room. He sped through the house, searched each room, but didn't find Hannah. He jammed his feet into his boots, grabbed his coat off the hook, and darted outside.

The strong winds decreased visibility to a few feet. He pulled his collar up higher on his neck and plowed a path through the crunching snow to the barn. A quick check of the calf pen and the horse stalls was futile. Hannah wasn't in the barn. But neither was Moose. The old gelding's stall was empty.

He pushed the barn door open, lowered his head, and trudged into the wind. Hannah lacked the skills necessary to find her way in these whiteout conditions. She also had no concept of time. It would be dark soon, and the temperature would plummet.

He spotted Lindie coming down the porch steps. "Go back inside."

"I want to help."

"Not this time. Wait for us in the house." He couldn't risk having her exposed to the subzero temperature. Mid-January wasn't the time of year to be outdoors for an extended period. Moreover, she would slow him down.

Lindie cringed, but she turned and went inside.

He followed what he hoped was a set of fresh tracks. With the snow blowing, he couldn't be certain they were tracks at all. His pant legs were covered in snow and his legs felt numb. He paused for a moment and pulled in a sharp breath. The crisp air cut into his lungs, leaving him winded and lightheaded. He continued his search, not stopping until the tracks vanished.

He scanned the field. Nothing. Had he not noticed Moose

missing from his stall, he would have assumed Hannah had fled to the woods again. The horse wouldn't make it under the low-reaching limbs. Even so, he didn't expect Hannah would have considered the horse's size. Josiah trudged on. By the time he reached the fence at the back of the pasture, he spotted them. Moose was lying on his side with Hannah clinging to the horse's neck.

Josiah bent to his knees beside Hannah and searched her for injury. "Were you riding Moose?"

She shook her head, then peeled off her mittens to sign. "He got loose. I followed him to bring him back."

He quickly examined Moose. No signs of distress. The old horse closed his eyes when Josiah stroked his neck. Over the years he'd owned plenty of animals that instinctively wandered off when it came time to die. At twenty-two, Moose likely was doing the same. Josiah's heart ached for Hannah.

"Go back to the house," he instructed.

Hannah looked at Moose, then back to him. She flung herself on Moose. Her body racked with sobs.

God, I need wisdom. His face had gone numb from the howling wind. He had to act quickly. He tapped Hannah's shoulder, but she ignored him and closed her eyes. Josiah pried her away from the horse's neck and lifted her into his arms. Leaving Moose was hard, but he couldn't let his daughter get frostbitten. Once she was inside where it was warm, he would come back. He expected Hannah to rebel when he carried her away from the horse, but she laid her head on his shoulder instead.

He reached the house, breathless and weary. Thankfully, Lindie was there to open the door.

Lindie helped Hannah out of her cape, then draped a blanket over her shoulders and walked her closer to the woodstove. Hannah's purplish lips quivered.

Josiah strode to the bedroom and removed his hunting rifle from the closet. He couldn't let Moose suffer.

Lindie gasped. "Why do you need a gun?" She followed him to the door.

"Make sure Hannah stays inside." He opened the door and stepped into the cold air. He pulled his glove off with his teeth, dug his hand into his pocket, and fished out the bullets. His fingers stiffened as he loaded the gun.

Lord, please give me a sign if I'm not to put Moose out of his misery. He didn't want to think about the pain Hannah would feel if Moose died.

❧

Lindie rocked Hannah in her arms. They both cried after Josiah left the house with the gun. "Moose didn't get up. He must—" Hannah couldn't finish signing before she broke down in tears. Lindie wasn't sure what she meant, but what mattered now was comforting Hannah. Rocking helped a little. When one of her nephews was upset, she would rock him and sing. But Hannah wouldn't be able to hear. Instead, she rubbed the child's back.

It wasn't long before Hannah went limp in her arms. Then as though something had startled the child, she jolted upright. Her eyes widened as she looked around the room. She scurried off Lindie's lap and bolted toward the door.

Lindie stopped her.

"Let me go to Moose," she signed.

Lindie shook her head.

"But Moose—"

The door opened and a blast of air entered with Josiah.

Turning toward her father, Hannah's hands moved so quickly that Lindie couldn't follow.

He stretched out his arm, holding the gun toward Lindie. "Would you hold this? It isn't loaded," he said.

She held the gun pointed at the floor as he signaled to Hannah to wait a minute, then took off his coat and hat.

Lindie turned so that Hannah wouldn't see her mouth moving. "Did you have to shoot him?"

"Nay." He faced Hannah. "Moose got up himself. He's in the barn."

She flung her arms around her father.

Josiah kissed the top of his daughter's *kapp*, then peered over her head at Lindie. "God answered *mei* prayer. By some miracle, the horse was on his feet when I reached him."

Lindie smiled. "You've certainly made Hannah happy."

"That was God. I had every intention of shooting him so he wouldn't suffer." He reached for the gun in her hands. "I'll put that away."

Lindie followed him to the bedroom. "What had happened to Moose? Hannah was so distraught she couldn't even sign."

"He's old. Animals often wander off to die." He placed the gun on the rack inside the closet. "I don't think he has much longer to live. The old horse had closed his eyes. Given up." He rubbed the spot under his arm where she had found the lump.

"You need to have that lump checked. Does it hurt?"

"Nay." He dropped his hand and smiled. But it masked nothing.

Chapter Twenty-Six

Y ou've relapsed."
Doctor Ethridge's words echoed as Josiah's mind refused to register the news. No. This wasn't so. God had healed him six years ago. The tests were wrong. A crushing sensation filled his chest. Stole his breath. He needed air. Josiah tugged his collarless shirt away from his skin. The room grew hot.

"Can I get you some water?"

Vaguely aware he nodded, he felt the room spin. Sweat beaded on his neck, dripped down his back. He gripped the edge of the cushioned exam table as dizziness swept over him.

"Here, drink this." Doctor Ethridge handed him a small paper cup filled with water.

Josiah gulped it down. It wasn't enough to replace the cottony taste in his mouth, but at least the room wasn't moving so fast.

"Maybe you better lie down a few minutes."

"No." He licked his parched lips. "I need to know how long I have."

"It's too early to know for sure," Doctor Ethridge said, his eyes full of sympathy.

"Are you talking weeks? Months?" Josiah needed solid information.

"Is Lindie in the lobby? I'll send for her."

Josiah shook his head; it throbbed as if lambasted by a shovel. "I came by myself." He hadn't even told Lindie last week about undergoing the biopsy on the lump.

Doctor Ethridge collected the empty cup, filled it with more water, then handed it back. "Josiah, I'm sorry to have to deliver such bad news."

Again. The doctor said that the last time too. He cited the odds of remission after relapse, but Josiah's mind raced with other thoughts. Days. He had days, not months. That must be why the results from the biopsy came back so quickly.

Josiah slugged down the water. "So it's only . . . a matter of days?"

"I'm not saying that. Until we see how you respond . . ."

Josiah shifted his eyes to the tile floor. His thoughts drifted to his family. How would he tell Hannah? She'd already lost her mother. He didn't want to leave Lindie either. Being alone with two children would be difficult for any woman. She wouldn't know how to run the lumberyard. Simon wasn't strong enough to keep it going. Would Lindie stay in contact with Simon if she moved back to Ohio with the children?

"Josiah?" Doctor Ethridge cleared his throat.

He lifted his head.

"I thought we could discuss a treatment plan. That is, if you're ready."

"Chemo again, right?" He wished there were other options. Anything but chemotherapy. Those treatments wiped him out physically. He still remembered how his veins burned during the infusion.

"We could follow the same regimen as the last time . . ."

"Or?" At least Josiah hoped there was another choice. The longer he stared at the doctor's grim expression, the more nervous he became. Josiah grasped his leg to calm it from bouncing.

"I'm afraid it's a long shot. Once you've come out of remission, as you have, the likelihood of going back into remission isn't great. I'm not saying it can't happen."

Josiah pulled in a deep breath. He didn't like the idea of receiving chemo treatments again, but he would take the harsh side effects over dying. "What about doing that transplant you talked about the last time?"

"Using high doses of chemotherapy agents followed up with a bone marrow transplant would increase your chances, but we didn't have luck finding a donor match the last time."

Josiah didn't need luck—he needed God. "What about doing just the chemo?"

"At the high dosage you need, it's risky. The medication will destroy the good cells along with the bad. Without following up the treatment with a bone marrow transplant, it isn't likely to be successful." He continued talking, something about his already adding Josiah's name to the transplant waiting list. The doctor's words disappeared into the background of Josiah's thoughts.

What will become of Hannah, God? Who will be able to communicate with her? Lindie treats her well, but she still isn't proficient in sign language. And, Lord, what about Lindie? I promised to do everything in my power to keep her safe. She trusted me . . .

"I'll let you talk this over with your wife."

Josiah jerked his head up. "What? No. I can't tell Lindie. I can't put more stress on her. Not while she's pregnant." His words ran together.

"I agree that her condition is delicate. We don't have to tell her *yet*." The doctor studied the chart. "We'll start the chemo at the same dosage as last time, increase it incrementally, and if the treatment fails, then we can discuss other options. The odds are not in your favor, but let's hope that's all you'll need to go into remission again."

Odds. The doctor was a godly man yet he still quoted odds.

Doctor Ethridge scribbled something on a prescription pad, tore it off, and handed the paper to him. "Take this to the hospital. It's an order to have an IV port inserted."

Josiah studied the scribbling, but the prescribed directions made no sense to him.

"I'll order the agents and once they arrive, we can set up a treatment schedule."

Josiah nodded without lifting his head.

"You're not going to be able to keep this from Lindie."

"This is February. She only has three months before the baby is due," Josiah said.

Doctor Ethridge lowered his eyes and nodded.

Josiah closed his eyes. "I don't have that much time, do I?"

❧

Lindie paced the kitchen floor. Josiah had been gone all day. It wasn't like him to leave and not tell her what time he would be back. She tried not to fret, but she couldn't keep from looking out the window. The sun had set an hour ago and his supper dish sat untouched on the table. She peered out the window again. Snowing. Would it ever stop?

Lord, please keep him safe. The roads were dangerous. The plows didn't always do a good job clearing the shoulders. He wouldn't have anywhere to steer the horse if a car spun out of control. So many things could go wrong. Molly could slip and fall on a patch of ice.

"Do not let your heart be troubled and do not be afraid," Lindie whispered. She wrung her dry, cracked hands together and repeated the verse from the book of John. "Let not your heart be troubled . . ." If it took all night to feel some sort of peace, she would keep quoting the Word. She crossed the room again. "Let not—"

Hannah's cry startled Lindie. She raced from the kitchen, down the hall, and into the child's room.

"Shh." Lindie sat on the edge of Hannah's bed.

A frightened, almost wild look overcame the girl. "He's dying," she signed, her hands moving fast.

Lindie swept Hannah's hair away from her face, then kissed her forehead. "You had a bad dream," she said slowly enough for Hannah to read her lips.

Hannah stared.

"*M-O-O-S-E*"—Lindie spelled out one letter at a time—"is okay." Josiah had checked on the horse multiple times in the last few days and he'd made a miraculous recovery. Lindie straightened the bedcovers.

"Not Moose." Hannah's hands paused. "Father."

Lindie crinkled her brow and, without prompting, Hannah repeated the hand gestures. Lindie pulled the child into her arms and hugged her tight. No wonder she was so upset. She pulled back so Hannah could see her lips. "Pray for him. God hears you."

Within seconds of Hannah closing her eyes, a light flashed outside the window.

Relief washed over Lindie. She tapped Hannah's arm. "Your father is home," she said, pointing to the window. "I just saw the buggy's lantern light." She patted the pillow. "Everything is okay. Go back to sleep."

After she tucked Hannah under the covers, Lindie hurried to the kitchen. She pushed the curtains aside and looked toward the barn. A dim glow from the lantern illuminated Josiah's buggy as he worked to unhitch the horse. Home at last. He was safe.

She put the coffeepot on the stove and his supper plate in the oven to reheat. A few minutes later she removed the plate from the oven, placed it and a freshly poured cup of coffee on the table, then waited.

And waited.

What was taking him so long? She picked up a damp dishcloth and scrubbed the counter. He was gone all day. What was he going to do, dally in the barn all night? It was already late.

Several minutes later the back door opened. Josiah stepped into the kitchen, removed his hat, and ran his hand across the back of his neck. "I thought you would have already gone to bed," he said.

"How could I sleep with you not home yet? I was worried."

He bowed his head.

"Your food is getting *kalt—again*." She applied more pressure on the cloth as she scoured the countertop.

He pulled the chair out from under the table and sat. He closed his eyes briefly, then picked up the fork.

"Were the roads bad?"

"Snowy, but not too slippery." He took a bite of potatoes, chewing them slowly.

"Are they *kalt* again? I'll warm them up."

She tossed the rag on the counter, picked up his plate, and took it to the stove.

"Are you feeling all right?" he asked, probably in response

to the sound of clanging pots and pans as she pulled out the fry pan she'd just washed.

"I feel fine." She slapped a heaping tablespoon of lard into the cast-iron pan.

He scooted his chair back. "I don't think I'm hungry."

She spun around, crossed her arms, and glared at him. If he wasn't hungry, he should have stopped her before she dirtied the pan.

"Okay, I'll eat." He raised his hands in surrender and returned to his seat. "Just didn't want you to go to all that trouble, is all."

"It's no trouble." She dumped the potatoes from his plate into the grease. Reheating them twice would probably dry them out more. The chicken's white meat was already dry and stringy.

"Did Hannah give you problems today?"

"*Nay*, why do you ask?"

He shrugged. "You don't seem to be in a *gut* mood."

She huffed. "Earlier you said you had some things to do. I thought you were going out to the barn, but you harnessed the horse and drove off. Then you were gone all day. I should have asked what you wanted reheated, your lunch or dinner, since you weren't home to eat either."

He bowed his head. "I'm sorry."

"It's snowing. And dark. And I was worried about you. What if something happened? Hannah and I wouldn't know what to do without you."

His shoulders slumped. "You would handle things fine," he said softly, then added, "Wouldn't you?" He scrutinized her from across the room. "Well?" His voice strengthened. "Would you be able to take care of Hannah?"

"Are you *still* judging my skills to look after your child? I didn't think I still had to prove myself."

"It was a what-if question. What if something happened to me?" He rubbed the back of his neck again as though trying to massage a knot loose.

"Oh." The potatoes sizzled and she turned to the stove. First Hannah dreamt he was dying and now he posed this question.

Josiah stood. "I'm sorry you went to all this trouble, but I'm really *nett* hungry." He left the room.

⁓

Josiah slipped out of bed and dressed quietly so as not to wake Lindie. Now that she was in her last trimester, she woke several times throughout the night to empty her bladder. He wanted her to sleep as long as possible. Plus, he wanted to get an early start on the lumber orders he needed to fill. After Eli received the first shipment of elm, he had placed another order. It was good that Josiah had enough wood and didn't need to chop more trees, since he had less than a week before the doctor wanted to start chemotherapy. Doctor Ethridge had warned him the dosage would start low and steadily increase, which would also increase the severity of the side effects. Because he only had three days, Josiah arranged for Jakob Troyer to help him complete the orders.

Josiah filled a cup with coffee and took it out with him to the workshop. He wanted to get a fire started in the woodstove. He also didn't want Lindie to hear him in the kitchen and get up. He still didn't know how to break the news to her.

Jakob Troyer arrived shortly after sunrise and they worked hard until late afternoon, breaking only for lunch. Then Josiah continued working after Jakob went home. Except for taking Sunday off to rest, the grueling schedule continued throughout the week. Josiah found planing lumber a means to smooth out his frustration. Not that anything could lessen his anxiety about what was ahead.

Lindie entered the workshop sometime after Jakob had gone home.

"Josiah, don't you want to eat supper?"

He set the hammer on the worktable. "I didn't know it was that late."

She shivered. "It's *kalt* in here."

"I guess I let the fire die out."

Lindie frowned. "You used to spend more time in the *haus*."

He missed those long afternoons too, when he didn't rush back to work after lunch.

She lifted her hand to his arm. "When are you going to get this lump checked?"

He backed away from her. "I'm sorry I haven't been around the *haus* much." He looked at the sawdust on the floor. "It'll probably be that way . . . for a while."

"Are the orders so urgent that you feel you must work day and *nacht*? Don't you think it's important that you find out about that lump?"

This was hard. He wanted more than anything to keep her from worrying and she was doing it anyway.

"Your *dochder* is concerned about you too."

He looked at her. "Does she know about the lump?"

Lindie shook her head. "*Nay*, I haven't said anything."

"Things are okay between you two, though, right?"

"*Jah*, but why do you keep asking me that?"

"I need to know that things are still working out. That she's accepted you as her *mamm*. That if something should happen—"

"Please, Josiah, you're frightening me." Lindie winced and, bending slightly, held her belly.

266

"What's wrong?"

"It isn't anything." After a moment, she straightened, her face strained with a smile.

"Are you sure?"

She nodded. "The *boppli* kicked, is all."

He placed his hands next to hers on her abdomen and smiled. "His kick is as strong as a horse." If he could freeze time, it would be in this moment. "Have I told you how much I love you?"

"*Nett* lately," she said, frowning. "I was beginning to think . . ."

"You were beginning to think what?"

"That I was too fat—too pregnant."

"What?" He chuckled until he realized her frown was real. He cupped her face in his hands and peered into her eyes. "I think you're beautiful pregnant." He kissed her forehead. "I love you. I should tell you so every day." He kissed the bridge of her nose. "Because I do."

She smiled. "I love you too."

"I'm going to tell you every day for the rest of *mei* life."

Chapter Twenty-Seven

The sun peeked over the horizon as Josiah reached the doctor's office. With the routine questions about how he was feeling and his blood pressure and pulse recorded, the infusion was started.

He was told the medication might burn and it did. Like someone jabbing a branding iron through his veins. Josiah closed his eyes. He refused to complain. He appreciated Doctor Ethridge agreeing to do the infusion in his office. Six years ago it took heavy convincing to receive the treatments in the office instead of at the hospital. Josiah couldn't afford what the hospital would charge for therapy then, nor could he now. At least Doctor Ethridge offered trade for payment. There weren't many small-town doctors like him, and the Amish were blessed to have such a caring and godly man.

"This will take a couple hours to infuse," the doctor said. "Would you like the lights turned off?"

"Yes, please."

Josiah rested as best he could on the stiff cot. Although his body relaxed, his mind didn't. Images of Hannah and Lindie flashed before him. He didn't want to leave them. *Lord, I want to live. I want to grow old with Lindie surrounded by our* kinner. A warm stream of tears spilled down his face and soaked into his beard.

It seemed forever before the doctor returned. He checked the IV fluids and disconnected the tubing. "I want you to stay another hour or two so we can monitor your blood pressure." He handed him a plastic basin. "In case you need to be sick."

It wasn't if, but when. The rolls of nausea had already started. He'd hoped to leave before his stomach revolted. He had skipped breakfast for that very reason. The nurse entered the room, took his blood pressure, and asked him a few questions. Shortness of breath, itching . . . he answered no to all of them. She left him alone, only to return an hour later to repeat them again. After the third recheck, the nurse removed the cuff from his arm.

"Your blood pressure is good," she said.

"Does that mean I can leave?"

"Let me ask the doctor." She left the room and returned a minute later. "He will see you at the same time tomorrow."

Josiah pushed off the cot. When he stood, his legs wobbled and his knees threatened to buckle. Driving home would be a challenge.

"Can I take this?" He lifted the plastic basin. He hadn't used it yet, but he wasn't sure he could hold back his ratcheting stomach once the buggy started down the bumpy roads.

"Yes, you can." The nurse walked beside him.

He was grateful for the help, until he came face-to-face with Ada Fisher.

"I noticed your horse out back." Ada scrutinized him a little closer. "*Ach*, Josiah, you don't look well."

He tried to smile but couldn't get his lips to curl upward.

"Is Lindie here with you?"

"*Nay*, she's home with Hannah." His stomach churned. If he didn't leave soon, she would figure out he wasn't here for the flu. He wouldn't be able to hide anything from Lindie now. He had to tell her today. Later. He couldn't do it looking or feeling like this. He ambled slowly out the door as Ada's newborn infant started to cry. Loud. His sensitive ears rang with the high-pitched shrill.

He stopped twice to vomit on the ride home. Both times his rib muscles ached as through they'd been pressed through a meat grinder. Once home, he unharnessed the horse but didn't have the strength to hang the equipment on the stud and left it lying on the barn floor in a heap. It didn't matter. He needed to lie down and wait for the queasiness to pass.

Josiah shuffled to Simon's place. The room reminded him of the *icehaus*. Cloudy breaths escaped his mouth as he opened the woodstove. He balled the newspaper around the kindling and chose a log with the most bark, hoping the fire would take off immediately. It did. The light-headedness would soon pass. Josiah pulled the covers back on the bed and collapsed.

༜

Bright afternoon sun glittered on the freshly fallen snow and provided the perfect amount of light in the sitting room by which to do the mending. Lindie demonstrated to Hannah how to thread the needle, then made a few stitches while Hannah watched. Lindie handed a sock that needed darning to Hannah and helped her weave the needle through the material.

"Very good," Lindie said.

Hannah beamed.

Lindie selected another sock from the pile. The material was so threadbare, even closing the holes wouldn't make the sock usable. She tossed it into the rag pile and grabbed another one as someone knocked on the door.

Rebecca stood at the door, holding a food dish.

"Gut afternoon." Lindie opened the door wider.

"I know this probably isn't a *gut* time, but I wanted to stop by and lend support."

"Denki." Normally people brought food *after* the baby was born. Lindie pushed a strand of hair over her ear. "I was just teaching Hannah how to sew."

Rebecca only glanced in Hannah's direction before looking back at Lindie. "How are you doing?"

"I feel fine." She straightened her dress apron.

"Is there anything I can help you with? I could take care of Hannah." Rebecca reached for Lindie's hand. "You don't have to go through this alone."

"What do you mean? *Mei boppli* isn't due yet."

Rebecca looked around the room. "Is Josiah resting? I don't want to wake him."

"He's out in the barn." Where he'd been all week.

"Ada said she saw him at the *doktah's* office. He had the same paleness as when . . ."

"When what?"

Rebecca cringed. "When he . . . first had lymphoma."

The air left Lindie's lungs in a whoosh. "Wha—" She choked on her words.

Rebecca pulled a chair out from the table and coaxed her to sit, then filled a glass with water. "I'm so sorry. I thought you knew," she said, handing Lindie the glass.

She sipped the water, too stunned to talk. After a moment, she rose from the chair. "I'm truly grateful," she said, going to the window. Josiah's buggy sat next to the barn. She hadn't thought anything about him working all day. But if he was sick, he shouldn't be in the drafty barn.

"The entire settlement feels bad. The last time he was sick we all had our blood tested to see if any of us could donate our bone marrow," Rebecca said. "But none of us were a match."

Lindie couldn't grasp the information. She continued to stare out the window.

Rebecca placed her hand on Lindie's back. "If he didn't say anything to you, then maybe it's just the flu."

"That's why you asked if he was feeling okay during the *nacht* of the sleigh ride? That was over a month ago."

"I thought he looked a little run-down."

"I didn't pick up on any of it," Lindie said softly.

"It still might only be the flu."

Whatever was ailing him, Lindie had to know. "Would you mind taking Hannah for the *nacht*?"

"I can take her longer if needed."

"*Denki*, let me go tell her." Lindie blotted her eyes with the corner of her dress. She didn't want any trace of tears to alarm Hannah. At least she wouldn't hear if her voice cracked. Lindie cleared her throat anyway and tapped Hannah's shoulder.

The girl looked up from her sewing.

Lindie faked a smile and made the hand gestures to pack some clothes. She motioned to Rebecca and explained that the bishop's wife wanted Hannah to spend the night.

Hannah stared a long moment. Lindie repeated the gestures, but Hannah shook her head slowly.

"I love you. But you must do as you're told."

Hannah stood, left the sock on the chair, and went toward her bedroom. A few minutes later she returned, clothes in hand. Rebecca placed her arm around the child's shoulders and guided her toward the door, but Hannah stopped in front of the desk. She stared at the picture she drew of the hands hanging on the wall.

Lindie's throat constricted. She willed herself not to cry. As Hannah walked with them to the buggy, she glanced over her shoulder. Her large brown eyed bore into Lindie's.

Once the buggy pulled out of sight, Lindie proceeded to the workshop. Josiah wasn't around. She called for him, but he didn't answer. She went to the rear of the building and tapped on the door. "Josiah?"

No answer.

She eased the door open and tiptoed inside.

Huddled under a heavy quilt and overcome by tremors, his eyes opened a crack, then closed.

"Josiah," she whispered. She sat on the edge of the bed and pushed his hair off his forehead. His ashen skin was dotted in sweat. She rested her hand above his brow. Hot. Clammy. "Josiah." Her voice cracked.

"Go back." Racked with shivers, his voice shook. "Too . . . *kalt*."

"What are you doing out here? Alone?" She buried her face in the pillow beside him and sobbed.

He pulled his arm out from under the covers and patted her back. "Don't cry."

She lifted her head. "Tell—me. What's—wrong—?" Her voice broke. "Is it true? Do you have lymphoma?"

His eyes welled with tears.

Chapter Twenty-Eight

Sometime during the night the adverse effects Josiah experienced from the medication wore off, but another sickness overcame him. The possibility of death. Leaving this woman he had come to love carried more fire through his veins than the toxic infusion of chemicals.

The bedsprings squeaked when he crawled out of bed. Lindie stirred.

"Go back to sleep," he whispered.

She moaned softly and rolled to her other side, then flipped back over. "You're *nett* going without me." She bounded out of bed before he could object.

"Lindie, I think it'd be best if—"

"I'm going to the *doktah's* appointment with you." She grabbed a dress from the closet. "Rebecca has already said she would watch Hannah longer."

"It's a long day."

"And I want to spend it with *mei* husband."

"Fine." It would take too much energy to stop her. Besides, she could drive home. "I'll get the buggy ready."

"Don't you want to eat something first?" She slipped on her dress and grabbed a handful of straight pins from the top of the dresser. "It'd only take a minute to make eggs."

He spoke over his shoulder as he left the room. "I'd rather *nett* eat." He didn't want to alarm her, but today's dose was supposedly stronger, which probably meant more violent side effects. After uncontrollable shakes had racked his body yesterday, he dreaded what effects the infusion would have today.

"You need your strength, Josiah," she called out behind him.

"If it makes you feel better, you can make me a sandwich to eat afterward." He shoved on his boots. He wouldn't be surprised if she made him four sandwiches to make up for no breakfast. She would find out soon enough why he had no appetite. He pulled on his coat and grabbed his hat from the hook.

Lindie had a knapsack packed and was outside by the time he had Molly harnessed. As they headed for town, neither spoke. He appreciated the silence.

The nurse entered the empty lobby. "If you'll follow me, we can get started."

Josiah nodded and he and Lindie trailed the nurse to the scale. He couldn't imagine that his weight had changed since she took it yesterday. But he removed his boots and stepped on the scale. The nurse recorded the weight without comment. She led him to the examination room, where he climbed on the paper-lined table. Lindie sat in the chair in the corner. The nurse took his blood pressure, pulse, and temperature and documented the results on the clipboard. She asked Josiah a few questions about how he'd tolerated yesterday's infusion and the amount he vomited. She held the same facial expression as she jotted notes in the chart.

The nurse closed the chart and directed her attention to Lindie. "Are you seeing the doctor today too?"

"Next week is my appointment."

"You don't have much longer to go."

"Three months." A soft glow radiated from Lindie's face as she smiled.

"Doctor Ethridge won't be long." On her way out, the nurse placed the clipboard in the tray on the door.

"It seems strange to be sitting here and not on the cot." Lindie folded and unfolded her hands. Finally, she stood and motioned to the cup dispenser on the wall. "Can I get you some water?"

"Sure." He agreed more to give her something to do than because he was thirsty.

She filled a small paper cup from the sink and handed it to him.

"Denki." He took a small sip, leery of having too much in his stomach.

"Do you want more?"

"I haven't finished this." He tipped the cup so she could see how much remained. He drank the rest as Doctor Ethridge entered the room. Josiah crushed the paper cup in his hand and passed it to Lindie, who tossed it into the trash before sitting down.

"Are you feeling up for another round?" the doctor asked.

"I suppose so."

Doctor Ethridge listened to Josiah's heart and then went through a list of questions ranging from what type of side effects Josiah had experienced to what color his urine was and how many bowel movements he'd had. After making a few notes, he set the clipboard on the counter. "Normally I don't mind if a family member sits in the room during the administration." He turned to Lindie. "But because you're pregnant, I'm going to ask that you wait in the lobby during the infusion."

Lindie nodded.

The look she gave Josiah tugged at his heart. He wanted to pull her into his arms and reassure her everything was fine. Instead, he winked, and enjoyed the brief satisfaction of making her smile.

❧

Lindie sat in the chair next to the lamp table. Finding out about Josiah's illness left her with so many unanswered questions. How long could someone in his condition live without a bone marrow transplant? Would he go into remission with just chemotherapy? She should have brought a pad to write a letter to Margaret. She wanted to ask Eli if he knew that Josiah had once had cancer.

A half hour later Doctor Ethridge crossed the lobby.

She stood. "Is he done?"

"No, it's going to be another hour or two yet." He motioned to the chair, then sat down on the one beside her. "Josiah is tolerating the infusion."

She blew out a breath. "You had me worried."

"I thought you might be." He patted Lindie's hand. "How are you feeling?"

"The baby kicks a lot during the night. I don't get much sleep, but I'm fine." She leaned forward. "Tell me about Josiah. Will this medicine that he's getting work?"

He looked at his folded hands. "It's a long shot," he said without lifting his head. "He needs a bone marrow transplant." He paused as though allowing her time to take it all in. "I'm sorry to say we haven't found a donor match."

"I haven't been tested."

"Even if you were a perfect match, I would not advise it while you're pregnant. It's a complex procedure. The marrow is taken from the hip area. It's not a good idea. I'm sorry."

Her shoulders slumped and she fell back against the chair. This pregnancy had a way of altering her life—again. First Moses's rejection, now the possible loss of the man she loved. "Please." She inched forward in the seat. "I have to do something to help him."

"We're doing everything possible. Even if he went to a cancer center, they couldn't do more without a donor. The regimen I've prescribed is aggressive," he said. "Josiah understood and agreed to the risks." He stood. "I need to check on how the infusion is going."

Lindie rushed to his side. "Couldn't I at least be tested?"

He stopped. "What if you're a match? Would you want me to induce labor so you deliver early?" He shook his head. "That would jeopardize the health of the baby. I won't do that. It's one thing for Josiah to take risks—it's his life—but I won't agree to risk the life of an unborn child."

"I might naturally deliver early. You said so yourself a few months ago."

"That isn't so much an issue now that you're gaining weight." He smiled. "But I suppose it wouldn't hurt to do the blood test. If you are a match—*and* the baby arrives early . . ."

"Can we do it now?"

He nodded. "I'll tell my nurse." His gray eyebrows formed a straight line. "There's still a risk that you won't be strong enough after giving birth. I'm not the one who will perform the bone marrow procedure, so you'll have to pass another doctor's specifications. There is no guarantee."

"I understand. But I believe in miracles. All things are possible."

Doctor Ethridge nodded. "Keep that hope alive."

Even as she nodded, doubt seeped in. *God's ways are not our ways. His thoughts are not like ours . . .*

Chapter Twenty-Nine

Josiah's condition deteriorated rapidly after he received the second infusion. Other than reheating the meals brought over by the womenfolk, Lindie hadn't left his bedside in three days. Between Ada and Rebecca, Hannah was well cared for. Lindie was grateful for their help. Neither she nor Josiah wanted Hannah to see how sick he'd become.

She lifted the soup spoon to Josiah's mouth and cupped her other hand under his chin. "Take a sip. You need your strength."

He opened his mouth wide enough for the spoon and accepted the broth. His eyes closed.

Don't stop. A few sips weren't much, but a start nonetheless. Doctor Ethridge had said the medication might suppress Josiah's appetite. She never thought it would vanish altogether.

"Will you try and eat more?" She readied another spoonful, but his eyes remained closed and his mumbling wasn't comprehensible. Lindie lowered the spoon and set it and the bowl on the table. She knelt at the side of the bed, rested her forehead against the mattress, and closed her eyes.

"Father, please, I don't want to see him suffer. He's a *gut* husband." Her plea turned whiny. "Don't take him from me. Please."

Josiah reached down and placed his hand on the side of her face.

She clasped his hand and pressed it tighter against her cheek. "Father, give him strength to fight."

"I won't give up."

Hope soared within her. "I'm holding you to that."

The corners of his lips creased upward a moment, then his eyes closed and his mouth returned to its neutral position.

"I love you, Josiah," she said, rising up from her knees.

His lips moved a little, but nothing audible came out.

꒰꒱

A few days later Josiah felt well enough to sit up in bed. He ran his hand through his hair and a clump of hair fell out. "It won't be long before I'm bald. You think *mei* hat will still fit?"

Lindie took the chunk from him. "If it doesn't, I'll knit you a cap to wear under it." She tossed it into a trash can beside the dresser. "Are you hungry?" She and Hannah had eaten earlier, but she'd saved him a plate to reheat.

"*Nay.*"

Five days he had spent in bed, lacking the energy to even swallow soup. He was wasting away. His shadowed eyes were sunken and so were his cheeks. She sat on the edge of the bed and reached for his hand. "Won't you at least try to eat something?"

He shook his head. "Maybe later. I'm *nett* hungry."

"You said that earlier."

He cracked a smile and her heart warmed. She had sorely

missed his company over the past few days. Now that he was more alert, she wanted to share his every waking minute.

Lindie wished her doctor's appointment wasn't today. Yet she'd held a glimmer of hope all week that she would hear news about the blood tests. Deep in her heart she was sure she was Josiah's donor match. Why else would God have put them together?

"Rebecca will be here soon. She's going to watch Hannah while I go into town for *mei* checkup." She hadn't told him about Simon's bus arriving today. He might insist on meeting him at the station.

The bell over the door jingled. "I better make sure that wasn't Hannah leaving." She crossed the room and stepped into the hallway. Hannah's door was open and she was busy drawing on her sketch pad and didn't look up. Lindie continued down the hall.

"I let myself in when no one answered," Rebecca said, shaking her arm out from her cape. "How is Josiah?"

"Better if I could get him to eat." She motioned toward the kitchen. "I have a pan of meatloaf in the oven. I don't know if he'll eat, but even if he only takes a bite or two it's better than nothing."

Rebecca followed Lindie into the kitchen. "And Hannah, how is she?"

"She knows he's sick, but she's not aware of the severity." Lindie opened the oven door and removed the pan of meatloaf. "I've waited for Josiah to say something, but he's been so sick that he hasn't wanted Hannah to see him."

"I'll pray God gives you and Josiah wisdom concerning Hannah. I know sometimes it's difficult for you to communicate with her, but God will open those doors too."

"Hannah and I are making progress. God has been *gut* about that." She sliced the meatloaf and placed it on a plate. "Pray that I'm a donor match. I should find out something today."

"Is it possible to donate while you're pregnant?"

"If the *boppli* arrives early." Lindie sighed. "I could use any suggestions you have for early delivery. I thought about spicy food, but maybe there is a tea I could drink?" She grabbed a fork from the drawer and a clean dish towel for him to use as a napkin. "I'll be back in a minute." Lindie carried the dish into the bedroom and set it on the bedside table. "Josiah," she whispered, "your plate is on the stand." His eyes remained closed. "I'm leaving *nau* for town. I won't be long." Lately it seemed she talked more to the wind than to him, he drifted in and out so much. She started to turn away and he grasped her arm.

"Be careful," he said.

"I will." She leaned down and kissed his forehead. "You eat something. Your plate is on the nightstand."

"Is it snowing?"

"It is, but *nett* hard." It had snowed some all week, six inches yesterday.

"You should ask someone to drive you to town."

"Don't worry about me. I'll be careful." Had he forgotten she grew up in Ohio? She'd driven in the snow plenty of times. Besides, on the way home for her appointment, she planned on picking up Simon. He could drive if the road conditions worsened.

He licked his cracked lips. "I should be the one to take you."

"You concentrate on eating and getting stronger." She squeezed his hand. "I'll see you when I get back. Hopefully I'll have *gut* news to share." Lindie opened the door and paused before leaving. "Make sure you eat."

She stopped at Hannah's room long enough to tell her to

be mindful of Rebecca, then instructed Rebecca to watch that Hannah didn't leave the house unattended. Lindie checked the wall clock. She would have to hurry.

Driving to town, joyfulness bubbled within Lindie. She practically bounced on the seat, certain she would hear the doctor say she was a match. Lindie understood now why God had allowed the vile attack. The past events, though painful, had a higher purpose. She had a husband who needed her bone marrow. Surely God had all of this planned. He provided a fine husband, a daughter who needed motherly guidance, and a soon-to-be-born baby. God provided a family to love. And God would use her bone marrow to save Josiah's life. Choked up with tears of joy, she peered up at the clear blue sky and praised the Lord.

꒯

The temperature had plummeted several degrees in the short time Lindie had been in the office. The weather wasn't nearly as numbing as hearing the news she wasn't a donor match. She cried, not caring that the gusty, bitter winds turned her face raw. The burning sting didn't matter, nothing did.

You're a closer match than anyone else in the district, but not close enough, the doctor's words echoed.

What was she supposed to do now? Stand by, urge Josiah to sip broth, and watch him die? *Why, God? Why couldn't you have used me? I thought I understood why I was here—why so many horrible things had happened to me. I never thought I could feel loved . . . until Josiah.*

Even wearing gloves, her hands were stiff by the time she reached the bus station. Simon's bus was delayed due to weather. Lindie slouched on the bench and closed her eyes. "God, I don't know how to accept this outcome, but I do know Hannah and Josiah need me to be strong. Help me, please." She whispered continuous prayers throughout her wait, not paying attention to the overhead announcements. Another hour passed before a bus pulled up to the platform. She wiped her face with the hem of her cape and waited as the passengers unloaded.

Simon's expression turned weary when their eyes connected. Carrying a small suitcase, he ambled across the platform. "Is something wrong?"

She nodded, then covered her face, overtaken in sobs.

Simon patted her shoulder. "I didn't mean to be gone so long. Has Josiah been sick this entire time?"

She shrugged, then, wiping her face and taking in a hitched breath, she asked, "How did you know?"

He grimaced. "Josiah wouldn't have sent you out in this weather if he could *kumm* himself. I knew something was wrong. What's happened?"

"His lymphoma is back. He's had a few chemotherapy treatments." She sniffled. "I just found out I'm *nett* a donor match." Her vision blurred and she fought to control her tears.

"Let's head home," he said. "You can tell me more on the way."

As Simon drove the buggy, Lindie filled him in on what the doctor had said about Josiah's condition. When they arrived home, Simon stopped the buggy next to the house. "I'll be in to see Josiah after I take care of Molly."

"It's *gut* to have you back." She meant it. Hannah needed the stability of her grandfather, and Lindie needed help convincing Josiah to eat. "I'm sorry. I haven't even asked you how your *bruder* is doing."

"He made improvement while I was there, but he's lost the use of his left side."

"I'm sorry."

"*Denki.*" His voice choked. "You should go inside where it's warm."

Lindie climbed out of the buggy. The snow crunched underfoot as she climbed the porch steps. She was tired of the snow and looking forward to spring when she could plant a garden.

Rebecca met her at the door. "Everything okay?"

"The *boppli* is fine." She removed her outer clothing and shivered. "Simon's home. He'll be in after he takes care of the horse."

"I'll put the kettle on," Rebecca said.

Lindie's toes were numb. She couldn't feel the floor as she walked into the kitchen. Lindie stood next to the woodstove.

Rebecca placed a tea bag in each cup. "Any news if you're a match or *nett*?"

Tears brimmed. "I'm *nett*."

Rebecca frowned. "I don't know what to say."

"Me either." She tapped her chest. "I felt it down deep that I was a match. I don't know what I'll do—" Hannah entered the room and Lindie quickly dried her eyes. She breathed a little easier when Hannah didn't seem to notice she'd been crying, but instead seemed eager to show off her drawing.

"Very nice," Lindie signed.

Rebecca praised Hannah's drawing. "Did she draw the pictures on the wall in the living room too?"

Lindie nodded. "She's talented, isn't she?"

"*Jah*, it's hard to believe an eight-year-old drew them." Rebecca smiled at Hannah. She stumbled with her hand gestures telling Hannah she liked the picture, but Hannah seemed to understand.

"I suppose I should be going," Rebecca said.

Lindie walked her to the back door. "*Denki* again for all your help."

"I'm glad to do it." She put on her cape. "You don't have to worry about the barn work. The men will continue taking care of the chores. I know Simon is home, but he doesn't need to do all the work himself. Of course, the womenfolk will supply the meals."

"You have all been so kind."

"We wish we could do more." Rebecca tied her winter bonnet strings. "But know our prayers are with you."

"That is a blessing." She made herself smile until Rebecca was gone. Then she shuffled over to the sink, her thoughts consumed with how quickly her hope had faded after receiving the test result. She filled a glass with water to take to Josiah. He would be worried if she didn't let him know she had made it home. But unable to face him yet, she set the glass on the table, sat down on a chair, and buried her face in her hands.

Faith moved the hand of God and faith was the substance of things hoped for. Faith as small as a mustard seed . . . She didn't even have that. How could she keep her hope alive when Josiah was dying?

"Do I have any faith at all?" Lindie pushed off the chair. She wanted to be near Josiah. Entering the room, her gaze moved from his sleeping form to the uneaten food on the plate. She set the glass of water on the nightstand.

Josiah patted the edge of the bed. "Will you sit with me?"

"I thought you were sleeping." Lindie sat next to him and reached for his hand, but realizing hers were much too cold, she released them.

"Tell me what's wrong."

"I didn't want *mei* hands to get you *kalt*." She rubbed hers on her dress.

"That's *nett* why you've been crying. Is something wrong with the *boppli*?"

"*Nay*." She smiled, feeling an inner nudge. "She must have heard us talking about her because she just gave me a *gut* kick."

Josiah lifted his hand to her belly and smiled. "*Jah*, he is active."

She liked that he was teasing her again about the baby's gender. If she had her wish, she would have two Josiahs around the house.

"Talk to me, Lindie."

"You haven't eaten anything."

"I did. A little."

She looked away as new tears began to form. Josiah tugged her arm and she faced him, but unable to find her voice, she fell into his arms. "We just fell in love. I don't want to lose you." She buried her face in the crook of his neck. "I'm *nett* your match. The test came back negative."

He wiped his palm against her face. "I didn't know you were tested."

"I was so sure I would be the one. You've done so much for me."

"It's okay." Tears welled in his eyes. "You wouldn't have been able to donate being pregnant. The *doktah* should have told you that."

She rested her head against his chest. His heart pumped strong measured beats.

A few minutes passed before he said, "We have some things to talk about that we shouldn't put off."

She froze.

"Lindie." He nudged her shoulder. "I want us to plan what will happen after I'm gone."

She bolted upright. "You promised to fight this."

"We both know I'm *nett* getting better. I can't get dressed. I can't even walk to the bathroom without help."

Lord, where is the hope? I need to hold on to something. A hard kick from the baby stole her breath. She clutched her belly.

"Lindie, what is it?"

"The *boppli*." She puffed out a few rapid breaths. "The *boppli* doesn't want to hear this talk either."

Hannah pushed the door open and bounded into the room, toting her sketch pad. She crawled up on the bed beside Josiah and handed him the artwork.

Lindie pushed off the bed. He needed some time alone with Hannah. "I'm going to get supper started." She didn't want to spoil the surprise of Simon's return. He should be in any moment.

She paused at the threshold and looked back at father and daughter. Hannah's hand was on Josiah. Her eyes were closed and her mouth moved without sound. Lindie's throat tightened. *Lord, as you answered Hannah's prayer for the injured deer, answer this request too. You've placed it on her heart to pray for Josiah, just as you placed it on her heart to lay hands on the wounded deer.*

Lindie slipped out of the room. She stopped in the sitting room to add another log to the woodstove. Hannah's drawing over the desk caught her eye. Something stirred within her as she stood looking at it. The different-sized hands reminded her that God had given her the perfect family, but the story of Job hit home also. *The LORD gives and the LORD takes away.*

Chapter Thirty

Lindie sat in the corner of the waiting room at the doctor's office, silently praying Josiah wouldn't discontinue the treatment. She had overheard him talking to Simon last evening and Josiah sounded very discouraged over the side effects.

Doctor Ethridge approached her, his hands buried in the pockets of his white coat. "The infusion is finishing up," he said, sitting in the chair next to hers. "I wanted to talk with you about his treatment."

Lindie gripped the arms of the chair, bracing for the news.

"He's currently receiving very high doses of chemotherapy."

She nodded. This wasn't new information.

"It isn't working. Not like it should for two rounds of treatment."

Her stomach churned and her ears buzzed with a high-pitched sound.

"I wanted to speak with you first and I would have mentioned this yesterday, but I didn't have all the information."

"Is it a new treatment?" *Lord, let it be so.*

"It's still somewhat investigational."

Lindie inched to the edge of her seat. "When can he start?"

"It's not that simple. Many factors must coincide and it involves you. And the baby. That's why I wanted to talk with you before mentioning anything to Josiah."

"Tell me what I need to do. I'll do anything."

"A former colleague of mine is working in stem-cell research using umbilical cords. Even without having a perfect match, there have been successful studies in transplant patients."

Her mind burst with questions, but none she could formulate to ask.

"There's no risk to the baby, but it would mean delivering the baby in the hospital where Doctor Cole is affiliated. Once the baby is born, the stem cells would be extracted from the cord."

"I don't care where I have the baby. Can we go tell Josiah now?" She stood.

"We can talk more after his infusion is completed."

She sat back down. "You'll send for me, right?"

He nodded. "It shouldn't be too much longer."

✧

Josiah blinked when the overhead light suddenly came on in the examination room. He must have dozed during the infusion. Unusual, since the fire fed to his veins made it difficult to relax.

The nurse inspected the IV bag. "You're almost finished. How are you feeling?" She shoved her hands into the rubber gloves.

"Tired." *Weak. Useless.*

She inspected his arm. "Any itching?"

"No."

"There's no redness or swelling around the site. That's good."

She disconnected the tubing from his IV port, tossed the empty bag along with her gloves into a red container, then washed her hands. "Any chest heaviness? Shortness of breath? Blood in the urine?" Her list of questions continued as she wrapped the blood pressure cuff around his arm.

He answered no to all of them, though he doubted she heard him since her ears were plugged with the stethoscope.

Doctor Ethridge poked his head inside the room. "How's our patient?"

"Ready to go home," Josiah said.

The air in the cuff deflated and the nurse pulled the earpieces out.

"Josiah, will you stop by my office when you're finished, please?"

"Sure." Josiah wanted to talk with him anyway. Every time he'd come in for an infusion, his blood had been drawn. Surely the doctor had an idea if the medication was working or not. If it wasn't, Josiah didn't see any reason to prolong the misery. Even Lindie should understand that.

He'd felt stronger—more alive—before starting the chemotherapy. He'd preferred the night sweats. Even the deep-seated cough that made his ribs feel bruised was better than being off-center from the chemo treatment. It was better than spending the day vomiting, or worse yet, having dry heaves that left him hoarse.

"Your blood pressure and pulse are within normal range," the nurse said. "Are you feeling nauseated?"

"Not yet." That usually happened on the ride home.

He rolled his sleeve down to cover his hairless arm. His beard and head would be next. As it was, the bald spots made him look as though he had mange. It bothered him more this time. It wasn't vanity, at least he prayed it wasn't. He didn't want his daughter to remember him without a beard. He'd started growing it after he and Caroline were married, and Hannah was too young to remember when the chemo caused it to fall out the last time. Perhaps his reasoning was vain after all. He stood. No light-headedness, balance seemed okay. He ambled to the door.

The doctor's office door was cracked and muffled voices filtered out. *Lindie.* Doctor Ethridge must have asked her to join them. Josiah sucked in a deep breath and tapped on the door. It opened on its own and the doctor waved him in.

Lindie bounded off the chair and was at his side the moment he stepped into the room. "Let me help you," she said.

Self-rendered in defeat, he didn't object to her circling her arm around his waist. As if things couldn't get more belittling, she told him where to sit. He wasn't blind. He could find the chair. He should be the one helping her. Her belly had grown to where she probably couldn't see her feet anymore.

"How are you feeling?" the doctor asked.

"I've felt better." *Understated.*

A light tap on the door preceded the nurse entering the room. "Here is Mr. Plank's chart. I recorded his vitals and lab results."

"Thank you." Doctor Ethridge opened the file.

Josiah studied the doctor's reaction as he reviewed the information. Stolid. Did Lindie notice the doctor's lack of expression too? Josiah didn't dare look her way. He gave the doctor a moment to review the chart, then cleared his throat. "Has my condition improved?"

"No, I'm afraid not." Doctor Ethridge rubbed his jaw. "Your platelet count is falling and so are the white blood cells."

None of that made sense to Josiah. He peeked at Lindie, who

was chewing her bottom lip. He turned away before her rapid blinking set loose a cascade of tears.

"Are you saying we should stop?" Josiah asked.

"You need a bone marrow transplant." He rubbed his forehead.

"But we know that isn't going to happen."

"Josiah." Lindie reached over for his hand. "Don't say that until you hear—"

"Lindie"—his tone was sharper than he wished, so he paused until he could control his voice—"we talked about this."

"You must keep hope alive."

The extent of hope he could muster now amounted to hoping for a peaceful passing. He didn't want to fight this battle. He leaned his head back against the chair and closed his eyes.

"Are you feeling sick?"

"Just resting." Mostly to avoid seeing the disappointment in her eyes.

"I've already mentioned this to Lindie," Doctor Ethridge said. "There has been some success with implanting stem cells from an umbilical cord."

Umbilical cord . . . He spoke with Lindie? His heart thumped against his ribs as the words registered. Josiah shot open his eyes. *"Nay!"* He shifted in his seat to face Lindie. "You're *nett* jeopardizing the *boppli*. How could you consider—"

"The baby won't be harmed," the doctor said. "Lindie was a partial match. Not good enough, but the baby's cord is a foreseeable alternative."

Lindie nodded.

Josiah stared at her. Hard. Did she forget he wasn't the baby's father? There wouldn't be a match. "I don't think you've thought this through," he said. He turned to Doctor Ethridge. "Perhaps

Lindie hasn't explained. I'm not the father." Her sharp intake of breath answered the question, but he continued anyway. "The baby wouldn't be a match."

Without the slightest reaction, Doctor Ethridge folded his hands and rested them on the desk. "I understand your concern. Of course given your Amish heritage and the rarity of your blood type, it would be better if the baby was yours, or at least from another Amish." He glanced at Lindie.

She shook her head.

"A significant amount of data shows that an embryonic stem-cell transplant is a viable option in cases where a bone marrow match hasn't been found. Even a marginal match has shown some success. It's an option to consider."

Josiah lowered his head and nodded even though his mind hadn't had time to sift all the information.

"There is a drawback," the doctor said.

Josiah lifted his head.

"Doctor Cole, who has agreed to take your case, doesn't practice in the state of Michigan. You would have to relocate."

"To where?"

"His clinic is in Cleveland, Ohio."

"That's perfect." Lindie's face lit. "That isn't too far from Middlefield. We can stay with Eli and Margaret and get an *Englisch* driver to take us to the clinic." She spoke fast and used animated hand gestures.

The cost hadn't dawned on her yet. It was highly unlikely that Doctor Cole would trade services for Amish-built furniture.

"Josiah, don't you think it's *wunderbaar*? An answer to prayer, *jah*?"

"Is there any way you can do it here?" he asked Doctor Ethridge.

He shook his head. "That's outside my scope of practice, but Doctor Cole is an excellent physician. He leads the research team."

"But he's probably expensive. I can't afford—"

Doctor Ethridge lifted his hand. "I've already explained that you don't have insurance and that your finances are limited."

"And he will work with me on a payment plan?"

"He plans to add you to his research study so grant money will cover your expenses, excluding transportation and living expenses. However, he isn't sure about the baby delivery. He said he would check with the hospital administration about their Good Samaritan program and see if there is something that can be done."

Lindie, perched on the edge of her seat, leaned forward. "We have midwives in my district. I don't have to go to the hospital."

Doctor Ethridge shook his head. "I'm sure Doctor Cole will want the umbilical cord immediately after delivery."

She wilted against the back cushion of the chair.

"That's a lot of details to work out before Lindie has the baby," Josiah said. "She's due in two and a half months."

"Doctor Cole requested you come now so they can do a pre-workup. It's also a good idea for Lindie to get established with a physician there as soon as possible in the chance she does deliver early." He tapped the closed file. "I'll have copies printed of both of your charts so you can take the records with you."

Lindie reached her hand out to Josiah's as though she sensed his apprehension. "This is *gut* news, *jah?*"

He forced a smile. "A lot to think about."

⁓

Time isn't a luxury we have. Lindie wanted to scream. Josiah needed a transplant. Why was he hesitating?

Doctor Ethridge tore a prescription off his pad and handed it to Josiah. "This will help stimulate your appetite."

Josiah folded the paper in half and shoved it into his pocket.

Doctor Ethridge slid his chair back from his desk and stood. "Talk it over and let me know what you decide."

She tried to prod him with her eyes to accept now, but he avoided her completely and merely nodded at the doctor.

"When can we pick up a copy of the records?" She wasn't wishy-washy. This news was the morsel of hope they needed.

"Check with my receptionist at the front desk before you leave. I'm sure she can have them ready by tomorrow."

Lindie stopped at the office window, signed the papers to release the records, and arranged to pick them up the following day. Josiah had gone ahead and was untying Molly from the post when she reached the buggy.

He handed her the reins. She'd driven home after the last infusion so it wasn't a surprise when he climbed into the passenger side. His silence rattled her.

"I'll stop at the drugstore so we can get the prescription filled."

"*Nay*," he said quietly. "Let's go home."

"It's going to help your appetite." He simply looked at her with a hardened stare and she clamped her mouth closed. Maybe his cottony-white complexion had something to do with his snappiness. She pulled back on the reins, slowing Molly. "You don't look well. Should I pull over?"

"*Jah*, you might better. I'm feeling queasy."

A spot opened along the curb in front of the drugstore and she stopped the horse.

He didn't jump out immediately. His eyes closed and he drew in a long breath and released it. "It might pass," he said.

"You rest a minute. I'm going to drop off your prescription." She scurried off the bench before he said something to stop her, but got to the door and had to turn around. "I need the prescription."

He made a muffled noise, something between a groan and growl, and dug his hand into his pocket. "It didn't work the last time."

"You've lost too much weight *nett* to try. Besides, I'm lonely eating without you."

The hardness in his eyes disappeared in a flash. He bowed his head. "I'm sorry you have to go through this, Lindie."

She reached for his hand. "Don't apologize. I'm your *fraa*. I love you."

᠉

Once Lindie helped Josiah into bed, she filled Simon in on the good news. With Hannah visiting her father, Lindie could speak openly.

"I think this treatment in Ohio will work, but Josiah is discouraged. He keeps telling me *nett* to get *mei* hopes up."

Simon nodded. "He knows how sick he is and he's concerned about you."

"He needs to be concerned about eating. He's *nett* going to regain his strength without proper nourishment."

Simon's smile looked strained. "You've taken *gut* care of Josiah and Hannah." He cleared his throat. "I'm sorry that I gave you a hard time when you first arrived."

"I understand. It would have been difficult to lose Caroline and then to lose your *fraa* less than a year later."

He nodded. "I didn't want to lose Josiah and Hannah too."

Lindie reached out and patted Simon's hand. "That won't ever happen."

"God had a reason for sending you." Simon nodded as though affirming his statement. "Josiah needed a helpmate."

"*Denki*, Simon." Denki, *God, for bringing us all together as a family.*

Hannah shuffled into the kitchen, her eyes blotchy and swollen.

Lindie wrapped the girl in a hug, then pulled back to ask what was wrong. The only thing she could decipher from Hannah's reply was her prayers didn't work. "*Mei* father is sick."

Simon confirmed what Hannah had signed.

Lindie released Hannah. "I better check on him."

Simon stretched out his arms toward Hannah and hugged his granddaughter as Lindie rushed out of the room.

"I wish you would have taken her out." Bent over the bed, Josiah dry heaved into the trash can. "I didn't want her to see me like this." His throat sounded hoarse. He flopped back on his pillow, sweat rolling down his face.

She removed the glass of water from the side table and sat down on the edge of the bed. "Take a sip of water. Your throat will feel better."

His hand trembled as he lifted the glass to his mouth.

Lindie made a mental to-do list. She would write Eli and Margaret tonight. Her brother and sister-in-law had plenty of room with the empty *grossdaadi haus*.

Josiah handed her back the glass. "*Denki.*"

"I'm going to let Eli know we're coming. Do you want me to have him go over to your parents' district and talk with them in person? Or should I send them a note to tell them when we will be arriving?"

"Neither."

"Josiah, you're *nett* changing your mind about going." Lindie's tone came out forceful.

"Wait until *after* I see *Doktah* Cole. I don't want them to get their hopes up too."

Lindie wasn't going to quarrel with him. First she had to get him on the bus. Until now, her sole focus had been on Josiah's new treatment option. She hadn't considered what it would be like to return to Middlefield—married.

Chapter Thirty-One

L indie leaned her head against the windowpane of the bus. It seemed as though they'd been traveling for days when they hadn't even crossed the Mackinac Bridge yet. Instead of blue open water, the straits appeared iced-over. So many things had changed since the northbound trip she made with Eli four months ago.

The baby's sharp kick to the ribs followed by a stiff blow to the bladder caused her to wince. Shifting on the seat proved only a temporary fix. The baby kicked again, this time harder. She repositioned herself once more.

"What are you so antsy about?" Josiah's eyes traveled over her and stopped on her hand holding her belly. "Is the *boppli* kicking?"

"*Jah.*" She smiled, hoping it covered her worry. Traveling such a long distance during her last trimester wasn't wise, but it wasn't avoidable either. The baby's activity had increased dramatically just recently. She rubbed her belly. *Don't arrive too early.* She whispered the same thing to the baby a few days ago when she'd grown so uncomfortable it seemed like she might deliver in

Cedar Ridge. Baby arrivals were unpredictable. Delivering on a bus would ruin everything.

The bus rattled over the bridge, jiggling her bladder. If memory served her, on the northbound trip they stopped about an hour before the bridge. She hoped her bladder could hold for another hour. She winced again. It didn't help that Hannah had fallen asleep with her head on Lindie's lap.

"I'll get her to move." Josiah nudged Hannah's shoulder.

Smiling sweetly, Hannah turned, but toward Lindie. If it weren't for the child being deaf, she would have thought Hannah was trying to listen to the baby the way she held her ear pressed against Lindie. The kicking stopped and Lindie's breathing eased.

Josiah closed his eyes. Since he had started taking the appetite-stimulating medicine and was eating three meals a day again, he'd regained some of his strength. Still, sitting upright for so long had to be difficult.

His seat beside the window was drafty even though the farther south they traveled, the less snow was on the ground. March was only days away. Margaret would need help tilling and planting the garden. Her sister-in-law usually sold seeds and rhubarb bulbs in early spring, so Lindie looked forward to helping with the roadside stand.

The mud-tinged snow from the heavy traffic always made it look gloomy. Still, the scenery wasn't as dismal today as she remembered it being on the day she rode the bus north. Dejected and unsure of her future, she'd wept most of that trip. Eli had tried so hard to reassure her about Josiah.

I promise my name, not my heart . . .

She remembered not wanting to look Josiah in the eye, and how he'd offered to buy her a ticket home. She had wanted to stay, but for the wrong reasons. Living another state away from her attacker was worth agreeing to any marital terms. An icy chill sped down her spine. She didn't want to remember why she left Ohio.

Focus on Josiah.

She inhaled as deeply as she could, held her breath, then released it slowly, letting her body go limp in the process.

Things were different. She was with Josiah. Married. In love. Safe.

꙰

The bus pulled into the station late. The sudden flash of over-head lights inside the bus caused Lindie to squint. She shielded her eyes from the glare, giving them time to adjust. Hannah did the same.

Lindie gathered Hannah's sketch pad and the cloth sack she'd packed their lunches in, along with the small quilt they'd shared to keep warm.

Josiah lumbered stiffly down the bus aisle, Hannah and Lindie following. Eli met them on the platform. Her brother took one look at Josiah and ushered him and Hannah to the *Englisch* neighbor's van. Lindie waited for the baggage.

Eli returned from the passenger pickup area. "It's hard to believe that is Josiah," he said, shaking his head.

"He's lost weight."

"Jah." Eli nodded. "I thought for a moment he was wearing some type of talc on his face he looked so white."

"Wait until you see him in better light." She eyed the baggage as the workers unloaded the underneath storage compartment of the bus.

"Margaret fixed up the *grossdaadi haus* so he will be able to rest uninterrupted."

"*Denki.*" She wished she could offer a happier greeting, but she was exhausted.

"How are you feeling?"

"Tired. Fat." She cracked a smile and tapped her belly. "Six weeks to go is all."

"It seems like you've been away longer."

"I suppose."

He scratched the back of his neck, shifted his feet, then took a few aimless steps in a large circle and stopped. He opened his mouth, but closed it. Instead of speaking, he stroked his beard.

She'd seen this look before, he was struggling to form his questions. "I suppose you're wondering if *mei* arranged marriage was the right decision," she said. "*Jah*, it was. You were right about Josiah. He is kind and gentle and has never once treated me harshly."

"Some of your letters were *nett* so . . ."

"I know. I was homesick and feeling out of place, but I adjusted eventually."

"No regrets?"

She shook her head. "*Nett* one." Her eyes widened. "Speaking of letters, I need to mail a note to Simon so he knows we arrived safely." She rummaged through her handbag and removed the letter she had already written and addressed.

"There's a mailbox next to the building," Eli said.

She spotted their bags as the attendant set them on the concrete slab and pointed them out to her brother, who collected the two suitcases. Lindie deposited the letter in the slot on their way to the van.

"Thanks for picking us up this late, George," Lindie said,

climbing in through the sliding side door. Judging from George's double take, her pending motherhood surprised him. If this was how the neighbors would react, what would the members say? She hadn't been gone that long. The math was simple enough to figure out that she was pregnant when she left. It wouldn't be easy to face everyone again. Would Josiah be strong enough to endure the gossip?

"Your husband mentioned you'll need a ride to Cleveland the day after next. That isn't a problem for me. Just let me know what time you need to be there and I'll pick you up."

"It's an early appointment." She would ask Josiah, but his head bobs indicated he was almost asleep. She would dig through the paperwork later for the exact time.

Their elderly neighbor merged into traffic.

Eli, sitting in the front seat, must have noticed Josiah trying to sleep. He said very little and mostly to George, asking about the road conditions.

The ground had only patches of snow. The roads shimmered as if they were wet. Probably slippery in patches too, if the freezing temperature blinking on George's dashboard was correct.

Lindie looked over her shoulder at Hannah buckled into the far backseat. Her heavy eyelids closed briefly, then shot open. The child wouldn't be able to fight sleep much longer with the vents blasting hot air. Lindie yawned. Hopefully Margaret would save her greetings until morning. Lindie wanted to go straight to bed.

Sometime later the hum of the engine cut off. The interior lights came on at the same time an opened door dinged. Josiah repositioned himself from the slumped angle he'd fallen asleep in. Lindie tapped Hannah. No use signing they'd arrived, since the girl's eyes were still closed.

"I'll carry Hannah," Eli offered.

Lindie was grateful. She wasn't supposed to lift anything, and even though Hannah was small for her age, Josiah wasn't steady on his feet.

Margaret met them outside for a brief hug. "I'll talk with you in the morning," she said. "I just wanted to say hello tonight."

George unloaded the baggage and they all ambled toward the *grossdaadi haus*.

Once inside, Eli lowered Hannah onto an already made-up cot in the bedroom. He and Josiah talked a little about the wood supply for the potbelly stove, then her brother and George left.

Lindie changed into her nightdress and slipped under the covers next to Josiah. She remembered closing her eyes, then waking to the rooster's crow.

⌁

It took a moment for Josiah's eyes to adjust to the sunshine streaming through the window. He glanced at the empty spot beside him. Across the room, the cot Hannah had slept on was also empty. He squinted at the wall clock. *Noon?* It must need batteries. He'd never slept this late.

Josiah climbed out of bed. His legs wobbled beneath him. He made it as far as the footboard and had to hold on to it for support. Pathetic. The long bus ride yesterday had left him weak. He scanned the room for his clothes and groaned under his breath. What did Lindie expect him to do, leave the *grossdaadi haus* in his long johns to find his clothes? He barely had the energy to climb out of bed.

The door creaked open and Lindie poked her head inside. "You're up?"

"And *nett* dressed."

She entered the room, a stack of clothes in her hands. "So I see." Her eyes twinkled as her careful inspection traveled from his eyes to his bare chest and down to his toes.

If he wasn't so drained, he would take advantage of her flirting and convince her to return to bed. Then again, weakness was only a state of mind. He crossed the room with more drive than he knew he had and cupped her face in his hands. "You think it's funny that you stole *mei* clothes?" He leaned closer and parted her lips with his.

He pulled away from the kiss. A whoosh of light-headedness threatened to buckle his knees. He reached for the ladder-back chair against the wall and sat. His muscles limp—spent.

"Are you okay?" she asked, her voice panicky.

No, he wasn't. What good was he if he couldn't spend a few intimate moments with his wife? He rubbed his face where his beard had been. His jaw's smooth texture mocked him as a husband.

"Josiah?"

"I'm fine," he said sharply.

Lindie set the stack of clothes on the bed and rushed to his side. She placed her hand on his shoulder and gave him a gentle pat. "Let me help you back to bed."

"Nay." Didn't she know how humbling it was already? A wretched state he was in, losing his breath this way. Had his knees buckled he would have fallen to the floor. She wouldn't have been able to get him up, and he would have been subjected to Eli picking him up in nothing but his long johns. He wasn't strong enough to stand for long, much less kiss her like he wanted.

Josiah pushed off the chair. Despite the piercing ringing in his ears, he lumbered to the bed and sat on the edge of the mattress. He took a deep breath and reached for his clothes.

Lindie crossed her arms in a self-hug, then spun toward the window, but not before he caught sight of her eyes glistening with tears.

He finished dressing and came up behind her, placing his hands on her arms. "I'm sorry."

"You didn't do anything wrong."

"I can't do anything right either." He kissed her ear, then rested his chin on her shoulder. "I haven't been much of a husband lately."

"Don't say that." Her voice squeaked and she tilted her head upward and stared at the ceiling.

Her bare neck elongated. Josiah leaned closer, taking in the fresh soap scent on her creamy skin. What was he going to do, start something he couldn't finish? He needed to talk with Eli and take care of why he allowed Lindie to convince him to come here in the first place.

Chapter Thirty-Two

The following day Josiah walked out of the doctor's office knowing what a pincushion felt like. Poked and prodded for what? The outcome never changed. He was still dying. Doctor Cole wasn't any more optimistic of the time Josiah had left than Doctor Ethridge had been.

The dismal prediction didn't surprise Josiah. His body grew more debilitated each day.

Lindie refused to believe what now two doctors had said.

"Doctor Cole's research statistics don't speak for God," Lindie argued as they left the office. "Abnormal test results mean nothing to God."

"We still need to talk about your future," Josiah said.

"*Our* future."

"Lindie, be reasonable. There's going to *kumm* a day when—"

"*Nay!* It won't *kumm* to that." The glass doors opened and she shot through them, walking swiftly down the sidewalk outside of the research center.

He didn't race to keep up. He couldn't.

She stopped and circled around. "I'm sorry," she said, returning to his side. "That wasn't thoughtful of me to rush ahead. Do you need help?"

"*Nay*. I want to help you. We must prepare for *mei* passing." He ignored her shaking her head and when she opened her mouth to object, he hammered home his point. "The *doktah* said the *boppli* probably won't arrive early. That's six weeks at the soonest."

"*Jah*, there is always hope. I could be induced."

"With medicine? *Nay*." He stepped off the curb and lumbered toward the parked van. "The *boppli* will come when it's ready."

"You *need* the stem cells."

"We need to trust God's will no matter what. Our time on earth is *nett* guaranteed."

"This *boppli* will arrive in time. I'll figure out something," she muttered under her breath.

He stopped and, reaching for her arm, used every fiber of energy he had to pivot her around to face him. "That's foolish." He used the sternest tone he could muster.

She swallowed hard enough that her eyes glazed, but said nothing.

"We'll talk about this later."

George had stepped out of the van and was sliding the door open. "You folks all set?"

Josiah nodded. "It's been a long day." He stepped aside and waited for Lindie to climb in first.

George seemed to understand they weren't up for chatting. He asked if they needed to stop anyplace else, and once Josiah responded, he turned the radio on to fill the silence.

Josiah closed his eyes. He hadn't meant to snap at Lindie.

Where was his compassion? This wasn't how he wanted her to remember him. She deserved better.

Without much traffic on the road, the drive back to Middlefield went by quickly. When George stopped the van in Eli's driveway, he turned to face them. "You folks let me know when you need another ride to the city."

"*Jah*, we'll be sure to." Josiah eased out slowly, then waited for Lindie. She muttered something about checking on Hannah and tromped up the porch steps.

George pulled away as Eli stepped out of the barn. His brother-in-law met him in the yard. "How did things go?"

Josiah shrugged. "I was pricked so much it feels like I wrestled a porcupine."

Eli frowned. "Sorry."

Josiah couldn't handle any more sympathy. "Can we talk in the *grossdaadi haus*, privately?" Feeling light-headed, he needed to sit before he collapsed. As they ambled the few feet, he collected his thoughts.

"What's on your mind?" Eli asked, holding the door open as Josiah entered.

Josiah shed his coat and kicked off his boots. "I wanted to talk with you about Lindie."

Eli fed a log to the bed of embers in the woodstove. "I guess I assumed you were happy."

"I am. I love Lindie with all *mei* heart." Josiah warmed his hands next to the stove. "I'm *nett* sure what all Lindie has told you . . . about why we're here."

"She said you needed a special stem-cell procedure."

Josiah cleared his scratchy throat. "Without it . . . I don't have much time to live."

RUTH REID

Eli's eyes widened, and for a long moment, he just stared. "She didn't say that."

"She's in denial."

"What did the *doktah* say today?"

"He confirmed everything." Josiah covered his hand over his mouth and closed his eyes. Lindie and Hannah flashed before his eyes. "I came here to make arrangements for after I'm—" His throat dried and he swallowed hard. Telling his best friend had proved more difficult than he'd expected. "I need to know Lindie, Hannah, and the new *boppli* will be all right after I'm gone."

Eli pulled a chair away from the small table and sat.

Josiah sat opposite him.

"They can move back here," Eli said. "This place is small, but adding a couple of bedrooms onto it won't be difficult."

A weight lifted from Josiah's chest. Northern Michigan was no place for Lindie and the children after he was gone. The community was too small to have the support she would need. "I thought about asking *mei* parents, but they're *nett* in *gut* health. I don't even want them knowing about *mei* relapse just yet."

"I know this must be difficult for both of you. Margaret and I have been praying since we found out, but we had no idea you were so sick."

"*Denki.*" Josiah bowed his head. "Lindie's been under a lot of stress, so I've tried to shelter her from as much as possible. The *doktah* doesn't know if the stem cells will work. I'm worried Lindie has convinced herself to have the *boppli* early. There's too much risk—for her, the *boppli*, and for the cord to be viable. You have to promise me that no matter how sick I get, you won't let her do anything foolish."

312

"Waiting is so hard." Lindie set the plates on the table.

"I know," Margaret said.

"Josiah hasn't left the *grossdaadi haus* in four days. I take meals out to him and he barely touches them. He sleeps mostly. I'm worried he's given up and I feel so useless."

"Just keep praying. The Bible says to pray constantly."

"I know."

"Be joyful in hope, patient in affliction, faithful in prayer." Margaret poured a glass of milk.

"I try. But doubt sets in." She set the glasses on the table. "What will happen if the *boppli* is late?"

"Be patient in affliction," Margaret said.

Lindie peered out the window at Hannah and Solomon, Eli and Margaret's youngest, playing tag. "I wish I had Hannah's faith. She's prayed for her *daed* and *nau* she runs around the yard like she doesn't have a concern." Lindie turned to Margaret. "I pray. But then I dwell on how gray his skin tone is and how his lips stay cracked no matter how many times I wet them with the rag or apply beeswax. I let things like that rob me of *mei* faith." Lindie swiped the tears from her eyes. "I try to encourage him to hold on, but I fear he isn't listening. He's miserable . . . and he's slipping away from me."

Margaret blinked and tears rolled down her cheeks. "God is in control of everything."

"I know that is true." Lindie dabbed the corners of her eyes with her sleeve. "Still, I can't stand by and do nothing." She rested her hand on her belly. The baby hadn't moved much since yesterday. At first, she appreciated that, but now it was beginning to worry her. "Should the *boppli* be kicking a lot?" She moved her hand over her abdomen. "How did you know when you were in labor?"

Margaret's face lit up. "Are you having cramps?"

"*Nay.*" Although she wished she was. "I'm just wondering."

"*Mei* labor started with cramps and quickly progressed to pressure." She chuckled. "You'll know."

"I haven't felt movement all day," Lindie said softly.

"All day!" Margaret set the lid to the boiling potatoes on the counter and swiftly crossed the room to the table. She pulled a chair out. "Here, sit down."

Lindie did so.

"When is your next appointment with the *doktah*?"

"In five days. This is normal, right?"

"You've been under a lot of stress." Margaret had never been good at concealing her emotions.

"What is it, Margaret?" Agitation crept into her voice. This was her first baby. She didn't know what to expect.

"I think Esther Ebersol should check you. I'm going to send Eli for her."

Her sister-in-law left the room before Lindie could object. Hearing the door snap, she pushed off the chair and went to the window. Margaret sprinted toward the barn.

The potato water bubbled over and sizzled on the stovetop. Lindie grabbed a pot holder and removed the frothing water. She shouldn't have said anything until after supper. Now the meal would get cold before anyone ate.

The back door opened and Margaret reentered. "Eli is on his way." She kicked her mud-clad shoes off at the door. She guided Lindie from the kitchen. "I think you should lie down. You can wait for Esther in *mei* room."

Lindie's thoughts flitted between Josiah's supper plate she hadn't fixed to what Hannah might think if she came in from playing and didn't find her.

Her sister-in-law opened the bedroom door, went immediately to her chest of drawers, and pulled out a nightdress. "Put this on, it'll be easier. I'll get the plastic covering for the mattress."

"Do you think it's time?" She ran her hand over her belly again. This wasn't anything like the time one woman doubled over in the middle of Sunday service and could barely walk on her own to the buggy.

"Esther will know."

Soon everyone in the district would know too. The back of Lindie's throat burned and an acidic taste filled her mouth. Why did it matter? Even if the members questioned the baby's date of birth and concluded that the timing had something to do with her disappearance, it wouldn't change anything. Josiah needed the stem cells and the sooner, the better.

Chapter Thirty-Three

A week had passed since Esther Ebersol predicted Lindie was still weeks away from delivery. Lindie hoped the midwife was wrong, but over the years Esther had delivered more than fifty babies in the district, and with all of them, she estimated their due date within a few days. And according to Esther, the baby wasn't in the proper position to indicate labor was imminent.

Lindie sat at Josiah's bedside and stitched quilt blocks as he slept. She wanted to be nearby should he need assistance. But over the last several hours, it seemed she couldn't finish even one square.

Josiah's eyes fluttered.

Lindie pushed her needlework aside and leaned forward. "Do you need something?"

"Did you hear the bell?" His words dragged.

"Nay."

"Look after Hannah . . . for me." His eyes closed.

Lindie stood. If Josiah wasn't so gaunt, maybe she wouldn't

worry that he talked in his sleep. Maybe instead of dreaming, he was delirious.

Look after Hannah for me.

Lindie walked over to the window. Hannah and Solomon were playing again in the yard while Margaret was hoeing in the garden. Lindie needed some fresh air. Being closed up in the small *grossdaadi haus* watching Josiah sleep had given her a backache. She grabbed her cape off the hook and went outside.

Margaret stopped hoeing and straightened her posture. "Are you feeling all right?"

Lindie nodded. She turned to watch Hannah dodge her cousin's outstretched hand as they chased each other around the clothesline. It was good to see her playing and the weather was so much warmer here in Ohio. "The children are playing *gut* together, *jah*?"

Margaret smiled. "I wondered how the two of them would get along *nett* being able to communicate. It seems they do quite well without words."

"That is a blessing." Lindie placed her hands on the small of her back for support. "I've been sitting so long that I'm stiff."

"How is Josiah?"

"Sleeping." Same as he'd done yesterday and the day before that. Lindie frowned. "He's too weak to do anything else." She stepped over the mound of dirt Margaret had just hoed, grabbed the rake leaning against the wheelbarrow, and began to work the ground.

"Do you think that's wise?"

"*Jah*." Lindie continued combing the ground. "I'm *nett* going past *mei* due date."

"You keep that pace and the *boppli* might *kumm* today."

"That's fine with me." She worked her way down the aisle

and stopped to rest. "What are you planting over there?" Lindie pointed to her left at the already tilled ground. Margaret rotated where she planted her seeds every year.

"Broccoli in the far row and brussels sprouts beside it. And in these first rows, I'm planting cabbage and cauliflower."

"I was looking forward to planting a garden in Cedar Ridge this year." She forced a smile but couldn't hold it. "Do you think I'll ever have *mei* own garden?" Lindie pulled in a ragged breath and peered up at the cloudy sky. "He's failing fast *nau*."

"Would you like to go inside and have a cup of tea?" She motioned to the children running up the porch steps. "It looks like they are going inside."

"Maybe in a few minutes." Lindie had spent so many hours indoors it felt good to be in the fresh air. She swung the rake, sank its prongs into the soil, and dragged it hard. The ground blurred at her feet, but she wasn't about to stop. Not now. Not when Josiah's life depended on her having this baby. She raked faster.

"Lindie, please don't wear yourself out." Margaret grasped Lindie's arm. "Esther is hardly ever wrong. It isn't time for the *boppli*."

Lindie continued breaking up the ground.

"You're bound to have hard labor if you try to force contractions unnaturally. Especially since the *boppli* isn't even in the right position."

That wasn't enough reason to stop. When Doctor Ethridge was concerned about her not gaining weight and possibly miscarrying, he said she needed to reach twenty-seven weeks and preferably to go past thirty. She was as thirty-two.

Horse hooves clip-clopped against the pavement in front of Margaret's house. Lindie lifted her hand to shield the sun for a better look. She wasn't familiar with the horse.

"That's Mary Schrock's buggy."

Lindie groaned under her breath. She assumed Esther would probably spread the news, but she hadn't expected Moses's sister to be the first visitor. Had her former best friend come to rebuke her again?

Margaret waved at Mary. "She's early. This is the day we go into town. I figured you would be sitting with Josiah or I would have mentioned it earlier. Did you want to *kumm* with us? I'm sure Eli would sit with Josiah."

"*Nay*. I have to stay close by."

"Will you tell her I'll be right out? I need to get *mei* purse."

"Okay." *Hurry*. Lindie faked a smile. She had a few childhood friends she had looked forward to seeing on church Sunday—Mary wasn't one of them.

Mary climbed out of her buggy. Her eyes widened and landed on Lindie's midsection. "I heard you were—"

Pregnant? News travels fast.

The door opened and Margaret skipped down the steps. "I just need another minute to close the vegetable stand and then we can go."

"I'll do it," Lindie said quickly. Her sister-in-law's stand this time of year wouldn't require heavy lifting.

The back door closed hard and Hannah bounded off the steps, toting a picture in her hand.

Lindie welcomed the distraction and signed, asking to see the drawing. Once Hannah held up the picture, Lindie wished she had asked in private. The wooded path in the picture looked identical to the trail behind Eli's house leading into the for-est. Lindie's hands trembled at the sight of where she had been attacked. She fumbled, signing to ask if Hannah had gone into the woods.

"This is Hannah," Margaret explained. "Her *dead* is Josiah Plank . . . Lindie's husband."

Mary smiled. "Hello."

"She's deaf," Margaret said.

Hannah ran toward the *grossdaadi haus*, the paper flopping in the breeze. "Maybe I'll see you on Sunday, Mary," Lindie said as she chased after Hannah. Although Lindie was grateful for a reason to avoid Mary, she didn't want Hannah waking her father.

Too late.

Hannah stood at Josiah's bed, signing something. Hannah was standing at an angle that made it hard for Lindie to see all the signals. She figured it had something to do with the picture, but as she stepped closer, she realized she was asking her father to believe.

"I pray, but you must believe," Hannah signed. She placed her hand on her father's chest and closed her eyes.

Lindie closed hers and prayed silently for his healing.

After a moment, Hannah turned to Lindie. "He's sleeping."

Lindie waved Hannah over to her and they tiptoed outside. At least Mary's buggy was gone. She could gather Margaret's stuff at the stand without being chased with questions.

Hannah walked with her to the roadside stand. Lindie pointed to the girl's drawing. "Did you go into the woods around here?"

With shifting eyes, Hannah nodded.

She hadn't meant to frighten the child. Still, after her brutal attack in those same woods, she shuddered at the thought of Hannah going off alone. Lindie pulled her into a hug.

The sound of crunching gravel drew Lindie's attention. A car came to a stop a few feet from the stand, and a man wearing jeans low on his hips stepped out. A cigarette dangled from the corner of his mouth as he strutted toward them. He didn't look like someone interested in buying rhubarb bulbs or seeds. He cast an eerie grin at Hannah.

Lindie's insides quaked. The hairs on her arms stood on end. Mustering as forceful a tone as she could, she said, "The stand is closed."

He continued toward them.

Lindie placed herself between the stranger and the child, then signed "run" behind her back. When Hannah didn't leave immediately, she repeated the hand gesture. This time Hannah bolted toward the house.

"Cute kid."

Don't fight me . . . Lindie's stomach knotted. She spun around and sprinted a few feet before his hand clamped her arm and stopped her midstep. He was quick to smother her scream.

"So you do remember me." He slammed her up against him. "I think we should go for a drive."

She dug her heels into the ground but was overpowered.

"Go quietly or I'll come back for the girl." His stale tobacco breath brushed over her face. "I might anyway."

Not again. God, please, not again.

His crushing grip over her face blocked her airflow while his other hand landed heavily on her belly where it roamed freely.

She rammed her elbow into his ribs, causing him to suck air. Even if it meant him killing her, she wouldn't let him take her. "Help me! Help—"

His hand closed off her mouth, this time with more force. Her chest tightened and she struggled to breathe. White spots filled her vision.

She lost her fight. He had her, was dragging her.

God, please . . . A sharp pain tore through her abdomen followed by enormous pressure against her pelvis.

"Let her go!" Eli shouted.

In turning to face Eli, the man lost his grip over her mouth and she gasped, taking in a lungful of air.

Eli aimed the pitchfork at them. "Silos Slabach, let her go."

Lindie didn't have time to register his name before she was thrust forward. She lost her footing and, by the grace of God, dodged the prongs of the pitchfork. She pushed up to her knees just as a sharp pain stole her breath.

Eli had followed Silos with the pitchfork to his car. The car door slammed, the engine roared. Eli tossed the fork on the ground and rushed to her side as gravel shot out from under the tires and the car fishtailed away.

Eli reached for her arm. "Are you all right?"

"*Jah*," she said through gritted teeth.

"That Silos is nothing but trouble."

Silos Slabach. He'd pounced on her so quick that day in the woods. While pinned to the ground and gagging on the *kapp*, she passed out before her mind registered knowing him. *No wonder he knew where I lived.*

"Lindie?" Josiah called in a frail voice from several feet away. His face grimaced as he ambled barefoot. His shirt was untucked and his suspenders hung loose around his pant legs.

"Go help him back to the *haus*, please," she told Eli. Josiah was too sick to be out of bed and barefoot. The snow had only melted a few weeks ago. Josiah wouldn't stop worrying unless she got up. Besides, she didn't want to still be on the ground when the contractions returned.

Lindie overheard Josiah refusing Eli's help, insisting he had to check on her. She pushed up to her feet. Her legs wobbled, but she found her balance.

"Josiah, you shouldn't be out of bed." He came alongside her.

"God has supplied me strength." He reached his arm around her waist. "Hannah said something about a man with mean eyes and that you told her to run."

"Jah." The cramps returned, this time with more intensity.

"Was that him?" he asked under his breath.

She spotted Eli bending down to pick up the pitchfork, then nodded to Josiah.

"He *kumm* to rob us," Eli said, shaking his head. "After he jumped the fence to live in the world, he got mixed up with drugs. You would think he would *kumm* to his senses having spent time in jail, but he hasn't even been out a year and he's already living wild."

"He needs to be locked up—forever," Josiah said.

"Jah. We've had a few break-ins in the settlement recently. Probably stealing stuff to sell for drugs. Someone thought they recognized him, but since they weren't certain, nothing was said to the authorities."

Josiah leaned closer to her. "Eli should know."

Eli's brows crinkled. "Know what?"

Another contraction tore through her. She doubled over and blew out a few rapid breaths. Fluid trickled down her legs. *"Mei* water—broke."

Chapter Thirty-Four

L indie willed herself not to bear down en route to the hospital, but the contractions were regular and lasting longer. Seated in the backseat of George's van and confined by the seat belt, she couldn't get into a comfortable position. Beads of sweat rolled down her forehead and stung her eyes. Just the motion of the van nauseated her. She closed her eyes but that didn't stop the acid from climbing to the back of her throat. Fortunately, the neighbor's wife had volunteered to watch Hannah until Margaret returned from town. Still, she didn't want Eli, Josiah, or George delivering her baby in the van.

"Ach!" She gripped the arms of the seat, leaving her finger impressions in the vinyl material.

"Another one?" Josiah asked.

She squeaked, *"Jah,"* sucked in a breath, and held it until tiny white spots floated over her vision.

"You have to breathe." Josiah pursed his lips and demonstrated how, but after two breaths, he became winded and stopped.

She tried, but the pressure was too great to concentrate. "I can't do this."

"*Jah*, you can."

She puffed out several rapid breaths. The contraction subsided. She slumped against the seat, exhausted. It wasn't long before another overcame her. Shifting in her seat, she clenched her teeth. *Not yet. Not in the van. Please, God . . .* She prayed for the contractions to stop.

They did.

Her breathing eased.

After several painless minutes, Josiah became antsy. "You should be having more contractions." He glanced at his pocket watch. "They were regular up until a few minutes ago." He reached across the bucket seats for her hand. "Your water broke, so it isn't false labor."

"Do you think something is wrong?" The moment she asked, she remembered Esther saying the baby wasn't in the proper delivery position.

"Just rest. We're almost there." He squeezed her hand and released it, then leaned his head against the seat and closed his eyes.

Traffic picked up the closer they came to the city. The hospital wasn't far now. But she couldn't rest. Visions of Silos Slabach invaded her mind. His dark eyes glared with evil intent, and a mixture of tobacco and alcohol coated his breath. She shifted on her seat.

Josiah stirred. "Another contraction?"

"*Nay*." She couldn't trouble him with recollections of the attack. She closed her eyes. What Satan had meant for evil, God had made good.

God, please forgive me for nett *wanting the* boppli *in the beginning. I was foolish to* nett *see that this was your will. I ask that you allow the stem cells to spare Josiah's life. In Jesus's name, amen.*

The van came to a stop under the awning of the emergency

---

room's entrance. Eli jumped out of the front seat and hurried into the hospital. A moment later he returned with a nurse pushing a wheelchair.

"Is this your first baby?" the nurse asked.

"Yes." Lindie lowered herself into the wheelchair, looked at Josiah, and gasped. He staggered out of the van, then struggled to walk beside her. "Josiah?"

"I'm all right." He winced.

Entering the building, the nurse called out for another wheelchair. Despite his protests, Josiah was rushed into a curtained-off area opposite Lindie's.

"My husband needs a stem-cell transplant. Doctor Cole is his doctor. Will you call him, please? Doctor Cole," she repeated. "His office isn't too far from here."

"I'll give the information to the emergency room physician." The nurse disappeared.

Lindie wrung her hands, waiting for news. A few moments passed before the curtain parted, and the nurse entered along with a man in a white lab coat. "How is my husband?"

"He's concerned about you," she said.

A hard contraction stole Lindie's breath. She puffed repeatedly, but it wasn't easing the pain. "Is someone calling Doctor Cole?"

"Yes, someone will." The nurse smiled.

"Your husband is in good hands," the man said, introducing himself as the ER doctor. He asked if her water broke, then made a quick assessment. He glanced at the nurse. "Call for a transport." He peeled off his gloves. "We'll get you up to the labor and delivery floor shortly, Mrs. Plank."

"Is the baby—" She gripped the handrails of the cot and bore down as pain like she'd never experienced shot through her.

"Try not to push. The baby isn't in the right position yet."
He turned to the nurse. "Give her 50 milligrams of Demerol and
start an IV."

Her body relaxed after the injection, but her mind raced.
What happens when a baby is in the wrong position?

⁊

Eighteen hours of hard labor passed in a blur once Lindie held
her newborn daughter for the first time. Drenched in sweat and
weeping with joy, she counted the tiny toes and fingers. *Perfect.*

"What are you going to name her?" the nurse asked.

"I want to wait and choose the name with my husband."
Lindie had considered several names, including Eva, after her
late mother. Now she wasn't so sure any of the names fit.

"I'm sure you'll choose a lovely name. Now," she said, reaching for the baby, "I need to take her into the nursery for some
measurements."

An odd sense of emptiness washed over Lindie as she released
the baby to the nurse's care. She hadn't held her daughter but a
few short minutes and already they'd formed a bond.

Another nurse moved her into a nondelivery room and helped
her into a clean hospital gown. A few minutes later the door
creaked open. Lindie recognized the fussing baby as her daughter
before the nurse rolled the portable bassinet past the curtain.

"It's feeding time," the nurse said. She lifted the baby out and
placed her in the crook of Lindie's arm.

"Are you hungry, my sweet one?" Lindie let the baby nurse,
stopping after a few minutes to pat her back. When the baby had
fallen asleep, Lindie held her close and marveled over the delicate
bundle.

Someone knocked softly on the door and then Eli entered the room.

He approached the bed with a big smile on his face. "Congratulations on your *dochder*."

"*Denki*. How is Josiah? Did he get the stem cells?"

Eli's expression sobered.

"What's wrong?"

"The doctor said he was . . ." He looked away.

"What? You must tell me."

"He should've been hospitalized days ago according to the *doktah*. They are worried even with the stem cells that he might not recover."

Lindie's eyes burned with tears. "He can't die."

Eli looked down at the floor.

"*Nay!*" She shook her head. "Hannah prayed and laid hands on him. God's given her a supernatural gift. He healed Josiah. You'll see." Her voice cracked.

Eli removed a tissue from the box on the nightstand and handed it to Lindie. "Lindie . . ." He turned and coughed into his hand. When he faced her again, his eyes were glossy. "Josiah loves you very much. He's made provisions for you and the *kinner*. Should something happen, he wants you to *kumm* back home."

Lindie shook her head. "*Mei* home is in Michigan *nau*. With *mei* husband and our children."

"I know you might *nett* want to return after what happened at the vegetable stand . . . and in the woods. But I'm going to see to it that Silos is punished."

"You know about that?"

He nodded. "I wish you would have said something at the time. I don't understand why you confessed to—"

"I didn't have a choice. He threatened to burn down every barn in the district. I believed him." He might start a fire yet.

"*Ach*, Lindie, I would have protected you."

"It's over *nau*." She gazed teary-eyed at her daughter. "I have a beautiful gift from God. Josiah and I do." She shifted the baby to her other arm and used her free hand to press the call button for a nurse. "I have to be with Josiah."

A tall, dark-haired nurse entered the room. "Did you need something?"

"I need to see my husband." She turned to Eli. "What floor is he on?"

"The seventh."

"I'm sure the doctor would want you to rest. It's only been a few hours since you delivered."

"I won't be able to rest unless I see him."

"Her husband is very ill," Eli said.

"Let me call your doctor and see what he says."

"Tell him that most Amish women have their babies at home. I know of some women who gave birth and later prepared the evening meal."

The nurse smiled. "You make a strong argument. Let me see what I can do." It wasn't long before the nurse returned. "You have permission to visit, *but* not the baby. Doctor Barns doesn't want the baby exposed to any other area in the hospital." She reached for the infant and gently lowered her into the nearby bassinet. "You'll want to return before her next feeding."

"I will."

"I'll take the baby to the nursery and then come back with a wheelchair." She rolled the bassinet out of the room.

"I know Josiah will be happy to see that you are all right," Eli said. "He was worried about you being alone during the delivery."

"God gave me a *gut* husband."

"I wish things were different in how the marriage came about."

Lindie shook her head. "God used the evil situation for his glory." She bowed her head. "At first I prayed God would take the *boppli*. I'm ashamed to admit that, but I didn't know how I could look at the child without being reminded of what had happened. I'm glad *nau* God doesn't give us everything we ask for. Without the *boppli's* stem cells, Josiah might—"

"Don't speak it." Eli reached for her hand. "This is part of God's plan too."

"You're right." She couldn't panic now. She had to stay strong. Besides, she believed with all her heart that everything that had happened was God's plan. And his plan included directing Hannah to lay hands on her father. Josiah needed to know he was healed. He needed to stay strong.

The nurse returned with a wheelchair and helped Lindie into it. Lindie looked down at the thin hospital-gown material. She hated the idea of wearing such a skimpy covering, but at least the second gown worn backward covered her backside. The nurse must have noticed Lindie's insecurity because she laid a thin blanket over Lindie's legs.

Eli pushed the wheelchair out of the room and down the hall and stopped at the elevators. Fortunately, the elevator was empty and she didn't have to feel the weight of people's stares at the way she was dressed.

The elevator doors opened and Eli pushed her to the end of the corridor. Josiah's room was dark when they entered and his eyes were closed.

"Maybe we should *kumm* back later," Eli whispered.

She shook her head. "I want to sit next to him a few minutes."

Josiah opened his eyes. "Only a few?" He smiled, though weakly.

Her heart skipped. Focused on Josiah, she was scarcely aware of Eli slipping out of the room. She reached for Josiah's hand through the bedrail and held it. "I want to stay with you forever. Tell me how you're feeling."

He smiled. "Tell me about the *boppli* first. Does she have red hair like yours?"

"*Jah,* and lots of it. Her eyes are blue and she has tiny fingers and toes."

"Did you count them?"

"Of course! Is there a new *mamm* that wouldn't?"

His smile widened.

"*Nau* tell me how you're feeling."

"Weak, but the *doktah* said that's expected." He paused, staring at her a moment. "Lindie, I spoke with Eli—"

"Don't." She lifted her hand. "Your *dochder* prayed for you."

"I know. She told me I had to believe."

"Then don't doubt. Don't speak about *mei* future unless it involves you."

"But, Lindie—"

"They asked me what name I wanted on the birth certificate. I like Hope or Joy Plank. Do you like either of those names?"

"I like them both."

She leaned closer to the bed. "You're *nett* going to ask me why I like those names?"

"I am a little surprised. I thought you would name her after your mother."

She shook her head. "I placed *mei* hope in the Lord and he made *mei* joy complete."

"I think either name is perfect." He paused a moment and

gazed into her eyes. "I love you, Lindie. You've filled *mei* heart with joy too."

She stood, bent over the railing, and kissed him. "You have to get better soon so you can see your new *dochder*."

He raised his head a couple of inches off the pillow, looked beyond her toward a built-in cabinet, then plopped back down.

"What are you looking for?"

"*Mei* clothes," he said.

"You can't leave *nau*."

"Will you find *mei* pants?"

She didn't budge.

"There's a letter for you inside the pocket." He lifted his head once more, but dropped it back down on the pillow. "*Mei* clothes are probably in that closet."

Lindie found his pants on a hanger and dug her hand into the pocket. She removed a small envelope with her name scrawled on the front. "Did you want me to open it *nau*?"

"Later," he said. "I just wanted to make sure you had it."

Chapter Thirty-Five

Five Months Later

The bedroom's blue cotton curtains fluttered in the morning breeze, a refreshing break from the August heat wave. Still, Lindie couldn't sleep. She tossed the covers back and crawled out of bed. She padded barefoot down the hall and into the kitchen. It wouldn't be long before Hope woke up. Since the infant started teething, she hadn't slept through the night.

Lindie set the kettle on the stove and stood by the window as she waited for the water to heat. They needed rain, just not today. Within a few hours, buggies would line the lawn, and the members would gather for Sunday service. Lindie didn't want anything to spoil this day. She also didn't want anything out of place. She turned away from the window and scanned the room. The floors were spotless, the curtains pressed. She gathered the *Budget* from the table and walked the newspaper into the sitting room. For now, she would shove it in one of the desk drawers.

Inside the drawer, Lindie spotted the envelope Josiah had given her in the hospital. Although she didn't need to reread the letter, she could recite every word. She sat down at the desk and pulled the tattered pages out of the envelope.

My Dearest Lindie,

As I take this moment to gather my thoughts, I cannot help but recall the feeling of breathlessness I had the first time I saw you. You stepped off the bus, pretending to be more interested in your rumpled dress than at looking me in the eye.

I never told you, but I was just as nervous. I'm not sure my hands had ever been so clammy. You must've noticed when Bishop Troyer told us to join hands at the ceremony. All I remember is how soft your hand felt in mine. And how frightened I was that I could never make you happy.

I regret now that you didn't have the wedding of your dreams. But I don't regret marrying you. If I live one day or a hundred years, I'll always be grateful that you've come into my life.

In the first letter I wrote to you, I said I would give you my name, but I could never give you my heart. That was a lie. My heart belongs to you. God has blessed me in that he's made my joy complete by giving me you.

I say all this because we don't know the plans of God. Should tomorrow never come, I don't want to miss telling you how much you mean to me. How much I love you.

Your husband,
Josiah

Lindie dabbed the corners of her eyes with her hankie. Josiah's letter moved her to tears every time she read it.

The floor creaked behind her and strong arms came around

her shoulders. "Mrs. Plank, you're going to have a houseful of people in a few hours. What are you doing rereading this old letter?"

She looked up and smiled at Josiah. "Your love letter will never be old to me."

Josiah brought her into his arms. "I need to write you a note every day and tell you how much I love you."

Lindie rested her head on Josiah's chest. "I'm so glad God gave me you."

He kissed the top of her head. "And in a few hours, God's going to give you a houseful of people, Mrs. Plank."

Lindie gasped. "I still have things to get ready."

Hannah yawned as she shuffled into the sitting room. Already dressed for church, she was closer to being ready than Lindie was.

Lindie gave Hannah a morning hug. "I'll make breakfast after I get changed." Lindie thought that since today was the first time she and Josiah were hosting the Sunday services, she would wear the pretty blue dress Simon had given her for Christmas.

Lindie quickly changed and headed into the kitchen, pinning her *kapp* in place. She reviewed the mental list of things still to do. Yesterday Josiah and Simon had cleaned the workshop, arranged the benches, and set up long wooden tables outside. She had the tablecloths pressed and ready. Josiah had found her a few rocks by the edge of the garden to help keep them from flapping in the wind. She still needed to make up the vegetable dip. Yesterday she and Hannah had gathered, washed, and cut broccoli, carrots, celery, and zucchini from the garden.

"*Guder mariye.*" Simon entered the kitchen.

"*Mariye,*" Lindie and Josiah said in unison.

Lindie poured him a mug of *kaffi*. "I'll have breakfast done in a few minutes."

Hope started to fuss just as Lindie cracked the first egg into the skillet.

"I'll get her," Josiah said. When he returned, the *boppli* reached her arms out toward Hannah.

Lindie glanced over her shoulder and smiled. Hannah, Josiah, and even Simon were all doting on little Hope, trying to keep her from crying long enough for Lindie to finish cooking.

Hope didn't stop fussing until she reached up and grasped Simon's beard. That made her smile.

Hannah laughed.

"You used to do that too," Simon said to Hannah as he worked to free his beard. "*Mei* new granddaughter doesn't want to let go of me."

Josiah helped Simon, but it wasn't until Hannah clapped her hands and said, "Hope," that the baby released Simon's beard, turned to her sister, and spread out her arms for Hannah to take her.

Laughter filled the room as Lindie placed the food on the table. She smiled. This was her dream come true.

⁓

Josiah stood at the window and watched Simon and Hannah walk hand in hand across the green lawn. Several of the members had arrived and other buggies were pulling into the driveway. He hadn't realized how excited Lindie was to host Sunday services until he watched her and Hannah buzzing around the house the past few days, cooking and cleaning. It made him happy to see them excited. He was a blessed man. He wasn't sure if it was

Hannah's laying hands on him or the miracle of Hope's stem cells that God used to heal him. Maybe it was Lindie's faith. It didn't matter. God had given him his life back.

Lindie came up beside him, Hope cradled in her arms. "Now that she's fed, she should sleep for a while." She craned her neck to see out the window. "*Ach*, I'm late. I wanted everything perfect before the others arrived."

He placed his arm around Lindie's waist and kissed her temple. "Everything is perfect."

Reading Group Guide

1. Lindie and Josiah entered into a marriage arrangement that didn't include falling in love. Do you think it would be easier, about the same, or harder for a non-Amish couple to make the same arrangement? Why?
2. Lindie believed she had nothing to offer a husband but a marred life. How did the enemy convince her she was unworthy? What role did her family and community play in reinforcing these negative beliefs?
3. How did Hannah respond to her father's remarriage? What eventually brought Hannah and Lindie closer?
4. Why was Josiah upset when Lindie rearranged the kitchen cabinets? Was his reaction reasonable? How did he try to mend the situation?
5. How did Lindie discover Hannah's God-given gift? Were Lindie and Josiah skeptical or supportive?
6. In what ways did God use Hannah's gift?
7. Although Hannah was deaf, she said she could hear God's voice. What are some other ways God uses the weak in the Bible to accomplish his purpose?

8. Do you think Lindie's struggle to accept her pregnancy was unrealistic given that most Amish women are thrilled to be pregnant? How did she accept Josiah pointing out she wasn't eating enough for two?

9. Lindie prayed for her situation to change, but to no avail. Later, she was grateful for her unanswered prayer. Have you prayed about a certain situation only to question if God was really listening?

10. How does Romans 8:28 apply to Lindie's situation?

11. How did God use what the enemy meant for evil as a blessing that gave God the glory?

12. Can you think of any situations in the Bible where God used a difficult situation for His glory?

Acknowledgments

I would like to thank my friends and family for their ongoing support and encouragement. I thank the Lord for giving me the opportunity to work with a wonderful publisher, Daisy Hutton, and her staff.

I could never fully express my gratitude for my editors: Natalie Hanemann and Becky Philpott. You've blessed me tremendously, working with me from development through line editing. Thank you!

"Ruth Reid captivates with a powerful new voice and vision."

—Kelly Long, best-selling author of *Lilly's Wedding Quilt*

About the Author

AUTHOR PHOTO BY LEXIE REID

Ruth Reid is a full-time pharmacist who lives in Florida with her husband and three children. When attending Ferris State University School of Pharmacy in Big Rapids, Michigan, she lived on the outskirts of an Amish community and had several occasions to visit the Amish farms. Her interest grew into love as she saw the beauty in living a simple life.